THE SATURDAY EVENING POST
Christmas Treasury

Two Volumes in One

Norman Rockwell

BONANZA BOOKS   **New York**

Originally published in separate volumes under the titles
The Saturday Evening Post Christmas Book
copyright © 1976 by the Curtis Publishing Company and
The Saturday Evening Post Christmas Stories
copyright © 1980 by the Curtis Publishing Company

This 1986 edition is published by Bonanza Books,
distributed by Crown Publishers, Inc.,
225 Park Avenue South, New York, New York 10003,
by arrangement with the Curtis Publishing Company.

Printed and Bound in the United States of America

Library of Congress Cataloging in Publication Data

The Saturday evening post Christmas treasury.

   Originally published as 2 separate works under the
titles: The Saturday evening post Christmas book and
The Saturday evening post Christmas stories.
   1. Christmas—Literary collections.   I. Saturday evening
post.   II. Saturday evening post Christmas book.   III.
Saturday evening post Christmas stories.
PN6071.C6S28   1986   810.8′033   86-19326

ISBN: 0-517-62926-7

h g f e d c b a

Volume One

THE SATURDAY EVENING POST

Christmas Book

Now is the season of the holly and the mistletoe;
the days are come in which we hang our rooms with the sober green of December
and feel it summer in our hearts.

THE SATURDAY EVENING POST, DECEMBER 29, 1866

It is a good thing to observe Christmas day.
The mere marking of times and seasons, when men agree to stop work
and make merry together, is a wise and wholesome custom.
It helps one to feel the supremacy of the common life over the individual life.
It reminds a man to set his own little watch, now and then,
by the great clock of humanity which runs on sun time.

But there is a better thing than the observance of Christmas day,
and that is keeping Christmas.

Are you willing to forget what you have done for other people,
and to remember what other people have done for you;
to ignore what the world owes you, and to think what you owe the world;
to put your rights in the background, and your duties in the middle distance,
and your chances to do a little more than your duty in the foreground;
to see that your fellowmen are just as real as you are,
and try to look behind their faces to their hearts hungry for joy;
to own that probably the only good reason for your existence
is not what you are going to get out of life, but what you are going to give to life;
to close your book of complaints against the management of the universe,
and look around you for a place where you can sow a few seeds of happiness—
are you willing to do these things even for a day?
Then you can keep Christmas.

Are you willing to stoop down and consider the needs and the desires of little children;
to remember the weakness and loneliness of people who are growing old;
to stop asking how much your friends love you,
and ask yourself whether you love them enough;
to bear in mind the things that other people have to bear in their hearts;
to try to understand what those who live in the same house with you really want,
without waiting for them to tell you;
to trim your lamp so that it will give more light and less smoke,
and to carry it in front so that your shadow will fall behind you;
to make a grave for your ugly thoughts and a garden for your kindly feelings,
with the gate open—
are you willing to do these things even for a day?
Then you can keep Christmas.

Are you willing to believe that love is the strongest thing in the world—
stronger than hate, stronger than evil, stronger than death—
and that the blessed life which began in Bethlehem nineteen hundred years ago
is the image and brightness of the Eternal Love?
Then you can keep Christmas,

And if you can keep it for a day, why not always?
But you can never keep it alone.

HENRY VAN DYKE

Volume One

Contents

THE MIRACLE

STORIES

TREASURES

CELEBRATION

Introduction

Christmas is the happiest day of the year and the shortest (almost—the actual winter solstice, when the sun reaches its greatest declination north and south, is December 21). It is such a happy day that the most popular Christmas stories are the saddest, the ones about poor little match girls in the snow or crippled children ignoring their afflictions; it is almost as though there were a conspiracy to discourage the natural ebullience of the day, the day when, since Christmas has its origins in pagan festivals, primitive man realized the world was not coming to an end, only the year, that the days would get no shorter, would indeed begin to get longer and warmer and that beneath the frozen, iron-hard earth life was stirring, bulbs swelling, sap rising and from these signs of nature, men's spirits soared.

In the celebration of a birthday we rejoice in the promise, the possibility of existence, for the little boy whose birth we mark fought against time and man's very nature to prove that the other man, the neighbor, is more valuable than the concept of good or any abstract perfection. Of himself he thought nothing; of the sick, the poor, the social outcast he thought everything, lived with them, and at the end died for them. His life was a cheerful life though, and in his teachings and example we are urged not to pull any long faces. Christmas is the essence of what he prescribes; giving, loving and pausing to reflect on the passage of time and our place in a grander scheme.

Christmas was not always December 25; early church fathers felt that the Epiphany, or the showing forth (usually commemorated January 6), was a much greater feast than Christmas and other early writers and theologians felt that, since the world was created perfect, flowers in bloom, trees in leaf, moon full, Jesus was therefore born in the spring, sometime in March when we now celebrate Easter.

It was the Roman Emperor Constantine (288-337) who is believed to have standardized the celebration of Christmas on December 25th, choosing the season of the pagan festival of the Unconquered Sun (*sol invictus*) so as to ensure peace between his political constituency and his newly found faith. In the year 330 he removed the capital of the Roman Empire to Byzantium so as to dissociate Christianity from Roman tradition. The church he founded, Hagia Sophia, may still be seen in Istanbul. It is a stupendous monument to the new religion, much of it built with remnants of pagan cults, including the columns from the temple of Diana at Ephesus where St. Paul preached. The temple was one of the wonders of the ancient world, but its columns are dwarfed by the magnificence of the new church.

Old Germanic midwinter customs have contributed to the keeping of Christmas, too, the lighting of the Yule log, the tree and decorations with evergreens. St. Francis of Assisi introduced the manger or creche with the figures of animals, shepherds and wise men adoring the newborn Christ. St. Nicholas (circa 340) was believed to visit children, admonishing them to be a credit to their parents, threatening them with empty stockings and rewarding them in good-natured reconciliation upon evidence of even mild repentance. The Dutch brought Sinter Klaas (Santa Claus) to the new world when they settled in the colony of New Amsterdam (New York). The English established the tradition of sending cards at Christmas and from all over the world, the non-Christian world included, people have contributed to the making of the most popular of festivals.

Most of these traditions remain. Above them is the spirit of peace and goodwill, the unexplained euphoria that comes upon us, Scrooge included, even against our will. We forget for a day the competition, the turmoil of day-to-day existence, and find in this moment of stock-taking that we will ever make new resolutions to improve, will fail in the larger portion, but may succeed in one or two promises and will always lose in our arguments against hope.

Christmas is the feast of children. It is their natural innocence that believes, not what adults have told them, but the evidence of their pure and unjaundiced eyes. In time, children grown old come to look on their beliefs as foolish, but in time again they look back on them as wise. Christmas urges us to believe and to make concrete our beliefs in our lives.

STARKEY FLYTHE, JR.

THE MIRACLE

THE CHRISTMAS

Saint Luke

In Bethlehem

A Greek physician who learned about Jesus only after the Crucifixion, Luke was not one of the Twelve Apostles. He never even saw Jesus, so no part of his Gospel is an eyewitness account. He had, however, good sources of information. He knew well men who knew Jesus well. He heard them tell, over and over, the stories of Jesus' life and teachings, his travels, and the miracles he performed.

When Luke wrote his Gospel, probably between A.D. 60 and 70, he included many details that authors Matthew, Mark and John left out of their accounts. Interestingly, some of these details are the kind a doctor would think worth recording. For example, when Luke tells of Jesus healing a man's withered hand, he tells us it was the man's right hand. When he tells of a man "possessed of a demon" he adds a detail about the man's condition—the man had refused to wear clothing—that points clearly to mental illness.

We know that Luke was well educated, and we know that he was a sympathetic, sensitive person. He is described as a "beloved" physician, and he reappears in Acts as the trusted friend and traveling companion of Paul and Timothy. More often than the other authors of the Gospels, he mentions the emotional responses of people he writes about. For example, he mentions tears and weeping more often than the other writers.

From whom did Luke hear the story of Jesus' birth? He might have heard it from Mary herself. It is known that Mary lived on after the death of Christ, quite possibly with John in Jerusalem. Luke spent two years in Caesarea, just a few miles away, at a time when she might still have been living. It seems likely that he would have gone to visit her, and asked her to tell all she could remember of the great events that had touched her life.

However Luke learned the story, he retold it well. His account is lyrical, touched with mystery, and yet a very real story of flesh-and-blood human beings who lived in a world where there was discomfort, cold, and darkness. Luke's account of the first Christmas as it appears in the King James Version may be the best known and most loved passage in all the world's literature.

AND IT CAME TO PASS IN THOSE DAYS, THAT there went out a decree from Caesar Augustus, that all the world should be taxed.

(*And* this taxing was first made when Cyrenius was governor of Syria.)

And all went to be taxed, every one into his own city.

And Joseph also went up from Galilee, out of the city of Nazareth, into Judaea, unto the city of David, which is called Bethlehem (because he was of the house and lineage of David);

To be taxed with Mary his espoused wife, being great with child.

And so it was, that, while they were there, the days were accomplished that she should be delivered.

And she brought forth her firstborn son, and wrapped him in swaddling clothes, and laid him in a manger; because there was no room for them in the inn.

And there were in the same country shepherds abiding in the field, keeping watch over their flock by night.

And, lo, the angel of the Lord came upon them, and the glory of the Lord shone round about them; and they were sore afraid.

And the angel said unto them, Fear not: for, behold, I

*A fifteenth-century Italian street scene
circles Fra Angelico's and Fra Filippo Lippi's
Adoration of the Magi. The two monks labored
for five years on their masterpiece.*

To escape the fury of King Herod, Joseph and Mary fled into Egypt, a journey (then) of some 200 miles. Herod, the lifelong friend of

bring you good tidings of great joy, which shall be to all people.

For unto you is born this day in the city of David a Saviour, which is Christ the Lord.

And this *shall* be a sign unto you: Ye shall find the babe wrapped in swaddling clothes, lying in a manger.

And suddenly there was with the angel a multitude of the heavenly host praising God, and saying,

Glory to God in the highest, and on earth peace, good will toward men.

And it came to pass, as the angels were gone away from them into heaven, the shepherds said one to another, Let us now go even unto Bethlehem, and see this thing which is come to pass, which the Lord hath made known unto us.

And they came with haste, and found Mary, and Joseph, and the babe lying in a manger.

And when they had seen *it*, they made known abroad the saying which was told them concerning this child.

And all they that heard *it* wondered at those things

Marc Antony and Caesar, was plagued in his last years by madness and the cruelty which ordered the murder of all Jewish boy babies.

which were told them by the shepherds.

But Mary kept all these things, and pondered *them* in her heart.

And the shepherds returned, glorifying and praising God for all the things that they had heard and seen, as it was told unto them.

And when eight days were accomplished for the circumcising of the child, his name was called JESUS, which was so named of the angel before he was conceived in the womb.

And when the days of her purification according to the law of Moses were accomplished, they brought him to Jerusalem, to present *him* to the Lord;

As it is written in the law of the Lord. . .

And to offer a sacrifice according to that which is said in the law of the Lord, a pair of turtledoves, or two young pigeons. . .

And when they had performed all things according to the law of the Lord, they returned into Galilee, to their own city of Nazareth.

The Coming of Three Kings

Matthew, who wrote this account of the Nativity, was a tax collector before he became one of the Twelve Apostles. He was at his desk in the tax office when Jesus, passing, said to him, "Follow Me," and changed his life. Why did Jesus choose a representative of the hated Roman government? Perhaps for his professional skills. A tax man would be used to keeping accurate records; and perhaps Jesus intended Matthew to make notes and record, for posterity, the story of his travels and teaching.

Matthew was not, of course, an eyewitness to the events recounted here. From whom did he hear this story? Some scholars think Matthew may have questioned Joseph and based this account on his memories of the magic night when a star stood over a stable and made Bethlehem the center of the world.

NOW THE BIRTH OF JESUS CHRIST WAS ON this wise: When as his mother Mary was espoused to Joseph, before they came together, she was found with child of the Holy Ghost.

Then Joseph her husband, being a just *man*, and not willing to make her a public example, was minded to put her away privily.

But while he thought on these things, behold, the angel of the Lord appeared unto him in a dream, saying, Joseph, thou son of David, fear not to take unto thee Mary thy wife: for that which is conceived in her is of the Holy Ghost.

And she shall bring forth a son, and thou shalt call his name JESUS: for he shall save his people from their sins.

Now all this was done, that it might be fulfilled which was spoken of the Lord by the prophet, saying,

Behold, a virgin shall be with child, and shall bring forth a son, and they shall call his name Emmanuel, which being interpreted is, God with us.

Then Joseph being raised from sleep did as the angel of the Lord had bidden him, and took unto him his wife:

And knew her not till she had brought forth her firstborn son: and he called his name JESUS.

Now when Jesus was born in Bethlehem of Judea in the days of Herod the king, behold, there came wise men from the east to Jerusalem,

Saying, Where is he that is born King of the Jews? for we have seen his star in the east, and are come to worship him.

When Herod the king had heard *these things*, he was troubled, and all Jerusalem with him.

And when he had gathered all the chief priests and scribes of the people together, he demanded of them where Christ should be born.

And they said unto him, In Bethlehem of Judaea: for thus it is written by the prophet,

And thou Bethlehem, *in* the land of Judah, art not the least among the princes of Judah: for out of thee shall come a Governor, that shall rule my people Israel.

Then Herod, when he had privily called the wise men, inquired of them diligently what time the star appeared.

And he sent them to Bethlehem, and said, Go and search diligently for the young child; and when ye have found *him*, bring me word again, that I may come and worship him also.

When they had heard the king, they departed; and, lo, the star, which they saw in the east, went before them, till it came and stood over where the young child was.

When they saw the star, they rejoiced with exceeding great joy.

And when they were come into the house, they saw the young child with Mary his mother, and fell down, and worshipped him: and when they had opened their treasures, they presented unto him gifts; gold, and frankincense, and myrrh.

And being warned of God in a dream that they should not return to Herod, they departed into their own country another way.

And when they were departed, behold, the angel of the Lord appeareth to Joseph in a dream, saying, Arise, and take the young child and his mother, and flee into Egypt, and be thou there until I bring thee word: for Herod will seek the young child to destroy him.

When he arose, he took the young child and his mother by night, and departed into Egypt.

Hieronymus Bosch's Nativity scene places Bethlehem in a cold northern landscape where shepherds warm their hands over a tiny fire.

Billy Graham

Angels

Dr. S. W. Mitchell, a celebrated Philadelphia neurologist, had gone to bed after an exceptionally tiring day. Suddenly he was awakened by someone knocking on his door. Opening it he found a little girl, poorly dressed and deeply upset. She told him her mother was very sick and asked him if he would please come with her. It was a bitterly cold, snowy night, but though he was bone tired, Dr. Mitchell dressed and followed the girl.

He found the mother desperately ill with pneumonia. After arranging for medical care, he complimented the sick woman on the intelligence and persistence of her little daughter. The woman looked at him strangely and then said, "My daughter died a month ago." She added, "Her shoes and coat are in the clothes closet there." Dr. Mitchell, amazed and perplexed, went to the closet and opened the door. There hung the very coat worn by the little girl who had brought him to tend to her mother. It was warm and dry and could not possibly have been out in the wintry night.

The Reverend John G. Paton, a missionary in the New Hebrides Islands, tells a thrilling story involving the protective care of angels. Hostile natives surrounded his mission headquarters one night, intent on burning the Patons out and killing them. John Paton and his wife prayed all during that terror-filled night that God would deliver them. When daylight came they were amazed to see the attackers unaccountably leave. They thanked God for delivering them.

A year later, the chief of the tribe was converted to Christianity, and Mr. Paton, remembering what had happened, asked the chief what had kept him and his men from burning down the house and killing them. The chief replied in surprise, "Who were all those men you had with you there?" The missionary answered, "There were no men there; just my wife and I." The chief argued that they had seen many men standing guard—hundreds of big men in shining garments with drawn swords in their hands. They seemed to circle the mission station so that the natives were afraid to attack. Only then did Mr. Paton realize that God had sent His angels to protect them. The chief agreed that there was no other explanation.

Angels announce, warn, protect. Wings symbolize their incorporeality, go back to the winged Egyptian sun god, Horus.

A north German painter used his own daughter as a model for these angels.

During World War II, Captain Eddie Rickenbacker was shot down over the Pacific Ocean. For weeks nothing was heard of him. The newspapers reported his disappearance and across the country thousands of people prayed. Mayor LaGuardia asked the whole city of New York to pray for him.

Then he returned. The Sunday papers headlined the news, and in an article, Captain Rickenbacker himself told what had happened. "And this part I would hesitate to tell," he wrote, "except that there were six witnesses who saw it with me.

"A gull came out of nowhere, and lighted on my head—I reached up my hand very gently—I killed him and then we divided him equally among us. We ate every bit, even the little bones. Nothing ever tasted so good." This gull saved the lives of Rickenbacker and his companions.

Years later I asked him to tell me the story personally, because it was through this experience that he came to know Christ. He said, "I have no explanation except that God sent one of His angels to rescue us. . . ."

Does it not seem mysterious that God brought the first message of the birth of Jesus to ordinary people rather than to princes and kings? In this instance, God spoke through His holy angel to the shepherds who were keeping sheep in the fields. This was a lowly occupation, so shepherds were not well educated. But Mary in her song, the Magnificat, tells us the true story: "He hath put down the mighty from their seats, and exalted them of low degree. He hath filled the hungry with good things, and the rich he hath sent empty away" (Luke 1:52, 53). What a word for our generation!

What was the message of the angel to the shepherds? First, he told them not to be afraid. Over and over again the presence of angels was frightening to those to whom they came. But unless they came in judgment, the angels spoke a word of reassurance. They calmed the people to whom they came. This tells us that the appearance of an angel is awe-inspiring, something about them awakening fear in the human heart. They represent a presence that has greatness and sends a chill down the spine. But when the angel had quieted the fears of the shepherds, he brought this message, one forever to be connected with the evangel:

"For behold I bring you good tidings of great joy, which shall be to all people. For unto you is born this day in the city of David a Saviour, which is Christ the Lord."

Arthur C. Clarke

What Was the Christmas Star?

Was it a comet, or two planets in conjunction? Or could it have been a blinding flash that started its trip toward the earth 3,000 years before?

Go out of doors any morning this December, an hour or so before dawn, and look up at the eastern sky. You will see there one of the most beautiful sights in all the heavens, a blazing, blue-white beacon, ten times brighter than Sirius, the most brilliant of the stars. Apart from the moon itself, it is the brightest object you will ever see in the night sky. It will still be visible even when the sun rises; indeed, you can find it at midday if you know exactly where to look.

Ours is an age in which the glare of electric lights has hidden the stars, so that men have forgotten many things that were familiar to their ancestors. If you take the average city dweller away from his floodlit canyons, lead him out to some hill in the country, and show him this brilliant herald of the dawn, he probably will have no idea what it is. Indeed, it is safe to predict that through December there will be a flood of flying-saucer reports from ignorant or credulous observers seeing this dazzling point of light against the sunrise.

It is our sister world, the planet Venus, reflecting across the gulf of space the sunlight glancing from her unbroken cloud veils. Every eighteen months she appears in the morning sky, rising shortly before the sun.

It has been seriously suggested that Venus was the Star of Nativity, and at least one massive book has been written in an effort to prove this theory. However, it is a theory that makes very little sense when examined closely. To all the peoples of the Eastern world, Venus was one of the most familiar objects in the sky. Even today, she serves as a kind of alarm clock to the Arab nomads. When she rises, it is time to start moving, to make as much progress as possible before the sun begins to blast the desert with its heat. For thousands of years, shining more brilliantly than we ever see her in our northern skies, she has watched the camps struck and the caravans begin to move.

Even to uneducated Jews, there could have been nothing in the least remarkable about Venus. And the Magi were no ordinary men; they were certainly experts on astronomy, and knew the movements of the planets.

What, then, was the Star of Bethlehem—assuming that it was a natural phenomenon and not a miraculous apparition? The Bible gives us very few clues; all we can do is consider some possibilities that at this distance in time can be neither proved nor disproved. One of those possibilities—the most spectacular and awe-inspiring of all—has been suggested only in the past few years. But let us first look at some of the earlier theories.

In addition to Venus there are four other planets easily visible to the naked eye—Mercury, Mars, Jupiter and Saturn. During their movements across the sky, two planets may sometimes appear to pass very close to one another, though in fact they are millions or hundreds of millions of miles apart. Such occurrences are called "conjunctions."

On very rare occasions, the conjunctions may be so close that the planets cannot be separated by the naked eye. This happened to Mars and Venus on October 4, 1953, when for a short while the two planets appeared to be fused into a single star. Such a spectacle is rare enough to be very striking, and the great astronomer Kepler devoted much time to proving that the Star of Bethlehem was a conjunction of Jupiter and Saturn. The two planets passed very close together (remember, this was purely from Earth's point of view—in reality they were half a billion miles apart!) in May, 7 B.C., not long before the date set by some authorities for the birth of Christ. Others set it as late as 4 B.C.

Kepler's ingenious proposal, however, is as unconvincing as the Venus theory. Better calculations than he could make in his day have shown that, after all, this conjunction was not a very close one, and the planets were always far enough apart to be separated easily by the eye. Moreover, there was a still closer conjunction in 66 B.C., which, following Kepler's theory, should have brought a delegation of wise men to Bethlehem fifty-nine years too soon!

In any case, the Magi could be expected to be as familiar with such events as with all other planetary movements, and the Biblical account also indicates that the Star of Bethlehem was visible over a period of weeks (it must have taken the Magi a considerable time to reach Judea, have their interview with Herod and then go on to Bethlehem). The conjunction of two planets lasts only a few hours, since they soon separate in the sky and go on their individual ways again.

We can get around this difficulty if we assume that the Magi were astrologers and had somehow deduced the birth of the Messiah from a particular configuration of the heavens. Suppose, for example, they had decided, by some esoteric reasoning of the type on which this pseudo science is based, that Venus or some other planet, perhaps Jupiter or Saturn, had taken a position in the Zodiac that foretold the birth of Christ. Then even when the planet concerned moved from this position, they might still refer to it as "His" star and continue to use it as a guide.

This theory is simple and plausible, for in ancient times most wise men did believe in astrology and, in consequence, many of them led somewhat precarious lives as court prophets. Because of its very simplicity, this theory can never be proved or disproved, but one would like to think that the facts are somewhat more exciting.

They may well be. It seems much more likely that the Star of the Nativity was something quite novel and unusual, and not one of the familiar planets whose behavior had been well known for thousands of years before the birth of Christ. Of course, if one accepts as literally true the statement that "the star, which they saw in the east, *went before them, till it came and stood over where the young Child was,*" no natural explanation is possible. Any heavenly body—star, planet, comet or whatever it may be—must share in the normal movement of the sky, rising in the east and setting some hours later in the west. Only the Pole Star, because it lies on the invisible axis of the turning Earth, appears unmoving in the sky and can act as a fixed and constant guide.

But the phrase "went before them," like so much else in the Bible, can be interpreted in many ways. It may be that the Star, whatever it might have been, was so close to the Sun that it could only be seen for a short period near dawn, and so would never have been visible except in the eastern sky. Like Venus when she is a morning star, it might have risen shortly before the Sun, then been lost in the glare of the new day before it could climb very far up the sky. The wise men would thus have seen it ahead of them at the beginning of each day, and then lost it in the dawn before it had veered round to the south. Many other readings are equally possible.

Very well then, can we discover some astronomical phenomenon that fits the Biblical text and is sufficiently startling to surprise men completely familiar with the movements of the stars and planets?

Let's see if a comet answers the specification. Most comets have a bright, starlike core or nucleus that is completely dwarfed by an enormous tail, a luminous appendage which may be in the shape of a narrow beam or a broad, diffuse fan. At first sight it would seem very unlikely that anyone would call such an object a star, but in old records comets are sometimes referred to, not inaptly, as "hairy stars."

It is perfectly possible that a comet appeared just before the birth of Christ. Attempts have been made, without success, to discover whether any of the known comets were visible around that date. But the number of comets whose paths and periods we do know is very small compared with the colossal number that undoubtedly exists. If a comet did shine over Bethlehem, it may not be seen again from Earth for a hundred thousand years.

We can picture it in that Oriental dawn, a band of light streaming up from the eastern horizon, perhaps stretching vertically toward the zenith. The tail of a comet always points away from the sun; the comet would appear, therefore, like a great arrow, aimed at the east. As the sun rose, the comet would fade into invisibility; but the next morning, it would be in almost the same place, still directing the travelers to their goal. It might be visible for weeks before it disappeared once more into the depths of space. The picture is a dramatic and attractive one. It may even be the correct explanation; one day, perhaps, we shall know.

But there is another theory, and this is the one most astronomers would probably accept today. It makes the

The great Post artist, J.C. Leyendecker, portrays a wimpled medieval Lady Bountiful making her rounds with page, mistletoe and gifts.

other explanations look trivial and commonplace indeed, for it leads us to contemplate the most astonishing and terrifying events yet discovered in the whole realm of Nature.

We will forget now about planets and comets and the other denizens of our own tight little solar system. Let us go out across *real* space, right out to the stars—those other suns, many of them far greater than our own sun.

Most stars shine with unwavering brilliance, century after century. Sirius appears now exactly as it did to Moses, as it did to Neanderthal Man, as it did to the dinosaurs, if they ever bothered to look at the night sky. Its brilliance has changed little during the entire history of Earth, and will be the same a billion years from now.

The Wise Men may have come from Alexandria.

But there are some stars, the so-called "novae" or new stars, that for no ascertainable reason suddenly turn themselves into celestial atomic bombs. Such a star may explode so violently that it leaps a hundred-thousand-fold in brilliance within a few hours. One night it may be invisible to the naked eye; on the next, it may dominate the sky.

Novae are not uncommon; many are observed every year, though few are near enough to be visible except through telescopes. They are the routine disasters of the universe.

Two or three times in every thousand years, however, there occurs something that makes a mere nova about as inconspicuous as a firefly at noon. When a star becomes a *super*nova its brilliance may increase not by a hundred thousand but by a *thousand million* times in the course of a few hours. The last time such an event was witnessed was in A.D. 1604; there was another supernova in A.D. 1572 (so brilliant that it was visible in broad daylight);

and the Chinese astronomers recorded one in A.D. 1054. It is quite possible that the Star of Bethlehem was such a supernova, and if so one can draw some very surprising conclusions.

We'll assume that Supernova Bethlehem was about as bright as the nova of A.D. 1572, often called Tycho's star after the great astronomer who observed it at the time. Since this star could be seen by day, it must have been as brilliant as Venus. As we also know that a supernova is, in reality, at least a hundred million times more brilliant than our own sun, a simple calculation tells us how far away it must have been for its *apparent* brightness to equal that of Venus.

The calculation shows that Supernova Bethlehem was more than 3,000 light-years or, if you prefer, 18,000,000,000,000,000 miles away. That means its light had been traveling for at least three thousand years before it reached Earth and Bethlehem, so that the awesome cataclysm of which it was the evidence really took place five thousand years ago, when the great Pyramid was still fresh from the builders.

Let us, in imagination, cross the gulfs of space and time and go back to the moment of the catastrophe. We might find ourselves watching an ordinary star—a sun perhaps no different from our own. There may have been planets circling it; we do not know how common planets are in the Universe nor how many suns have such small companions. But there is no reason to think they are rare, and many novae must be the funeral pyres of worlds, and perhaps races, greater than ours.

There is no warning at all, only a steadily rising intensity of the sun's light. Within minutes the change is noticeable: within an hour, the nearer worlds are burning. The star is expanding like a balloon, blasting off shells of gas at a million miles an hour as it blows its outer layers into space. Within a day, it is shining with such supernal brilliance that it gives off more light than *all the other suns in the universe combined.* If it had planets, they are now no more than flecks of flame in the still expanding shells of fire. The conflagration will burn for weeks before the dying star collapses into quiescence.

But let us consider what happens to the light of the nova, which moves a hundred times more swiftly than the blast wave of the explosion. It will spread out into space, and after four or five years it will reach the next star. If there are planets circling that star, they will suddenly be illuminated by a second sun. It will give them no appreciable heat, but will be bright

To the lowly shepherds, the star brought hope.

enough to banish night completely, for it will be more than a thousand times more luminous than our full moon. All that light will come from a single blazing point, since even from its nearest neighbor Supernova Bethlehem would appear too small to show a disc.

Century after century, the shell of light will continue to expand around its source. It will flash past countless suns and flare briefly in the skies of their planets. Indeed, by the most conservative estimate, this great new star must have shone over thousands of worlds before its light reached Earth, and to all those worlds it appeared far, far brighter than it did to the men it led to Judea.

For as the shell of light expanded, it faded also. By the time it reached Bethlehem it was spread over the surface of a sphere six thousand light-years across. A thousand years earlier, when Homer sang of Troy, the nova would have appeared twice as brilliant to any watchers farther upstream, as it were, closer to the time and place of the explosion.

That is a strange thought: there is a stranger one to come. For the light of Supernova Bethlehem is still flooding out through space. It has left Earth far behind in the twenty centuries that have elapsed since men saw it for the first and last time. Now its light is spread over a sphere ten thousand light-years across, and must be correspondingly fainter. It is simple to calculate how bright the Supernova must be to any beings who may be seeing it now as a new star in *their* skies. To them, it will still be far more brilliant than any other star in their entire heavens, for its brightness will have decreased only by 50 percent on its extra two thousand years of travel. . . .

At this very moment, therefore, the Star of Bethlehem may still be shining in the skies of countless worlds, circling far suns. Any watchers on those worlds will see its sudden appearance and its slow fading, just as the Magi may have seen it two thousand years ago when the expanding shell of light swept past Earth. And for thousands of years to come, as its radiance ebbs out toward the frontiers of the universe, Supernova Bethlehem will still have power to startle all who see it, wherever and *what*ever they may be.

Astronomy, as nothing else can do, teaches men humility. We know now that our sun is merely one undistinguished member of a vast family of stars, and no longer think of ourselves as being at the center of Creation. Yet it is strange to think that before its light fades away below the limits of vision, we may have shared the Star of Bethlehem with the beings of perhaps a million worlds, and that to many of them, nearer to the source of the explosion, it must have been a far more wonderful sight than ever it was to human eyes. What did they make of it, and did it bring them good tidings, or ill?

Donald Culross Peattie

ᴡWinter ᴡWonder

When the skies are lowest, when the gray clouds hang heavy with a great stillness and the winter-locked world lies waiting for some reprieve from despair, then falls the miracle of snow. It falls like a blessing, softly, silently, making a white beauty where outlines were bleak and colors were dun. As it veils the stone and smut of the cities, or draws its gentle blanket over fences and frozen ruts in the country byways, we too know its softening influence; men go walking with faces uplifted to feel that feathery cold touch.

The air is filled with a numberless whiteness. Some purity is abroad that is not of this earth. And if you pause and examine some of those first, great flakes lying unmelted on your coat sleeve, you will see the most delicate and fleeting perfection that Nature ever creates.

For it is in such an hour, when clouds are low, humidity is great, and the air is still, that the finest of snowflakes are formed and reach us in their most flawless perfection.

Snow covers the defects of a man-scarred world.

Most of the snow in the world never descends to us. Vast quantities of it are created in lofty clouds even in warm latitudes, but it melts as it falls through the warmer air, and reaches us as rain. In the icy north, of course, snow is a frequent visitant, but in that dry and frosty air it does not attain the marvelous gemlike size and pattern you find in a damp snowstorm in a milder climate, but whirls along in tiny icy pellets driven by whiplike winds.

So it is in our temperate climate that winter makes its finest display. One snowstorm, and the sad and bad old world we know so well has turned a new page. All is fair and new and pure, waiting to be inscribed. The least step of a sparrow may be noted there, and the footprints of the deer mice, with the dragging tail mark between; you can see the very leap of a cottontail in the spacing of his pad prints on the white sheet.

Now all our trees come into new unearthly bloom; old scars are hidden, and cleanliness lies like healing over all. That it is transient makes it no less dear. It will grow old and gray and tiresome, like man himself. But the first snowstorm, even more, the first flakes of that first snow, are perfect as only the newborn are perfect, and bring with them that same innocent air of being messengers from heaven.

A snowflake, of course, is simply the water vapor in the air crystallized into a geometrical shape. Simply, I say—yet the bewildering multiplicity of forms which a snowflake may take is beyond the power of the most accomplished worker in metal or wood or stone.

Hundreds and hundreds of patterns have been recorded, endlessly varying in detail. But every one is built upon the same principle, the hexagonal or six-faced crystal, and every last complexity of its design may be divided by six or three.

The reason for this is fundamental. Water, as we learned in school, is composed of two gases—hydrogen and oxygen—in the proportion of two parts hydrogen to one part oxygen; its nuclear atoms are so arranged as to produce each crystalline structure on a triangular basis. Nothing in nature is lovelier, and nothing in art has been more enduring, than this simple plan, with the connotation of holiness which the trinity brings to mind.

And snowflakes, of all things, are most truly made in heaven. They crystallize while floating about in the air, so that the atoms and molecules, which are the building blocks of all things, have a unique freedom in which to arrange themselves. As they descend through varying strata of moisture and temperature and air current, they grow and change and take on variety, until their intricate

As it falls, snow lifts spirits
who hear its silence and know a peace
which passeth human understanding.

DRAWN BY
SARAH S. STILWELL WEBER

elaboration surpasses anything that comes from the fingers of the most skilled lacemaker of Europe.

What a fairylike business the study of snowflakes would seem! Yet it is a respected science, with a long history. Away back in 1555, Olaus Magnus, the brother of the Archbishop of Uppsala, published in Rome a book about natural curiosities. That book contains what seems to be the first published drawing of a snowflake. It is a crude woodcut, and but for the legend beneath it might be mistaken for some other of Olaus' collection of curiosa. But it reminds us, at least, how long men have looked up and wondered at this gift from the skies.

In 1820 the arctic explorer, William Scoresby, recorded in a superb collection of drawings a variety of flake patterns. But drawing is a slow and inexact method of reproducing their passing wonder.

It has remained for the modern method of microscopic photography to catch this accurately, and one enthusiast in particular, W.A. Bentley of Vermont, has spent a lifetime in pursuit of the snowflake. Even the X ray has been turned upon it, to learn the last secrets of its structure.

For most of us it is enough to take the snowflake for its sheer delight, or, if you want to dig philosophy out of it, for testimony that in nature, at least, there is sound organization down to the last and most delicate detail.

When the clouds have emptied their bag of goose-feather whiteness, it is the wind that takes a hand at making over the world.

Never was stuff so malleable as snow, so easy and quick to work, and never was artist so free as the wind.

Now over the last year's nest is cocked a peaked new roof, now every fence post is capped, and the baldest ditch is softened to a slope like the flank of some great crouching beast.

The very currents of the wind that helped to shape the flake are written, with the tracks of wildlife, on the fields of white. And tomorrow, if the wind blows all night long and more snow falls, the careless sculptor will have shaped the world all over again.

Snow, in this soft blanket form, is a kindly thing. Cold as it is, it forms a shelter for little creatures crouching in its lee; it conserves earth's banked warmth, and thus protects plant life as well.

The winter form of rainfall, it provides drink for birds and animals, and is a store, indeed, of water for future irrigation, when thaws unlock it.

But snow is a force, as well, and all that soft and comfortable kindliness can turn to cruel power.

Let it freeze in a hard crust, and groundlings like quail and mice and partridge may be imprisoned under it and starve to death. Or let rain turn that snow upon the boughs to ice, and the grandest old limbs may crack and break beneath the strain. Or sudden thaw after great snowfall can end in disastrous flood.

But these are what insurance policies carefully call "an act of God." More certain are the joys of winter, the sparkle and the crunch of snow beneath the heel, the tingle at the bottom of one's lungs and the sense of blood running warmer for the cold of air.

Now skiers find their wings again; now on the front lawn rises that art form surely older than the Parthe-

*The young see no colds or flu
in the magic drifts of crystal,
only the ecstasy of wind speed
and bell sounds, the rapture of
snowball-induced flying top hats.*

19

Kids make angels in the whiteness that reflects their innocence, hoping to puzzle adults who come later, upright or in other postures.

JOHN FALTER

non—the snow man, complete with pipe and lumps of coal for eyes. Now winter berries stand out red against the white, and birds are plain to see, and sunrise or sundown glow rose-colored, with shadows that are purple-blue. The feeding tray, these days, shows us who are our true friends—cardinal and jay, and chickadee, who, by his upside-down hilarity, demonstrates that he loves winter best of all.

Nights are deeply silent, unless the owl goes hunting. Days have a bite like that you'll get when you set your teeth in a winy apple. The sun is welcome as at no other time, and finds a million diamonds to dance on, and at night the stars step forth with a grandeur and brilliance unknown to summer's skies.

The first of winter comes to us as welcome as the first of spring, all fresh and full of sparkle. Indeed it is spring that it is hiding underneath that coverlet of snow.

Next year's bloom, the waterfalls that will refresh parched August, all our eagerness for April, are to be fed by these first snowflakes twirling down, gathering, crowding, whitening the gray sky, filling our eyes and mind with the sense of a marvelous richness.

20

Even folks who "dread the winter"
will still hanker for "a little snow on Christmas Eve."
And in those parts of the world, including much of our own Southland,
where snow seldom falls, people take the symbol of "white Christmas"
to their hearts and pay no attention
to their climate in selecting winter-wonderland Christmas cards.
Indeed, it is not irreverent to believe that the Little Boy, whose birthday we celebrate—
who never slid down a hill in Nazareth or made a Santa Claus snowman—
may give a special meaning and promise in sometimes covering the scars
of our sad old world with a white Christmas.

THE SATURDAY EVENING POST DECEMBER 27, 1958

In our hearts it is to the deep country we return in December even though we may have been born in the city.

23

What They Said About Christmas

My best of wishes for your merry Christmases and your happy New Years, your long lives and your true prosperities. Worth twenty pound good if they are delivered as I send them. Remember? Here's a final prescription added, "To be taken for life."

—*Charles Dickens, "Dr. Marigold's Prescriptions"*

Heigh ho! sing heigh ho! unto the green holly
Most friendship is feigning, most loving mere folly.
    Then heigh ho, the holly!
    This life is most jolly!

—*William Shakespeare*

It is good to be children sometimes, and never better than at Christmas, when its mighty Founder was a child Himself.

—*Charles Dickens*

Christmas is coming, the geese are getting fat,
Please to put a penny in the old man's hat;
If you haven't got a penny, a ha'penny will do,
If you haven't got a ha'penny, God bless you!

—*Beggar's rhyme, anonymous*

Are you going to send a flaming red necktie to a quiet man with pepper-and-salt taste in clothing? Are you going to give teaspoons to a woman who already has several unused pounds of them? Are you planning to give a set of Scott's novels to a man who already has every volume? Are you planning to give large objects to people who live in small rooms? Are you going to send a potted fern to a lady who lives near the woods? Are you planning to send a dyed goatskin to a hunter? Are you forgetting that an author will already have plenty of inkwells?

"God tells us to forgive our enemies," cried the fiercest of all the Medicis, "But nowhere does He tell us to forgive our friends!" And one may well suspect that he was moved to this exasperatory burst by the receipt of an ill-chosen gift for which he was expected to be thankful.

—*The Saturday Evening Post, December 21, 1907*

Loving Father, help us remember the birth of Jesus, that we may share in the song of the angels, the gladness of the shepherds, and the worship of the wise men.

Close the door of hate and open the door of love all over the world.

Let kindness come with every gift and good desires with every greeting.

Deliver us from evil by the blessing which Christ brings, and teach us to be merry with clear hearts.

May the Christmas morning make us happy to be Thy children, and the Christmas evening bring us to our beds with grateful thoughts, forgiving and forgiven, for Jesus' sake. Amen!

—*Robert Louis Stevenson*

At Christmas I no more desire a rose
Than wish a snow in May's newfangled mirth;
But like of each thing that in season grows.

—*William Shakespeare, Love's Labour's Lost*

And so, at this Christmas time, I greet you. Not quite as the world sends greetings, but with profound esteem and with the prayer that for you, now and forever, the day breaks and the shadows flee away.

—*Fra Giovanni*

England was merry England, when
Old Christmas brought his sports again,
'Twas Christmas broach'd the mightiest ale:
'Twas Christmas told the merriest tale;
A Christmas gambol oft could cheer
The poor man's heart through half the year.

—*Sir Walter Scott, "Lochinvar"*

One Christmas was so much like another, in those years around the seatown corner now and out of all sound except the distant speaking of the voices I sometimes hear a moment before sleep, that I can never remember whether it snowed for six days and six nights when I was twelve or whether it snowed for twelve days and twelve nights when I was six.

—*Dylan Thomas, "A Child's Christmas in Wales"*

Charles Dickens

A Christmas Carol

Marley was dead, to begin with. There is no doubt whatever about that. The register of his burial was signed by the clergyman, the clerk, the undertaker, and the chief mourner. Scrooge signed it. And Scrooge's name was good upon 'Change for anything he chose to put his hand to.

Old Marley was as dead as a doornail.

Scrooge knew he was dead? Of course he did. How could it be otherwise? Scrooge and he were partners for I don't know how many years. Scrooge was his sole executor, his sole administrator, his sole assign, his sole residuary legatee, his sole friend, his sole mourner.

Scrooge never painted out old Marley's name, however. There it yet stood, years afterwards, above the warehouse door—Scrooge and Marley. The firm was known as Scrooge and Marley. Sometimes people new to the business called Scrooge Scrooge, and sometimes Marley. He answered to both names. It was all the same to him.

Oh! But he was a tightfisted hand at the grindstone, was Scrooge! a squeezing, wrenching, grasping, scraping, clutching, covetous old sinner! External heat and cold had little influence on him. No warmth could warm, no cold could chill him. No wind that blew was bitterer than he, no falling snow was more intent upon its purpose, no pelting rain less open to entreaty. Foul weather didn't know where to have him. The heaviest rain and snow and hail and sleet could boast of the advantage over him in only one respect—they often "came down" handsomely, and Scrooge never did.

Nobody ever stopped him in the street to say, with gladsome looks, "My dear Scrooge, how are you? When will you come to see me?" No beggars implored him to bestow a trifle, no children asked him what it was o'clock, no man or woman ever once in all his life inquired the way to such and such a place, of Scrooge. Even the blind men's dogs appeared to know him, and when they saw him coming on, would tug their owners into doorways and up courts; and then would wag their tails as though they said, "No eyes at all is better than an evil eye, dark master!"

But what did Scrooge care! It was the very thing he liked. To edge his way along the crowded paths of life, warning all human sympathy to keep its distance, was what the knowing ones call "nuts" to Scrooge.

Once upon a time—of all the good days in the year, upon a Christmas eve—old Scrooge sat busy in his countinghouse. It was cold, bleak, biting, foggy weather; and the city clocks had only just gone three, but it was quite dark already.

The door of Scrooge's countinghouse was open, that he might keep his eye upon his clerk, who, in a dismal little cell beyond, a sort of tank, was copying letters. Scrooge had a very small fire, but the clerk's fire was so very much smaller that it looked like one coal. But he couldn't replenish it, for Scrooge kept the coal-box in his own room; and so surely as the clerk came in with the shovel, the master predicted that it would be necessary for them to part. Wherefore the clerk put on his white comforter, and tried to warm himself at the candle; in which effort, not being a man of a strong imagination, he failed.

"A Merry Christmas, uncle! God save you!" cried a cheerful voice. It was the voice of Scrooge's nephew, who came upon him so quickly that this was the first intimation Scrooge had of his approach.

"Bah!" said Scrooge; "humbug!"

"Christmas a humbug, uncle! You don't mean that, I am sure?"

"I do. Out upon merry Christmas! What's Christmastime to you but a time for paying bills without money; a time for finding yourself a year older, and not an hour richer; a time for balancing your books and having every item in 'em through a round dozen of months presented dead against you? If I had my will, every idiot who goes about with 'Merry Christmas' on his lips should be boiled with his own pudding, and buried with a stake of holly through his heart. He should!"

"Uncle!"

"Nephew, keep Christmas in your own way, and let me keep it in mine."

"Keep it! But you don't keep it."

"Let me leave it alone, then. Much good may it do you! Much good it has ever done you!"

Scrooge had drawn in upon himself until the mirror of his soul remarked no breath to indicate life. His coffers swelled; his heart shrank. Love, Christmas, friends—fixed stars in the gray guarantee of existence—were dark voids to him.

"There are many things from which I might have derived good, by which I have not profited, I dare say, Christmas among the rest. But I am sure I have always thought of Christmastime, when it has come round—apart from the veneration due to its sacred origin, if anything belonging to it can be apart from that—as a good time; a kind, forgiving, charitable, pleasant time; the only time I know of, in the long calendar of the year, when men and women seem by one consent to open their shut-up hearts freely, and to think of people below them as if they really were fellow-travellers to the grave, and not another race of creatures bound on other journeys. And therefore, uncle, though it has never put a scrap of gold or silver in my pocket, I believe that it *has* done me good, and *will* do me good; and I say, God bless it!"

The clerk in the tank involuntarily applauded.

"Let me hear another sound from you," said Scrooge, "and you'll keep your Christmas by losing your situation! You're quite a powerful speaker, sir," he added, turning to his nephew. "I wonder you don't go into Parliament."

"Don't be angry, uncle. Come! Dine with us tomorrow."

Scrooge said that he would see him—yes, indeed he did. He went the whole length of the expression, and said that he would see him in that extremity first.

"But why?" cried Scrooge's nephew. "Why?"

"Why did you get married?"

"Because I fell in love."

"Because you fell in love!" growled Scrooge, as if that were the only one thing in the world more ridiculous than a merry Christmas. "Good afternoon!"

"Nay, uncle, but you never came to see me before that

happened. Why give it as a reason for not coming now?"

"Good afternoon."

"I want nothing from you; I ask nothing of you; why cannot we be friends?"

"Good afternoon."

"I am sorry, with all my heart, to find you so resolute. We have never had any quarrel, to which I have been a party. But I have made the trial in homage to Christmas, and I'll keep my Christmas humour to the last. So a Merry Christmas, uncle!"

"Good afternoon!"

"And a Happy New Year!"

"Good afternoon!"

His nephew left the room without an angry word, notwithstanding.

At length the hour of shutting up arrived, and

"...not well dressed; their shoes were far from waterproof."

Scrooge, dismounting from his stool, tacitly admitted the fact to the expectant clerk in the tank, who instantly snuffed his candle out, and put on his hat.

"You want all day tomorrow, I suppose?"

"If quite convenient, sir."

"It's not convenient, and it's not fair. If I was to stop half a crown for it, you'd think yourself mightily ill used, I'll be bound?"

"Yes, sir."

"And yet you don't think *me* ill used, when I pay a day's wages for no work."

"It's only once a year, sir."

"A poor excuse for picking a man's pocket every twenty-fifth of December! But I suppose you must have the whole day. Be here all the earlier *next* morning."

The clerk promised that he would, and Scrooge walk-

ed out with a growl. The office was closed in a twinkling, and the clerk, with the long ends of his white comforter dangling below his waist (for he boasted no greatcoat), went down a slide, at the end of a lane of boys, twenty times, in honour of its being Christmas eve, and then ran home as hard as he could pelt, to play at blindman's buff.

Scrooge took his melancholy dinner in his usual melancholy tavern; and having read all the newspapers, and beguiled the rest of the evening with his banker's book, went home to bed. He lived in chambers which had once belonged to his deceased partner. They were a gloomy suite of rooms, in a lowering pile of building up a yard. The building was old enough now, and dreary enough for nobody lived in it but Scrooge, the other rooms being all let out as offices.

Now it is a fact that there was nothing at all particular about the knocker on the door of this house, except that it was very large; also, that Scrooge had seen it, night and morning, during his whole residence in that place; also, that Scrooge had as little of what is called fancy about him as any man in the city of London. And yet Scrooge, having his key in the lock of the door, saw in the knocker, without its undergoing any intermediate process of change, not a knocker, but Marley's face.

Marley's face, with a dismal light about it, like a bad lobster in a dark cellar. It was not angry or ferocious, but it looked at Scrooge as Marley used to look—ghostly spectacles turned up upon its ghostly forehead.

As Scrooge looked fixedly at this phenomenon, it was

a knocker again. He said, "Pooh, pooh!" and closed the door with a bang.

The sound resounded through the house like thunder. Every room above, and every cask in the wine merchant's cellars below, appeared to have a separate peal of echoes of its own. Scrooge was not a man to be frightened by echoes. He fastened the door, and walked across the hall, and up the stairs. Slowly too, trimming his candle as he went.

Up Scrooge went, not caring a button for its being very dark. Darkness is cheap, and Scrooge liked it. But before he shut his heavy door, he walked through his rooms to see that all was right. He had just enough recollection of Marley's ghostly face to desire to do that.

We hear the great glad tidings, the sounds of Christmas.

Sitting room, bedroom, lumber room, all as they should be. Nobody under the table, nobody under the sofa; a small fire in the grate; spoon and basin ready; and the little saucepan of gruel (Scrooge had a cold in his head) upon the hob. Nobody under the bed; nobody in the closet; nobody in his dressing gown, which was hanging up in a suspicious attitude against the wall. Lumber room as usual. Old fireguards, old shoes, two fish baskets, washing stand on three legs, and a poker.

Quite satisfied, he closed his door and locked himself in; double-locked himself in, which was not his custom. Thus secured against surprise, he took off his cravat, put on his dressing gown and slippers and his nightcap, and sat down before the very low fire to take his gruel.

As he threw his head back in the chair, his glance happened to rest upon a bell, a disused bell, that hung in the room, and communicated, for some purpose now forgotten, with a chamber in the highest story of the building. It was with great astonishment, and with a strange, inexplicable dread, that, as he looked, he saw this bell begin to swing. Soon it rang out loudly, and so did every bell in the house.

This was succeeded by a clanking noise, deep down below as if some person were dragging a heavy chain over the casks in the wine merchant's cellar.

Then he heard the noise much louder, on the floors below; then coming up the stairs; then coming straight toward his door.

It came on through the heavy door, and a spectre passed into the room before him. The dying flame leaped up, as though it cried, "I know him! Marley's ghost!"

The same face, the very same. Marley in his pigtail, usual waistcoat, tights, and boots. His body was transparent; so that Scrooge, observing him, and looking through his waistcoat, could see the two buttons on his coat behind.

Scrooge had often heard it said that Marley had no bowels, but he had never believed it until now.

No, nor did he believe it even now. Though he looked the phantom through and through, and saw it standing before him—though he felt the chilling influence of its death-cold eyes, and noticed the very texture of the folded kerchief bound about its head and chin—he was still incredulous.

"How now!" said Scrooge, caustic and cold as ever. "What do you want with me?"

"Much!"—Marley's voice, no doubt about it.

"Who are you?"

"Ask me who I *was*."

"Who *were* you then?"

"In life I was your partner, Jacob Marley."

"Can you—can you sit down?"

"I can."

"Do it, then."

Scrooge asked the question, because he didn't know whether a ghost so transparent might find himself in a condition to take a chair; and felt that, in the event of its being impossible, it might involve the necessity of an embarrassing explanation. But the ghost sat down on the opposite side of the fireplace, as if he were quite used to sitting there.

"You don't believe in me."

"I don't."

"What evidence would you have of my reality beyond that of your senses?"

"I don't know."

"Why do you doubt your senses?"

"Because a little thing affects them. A slight disorder of the stomach makes them cheats. You may be an undigested bit of beef, a blot of mustard, a crumb of cheese, a fragment of an underdone potato. There's more of gravy than of grave about you, whatever you are!"

Scrooge was not much in the habit of cracking jokes, nor did he feel in his heart by any means waggish then. The truth is that he tried to be smart, as a means of distracting his own attention, and keeping down his horror.

But how much greater was his horror when, the phantom taking off the bandage round its head, as if it were too warm to wear indoors, its lower jaw dropped down upon its breast!

"Mercy! Dreadful apparition, why do you trouble me? Why do spirits walk the earth, and why do they come to me?"

"It is required of every man that the spirit within him should walk abroad among his fellow men, and travel far and wide; and if that spirit goes not forth in life, it is condemned to do so after death. I cannot tell you all I would. A very little more is permitted to me. I cannot rest, I cannot stay, I cannot linger anywhere. My spirit never walked beyond our countinghouse—mark me!—in life my spirit never roved beyond the narrow limits of our money-changing hole; and weary journeys lie before me!"

"Seven years dead. And travelling all the time? You travel fast?"

"On the wings of the wind."

"You might have got over a great quantity of ground in seven years."

"O blind man, blind man! not to know that ages of incessant labour by immortal creatures for this earth must pass into eternity before the good of which it is susceptible is all developed. Not to know that any Christian spirit working kindly in its little sphere, whatever it may be, will find its mortal life too short for its vast means of usefulness. Not to know that no space of regret can make amends for one life's opportunities misused! Yet I was like this man; I once was like this man!"

"But you were always a good man of business, Jacob," faltered Scrooge, who now began to apply this to himself.

"Business!" cried the Ghost, wringing its hands again. "Mankind was my business. The common welfare was my business; charity, mercy, forbearance, benevolence, were all my business. The dealings of my trade were but a drop of water in the comprehensive ocean of my business!"

Scrooge was very much dismayed to hear the spectre going on at this rate, and began to quake exceedingly.

"Hear me! My time is nearly gone."

"I will. But don't be hard upon me! Don't be flowery, Jacob! Pray!"

"I am here tonight to warn you that you have yet a chance and hope of escaping my fate. A chance and hope of my procuring, Ebenezer."

"You were always a good friend to me. Thank'ee!"

"You will be haunted by Three Spirits."

"Is that the chance and hope you mentioned, Jacob? I—I think I'd rather not."

"It is required of every man that the spirit within him should walk abroad among his fellow men, if not in life then after death."

"Without their visits, you cannot hope to shun the path I tread. Expect the first tomorrow night, when the bell tolls one. Expect the second on the next night at the same hour. The third, upon the next night, when the last stroke of twelve has ceased to vibrate. Look to see me no more; and look that, for your own sake, you remember what has passed between us!"

It walked backward from him; and at every step it took, the window raised itself a little, so that, when the apparition reached it, it was wide open.

Scrooge closed the window, and examined the door by which the Ghost had entered. It was double-locked, as he had locked it with his own hands, and the bolts were undisturbed. Scrooge tried to say, "Humbug!" but stopped at the first syllable. And being, from the emotion he had undergone, or the fatigues of the day, or his glimpse of the invisible world, or the dull conversation of the Ghost, or the lateness of the hour, much in need of repose, he went straight to bed, without undressing, and fell asleep on the instant.

Scrooge wakes when the curtains of his bed are drawn aside by a strange figure, childlike but white-haired, who identifies himself as the Ghost of Christmas Past. "Your past," he explains to Scrooge, and he magically transports the old man to another place and time. He sees himself as a young clerk apprenticed to a jolly merchant named Fezziwig. When the business closes on Christmas Eve the apprentices help to clear the warehouse floor for a great party to which Fezziwig has invited both friends and employees. There is music and feasting, but the highlight of the evening is the merry dancing that goes on till nearly midnight.

Scrooge cannot help contrasting this kind man's treatment of his young apprentice with his own gruff words to his clerk a few hours earlier.

The next memory the ghost makes Scrooge relive is a less happy one. A somewhat older Scrooge, hard-working and beginning to taste success, hears a fair but sad-faced girl saying farewell to him.

"Another idol has displaced me," she says, ". . . I have seen your nobler aspirations fall off one by one, until the master passion, Gain, engrosses you. . . I release you. With a full heart, for the love of him you once were."

This is too painful; Scrooge begs the Ghost to leave him and he sinks back into heavy sleep.

The second spirit to visit Scrooge is a genial giant who carries a torch shaped like a horn of plenty, and who identifies himself as the Ghost of Christmas Present.

"Spirit, conduct me where you will," said Scrooge. "I went forth last night on compulsion, and I learnt a lesson which is working now. Tonight, if you have aught to teach me, let me profit by it."

"Touch my robe!"

Scrooge did as he was told, and held it fast.

The room and its contents all vanished instantly, and they stood in the city streets upon a snowy Christmas morning.

Scrooge and the Ghost passed on, invisible, straight to Scrooge's clerk's; and on the threshold of the door the Spirit smiled, and stopped to bless Bob Cratchit's dwelling with the sprinklings of his torch. Think of that! Bob had but fifteen "bob" a week himself; he pocketed on Saturdays but fifteen copies of his Christian name; and yet the Ghost of Christmas Present blessed his four-roomed house!

Then up rose Mrs. Cratchit, Cratchit's wife, dressed out but poorly in a twice-turned gown, but brave in ribbons, which are cheap and make a goodly show for sixpence; and she laid the cloth, assisted by Belinda Cratchit, second of her daughters, also brave in ribbons; while Master Peter Cratchit plunged a fork into the saucepan of potatoes, and, getting the corners of his monstrous shirt collar (Bob's private property, conferred upon his son and heir in honour of the day) into his mouth, rejoiced to find himself so gallantly attired, and yearned to show his linen in the fashionable Parks. And now two smaller Cratchits, boy and girl, came tearing in, screaming that outside the baker's they had smelt the goose, and known it for their own; and, basking in luxurious thoughts of sage and onion, these young Cratchits danced about the table, and exalted Master Peter Cratchit to the skies, while he (not proud, although

The heart is as visible as a dueler's mark, is the best dancer, the most often caught under mistletoe, the bearer of the yule log.

35

his collars nearly choked him) blew the fire, until the slow potatoes, bubbling up, knocked loudly at the saucepan lid to be let out and peeled.

"What has ever got your precious father then?" said Mrs. Cratchit. "And your brother Tiny Tim! And Martha warn't as late last Christmas day by half an hour!"

"Here's Martha, mother!" said a girl, appearing as she spoke.

"Here's Martha, mother!" cried the two young Cratchits. "Hurrah! There's *such* a goose, Martha!"

"Why, bless your heart alive, my dear, how late you are!" said Mrs. Cratchit, kissing her a dozen times, and taking off her shawl and bonnet for her.

"We'd a deal of work to finish up last night," replied the girl, "and had to clear away this morning, mother!"

"Well! Never mind so long as you are come," said Mrs. Cratchit. "Sit ye down before the fire, my dear, and have a warm, Lord bless ye!"

"No, no! There's father coming," cried the two young Cratchits, who were everywhere at once. "Hide, Martha, hide!"

So Martha hid herself, and in came little Bob, the father, with at least three feet of comforter, exclusive of the fringe, hanging down before him; and his threadbare clothes darned up and brushed, to look seasonable; and Tiny Tim upon his shoulder. Alas for Tiny Tim, he bore a little crutch, and had his limbs supported by an iron frame!

"Why, where's our Martha?" cried Bob Cratchit, looking round.

"Not coming," said Mrs. Cratchit.

"Not coming!" said Bob, with a sudden declension in his high spirits; for he had been Tim's blood horse all the way from church, and had come home rampant—"not coming upon Christmas day!"

Martha didn't like to see him disappointed, if it were only in joke; so she came out prematurely from behind the closet door, and ran into his arms, while the two young Cratchits hustled Tiny Tim, and bore him off into the wash house, that he might hear the pudding singing in the copper.

"And how did little Tim behave?" asked Mrs.

Cratchit, when she had rallied Bob on his credulity, and Bob had hugged his daughter to his heart's content.

"As good as gold," said Bob, "and better. Somehow he gets thoughtful, sitting by himself so much, and thinks the strangest things you ever heard. He told me, coming home, that he hoped the people saw him in the church, because he was a cripple, and it might be pleasant to them to remember, upon Christmas day, who made lame beggars walk and blind men see."

Bob's voice was tremulous when he told them this, and trembled more when he said that Tiny Tim was growing strong and hearty.

His active little crutch was heard upon the floor, and back came Tiny Tim before another word was spoken, escorted by his brother and sister to his stool beside the fire; and while Bob, turning up his cuffs—as if, poor fellow, they were capable of being made more shabby—compounded some hot mixture in a jug with gin and lemons, and stirred it round and round, and put it on the hob to simmer, Master Peter and the two ubiquitous young Cratchits went to fetch the goose, with which they soon returned in high procession.

Mrs. Cratchit made the gravy (ready beforehand in a little saucepan) hissing hot; Master Peter mashed the potatoes with incredible vigour; Miss Belinda sweetened up the applesauce; Martha dusted the hot plates; Bob took Tiny Tim beside him in a tiny corner at the table; the two young Cratchits set chairs for everybody, not forgetting themselves, and mounting guard upon their posts, crammed spoons into their mouths, lest they should shriek for goose before their turn came to be helped. At last the dishes were set on, and grace was said. It was succeeded by a breathless pause, as Mrs. Cratchit, looking slowly all along the carving knife, prepared to plunge it in the breast; but when she did, and when the long-expected gush of stuffing issued forth, one murmur of delight arose all round the board, and even Tiny Tim, excited by the two young Cratchits, beat on the table with the handle of his knife, and feebly cried, Hurrah!

There never was such a goose. Bob said he didn't believe there ever was such a goose cooked. Its tenderness and flavour, size and cheapness, were the themes of

universal admiration. Eked out by applesauce and mashed potatoes, it was a sufficient dinner for the whole family; indeed, as Mrs. Cratchit said with great delight (surveying one small atom of a bone upon the dish) they hadn't eaten it all at last! Yet everyone had had enough, and the youngest Cratchits in particular were steeped in sage and onion to the eyebrows! But now, the plates being changed by Miss Belinda, Mrs. Cratchit left the room alone—too nervous to bear witnesses—to take the pudding up, and bring it in.

Suppose it should not be done enough! Suppose it should break in turning out! Suppose somebody should have got over the wall of the backyard, and stolen it, while they were merry with the goose—a supposition at which the two young Cratchits became livid! All sorts of horrors were supposed.

Hallo! A great deal of steam! The pudding was out of the copper. A smell like a washing day! That was the cloth. A smell like an eating house and pastry cook's next door to each other, with a laundress's next door to that! That was the pudding! In half a minute Mrs. Cratchit entered—flushed but smiling proudly—with the pudding, like a speckled cannonball, so hard and firm, blazing in half of half a quartern of ignited brandy, and bedight with Christmas holly stuck into the top.

Oh, a wonderful pudding! Bob Cratchit said, and calmly too, that he regarded it as the greatest success achieved by Mrs. Cratchit since their marriage. Mrs. Cratchit said that now the weight was off her mind, she would confess she had had her doubts about the quantity of flour. Everybody had something to say about it, but nobody said or thought it was at all a small pudding for a large family. Any Cratchit would have blushed to hint at such a thing.

At last the dinner was all done, the cloth was cleared, the hearth swept, and the fire made up. The compound in the jug being tasted, and considered perfect, apples and oranges were put upon the table, and a shovelful of chestnuts on the fire.

Then all the Cratchit family drew round the hearth, in what Bob Cratchit called a circle, and at Bob Cratchit's elbow stood the family display of glass—two tumblers, and a small custard cup that was without a handle.

These held the hot stuff from the jug, however, as well as golden goblets would have done; and Bob served it out with beaming looks, while the chestnuts on the fire spluttered and crackled noisily. Then Bob proposed:

"A Merry Christmas to us all, my dears. God bless us!"

Which all the family reechoed.

"God bless us every one!" said Tiny Tim, the last of all.

He sat very close to his father's side, upon his little stool. Bob held his withered little hand in his, as if he loved the child, and wished to keep him by his side, and dreaded that he might be taken from him.

Scrooge raised his head speedily, on hearing his own name.

"Mr. Scrooge!" said Bob; "I'll give you Mr. Scrooge, the Founder of the Feast!"

"The Founder of the Feast indeed!" cried Mrs. Cratchit, reddening. "I wish I had him here. I'd give him a piece of my mind to feast upon, and I hope he'd have a good appetite for it."

"My dear," said Bob, "the children! Christmas day."

"It should be Christmas day, I am sure," said she, "on which one drinks the health of such an odious, stingy, hard, unfeeling man as Mr. Scrooge. You know he is, Robert! Nobody knows it better than you do, poor fellow!"

"My dear, " was Bob's mild answer, "Christmas day."

"I'll drink his health for your sake and the day's," said Mrs. Cratchit, "not for his. Long life to him! A merry Christmas and a happy New Year! He'll be very merry and very happy, I have no doubt!"

The children drank the toast after her. It was the first of their proceedings which had no heartiness in it. Tiny Tim drank it last of all, but he didn't care twopence for it. Scrooge was the Ogre of the family. The mention of his name cast a dark shadow on the party, which was not dispelled for full five minutes.

After it had passed away, they were ten times merrier than before, from the mere relief of Scrooge the Baleful being done with. Bob Cratchit told them how he had a situation in his eye for Master Peter, which would bring him, if obtained, full five and sixpence weekly. The two young Cratchits laughed tremendously at the idea of Peter's being a man of business; and Peter himself looked thoughtfully at the fire from between his collars, as if he were deliberating what particular investments he should favour when he came into the receipt of that bewildering income. Martha, who was a poor apprentice at a milliner's, then told them what kind of work she had to do, and how many hours she worked at a stretch, and how she meant to lie abed tomorrow morning for a good long rest; tomorrow being a holiday she passed at home. Also how she had seen a countess and a lord some days before, and how the lord "was much about as tall as Peter"; at which Peter pulled up his collars so high that you couldn't have seen his head if you had been there. All this time the chestnuts and the jug went round and round; and by and by they had a song, about a lost child travelling in the snow, from Tiny Tim, who had a plaintive little voice, and sang it very well indeed.

There was nothing of high mark in this. They were not a handsome family; they were not well dressed; their shoes were far from being waterproof; their clothes were scanty; and Peter might have known, and very likely did, the inside of a pawnbroker's. But they were happy, grateful, pleased with one another, and contented with the time; and when they faded, and looked happier yet in the bright sprinklings of the Spirit's torch at parting, Scrooge had his eye upon them, and especially on Tiny Tim, until the last.

It was a great surprise to Scrooge, as this scene vanished, to hear a hearty laugh. It was a much greater surprise to Scrooge to recognize it as his own nephew's, and to find himself in a bright, dry, gleaming room, with the Spirit standing smiling by his side, and looking at that same nephew.

It is a fair, evenhanded, noble adjustment of things, that while there is infection in disease and sorrow, there is nothing in the world so irresistibly contagious as laughter and good humour. When Scrooge's nephew laughed, Scrooge's niece by marriage laughed as heartily as he. And their assembled friends, being not a bit behindhand, laughed out lustily.

"He said that Christmas was a humbug, as I live!" cried Scrooge's nephew. "He believed it too!"

"More shame for him, Fred!" said Scrooge's niece, indignantly. Bless those women! they never do anything by halves. They are always in earnest.

She was very pretty; exceedingly pretty. With a dimpled, surprised-looking, capital face; a ripe little mouth that seemed made to be kissed—as no doubt it was; all kinds of good little dots about her chin, that melted into one another when she laughed; and the sunniest pair of eyes you ever saw in any little creature's head. Altogether she was what you would have called provoking, but satisfactory, too. Oh, perfectly satisfactory.

"He's a comical old fellow," said Scrooge's nephew, "that's the truth; and not so pleasant as he might be. However, his offenses carry their own punishment, and I have nothing to say against him. Who suffers by his ill whims? Himself, always. Here he takes it into his head to dislike us, and he won't come and dine with us. What's the consequence? He doesn't lose much of a dinner."

"Indeed, I think he loses a very good dinner," interrupted Scrooge's niece. Everybody else said the same, and they must be allowed to have been competent judges, because they had just had dinner; and, with the dessert upon the table, were clustered round the fire, by lamplight.

"Well, I am very glad to hear it," said Scrooge's nephew, "because I haven't any great faith in these young housekeepers. What do you say, Topper?"

Topper clearly had his eye on one of Scrooge's niece's sisters, for he answered that a bachelor was a wretched outcast, who had no right to express an opinion on the subject. Whereat Scrooge's niece's sister—the plump one with lace tucker; not the one with the roses—blushed.

After tea they had some music. For they were a musical family, and knew what they were about, when they sang a Glee or Catch, I can assure you—especially Topper, who could growl in the bass like a good one.

When this scene vanishes the Ghost of Christmas Yet to Come—a stooped figure shrouded in black—arrives to

". . . while there is infection in disease and sorrow, there is nothing in the world so irresistibly contagious as good humor."

39

conduct Scrooge on yet another tour. This time, Scrooge knows, he will be shown glimpses of his own future. He shudders at the ghost's touch.

"I fear you more than any spectre I have seen," Scrooge says. *"But I know your purpose is to do me good, and as I hope to live to be another man from what I am, I am prepared to bear you company, and do it with a thankful heart."*

Then the spirit transports Scrooge to a city street where he hears men discussing a death, then to a pawn shop where thieves are selling the clothing and bedding of the dead man, and finally to a plundered bedroom where the dead man lies alone, for there is no one to mourn him or sit with the body. The face is concealed but Scrooge guesses that if it were visible he might see his own features.

"Spirit!" he cries. "This is a fearful place. In leaving it, I shall not leave its lesson."

Scrooge is saddened by this grim vision, and he begs the spirit to show him some tenderness connected with death. In response. . . .

The Ghost conducted him to poor Bob Cratchit's house—the dwelling he had visited before—and found the mother and the children seated round the fire.

Quiet. Very quiet. The noisy little Cratchits were as still as statues in one corner, and sat looking up at Peter, who had a book before him. The mother and her daughters were engaged in needlework. But surely they were very quiet!

" 'And he took a child, and set him in the midst of them.' "

Where had Scrooge heard these words? He had not dreamed them. The boy must have read them out, as he and the Spirit crossed the threshold. Why did he not go on?

The mother laid her work upon the table, and put her hand up to her face. "The colour hurts my eyes," she said.

The colour? Ah, poor Tiny Tim!

"They're better now again. It makes them weak by candlelight; and I wouldn't show weak eyes to your

father when he comes home. It must be near his time."

"Past it rather," Peter answered, shutting up his book. "But I think he has walked a little slower than he used, these few last evenings, mother."

"I have known him walk with—I have known him walk with Tiny Tim upon his shoulder, very fast indeed."

"And so have I," cried Peter. "Often."

"And so have I," exclaimed another. So had all.

"But he was very light to carry, and his father loved him so, that it was no trouble—no trouble. And there is your father at the door!"

She hurried out to meet him; and little Bob in his comforter—he had need of it, poor fellow—came in. His tea was ready for him on the hob, and they all tried who should help him to it most. Then the two young Cratchits got upon his knees and laid, each child, a little cheek against his face, as if they said, "Don't mind it, father. Don't be grieved!"

Bob was very cheerful with them, and spoke pleasantly to all the family. He looked at the work upon the table, and praised the industry and speed of Mrs. Cratchit and the girls. They would be done long before Sunday, he said.

"Sunday! You went today, then, Robert?"

"Yes, my dear," returned Bob. "I wish you could have gone. It would have done you good to see how green a place it is. But you'll see it often. I promised him that I would walk there on a Sunday. My little, little child! My little child!"

He broke down all at once. He couldn't help it. If he could have helped it, he and his child would have been further apart, perhaps, than they were.

"Spectre," said Scrooge, "something informs me that our parting moment is at hand. I know it, but I know not how. Tell me what man that was, with the covered face, whom we saw lying dead?"

The Ghost of Christmas Yet to Come conveyed him to a dismal, wretched, ruinous churchyard.

The Spirit stood amongst the graves, and pointed down to One.

"Before I draw nearer to that stone to which you

"It was always said of him that he knew how to keep Christmas well, if any man possessed that knowledge. May that be said of us."

41

point, answer me one question. Are these the shadows of the things that Will be, or are they shadows of the things that May be only?"

Still the Ghost pointed downward to the grave by which it stood.

"Men's courses will foreshadow certain ends, to which, if persevered in, they must lead. But if the courses be departed from, the ends will change. Say it is thus with what you show me!"

The Spirit was immovable as ever.

Scrooge crept towards it, trembling as he went; and, following the finger, read upon the stone of the neglected grave his own name—*Ebenezer Scrooge.*

"Am *I* that man who lay upon the bed? No, Spirit! Oh no, no! Spirit! hear me! I am not the man I was. I will not be the man I must have been but for this intercourse. Why show me this, if I am past all hope? Assure me that I yet may change these shadows you have shown me by an altered life."

For the first time the kind hand faltered.

"I will honour Christmas in my heart, and try to keep it all the year. I will live in the Past, the Present, and the Future. The Spirits of all three shall strive within me. I will not shut out the lessons that they teach. Oh, tell me I may sponge away the writing on this stone!"

Holding up his hands in one last prayer to have his fate reversed, he saw an alteration in the Phantom's hood and dress. It shrank, collapsed, and dwindled down into a bedpost.

Yes, and the bedpost was his own. The bed was his own, the room was his own. Best and happiest of all, the Time before him was his own, to make amends in!

He was checked in his transports by the churches ringing out the lustiest peals he had ever heard.

Running to the window, he opened it, and put out his head. No fog, no mist, no night; clear, bright, stirring, golden day.

"What's today?" cried Scrooge, calling downward to a boy in Sunday clothes, who perhaps had loitered in to look about him.

"*Eh?*"

"What's today, my fine fellow?"

"Today! Why, *Christmas day*."

"It's Christmas day! I haven't missed it. Hallo, my fine fellow!"

"Hallo!"

"Do you know the Poulterer's, in the next street but one, at the corner?"

"I should hope I did."

"An intelligent boy! A remarkable boy! Do you know whether they've sold the prize Turkey that was hanging up there? Not the little prize turkey—the big one?"

"What, the one as big as me?"

"What a delightful boy! It's a pleasure to talk to him. Yes, my buck!"

"It's hanging there now."

"Is it? Go and buy it."

"Walk-*er*!" exclaimed the boy.

"No, no, I am in earnest. Go and buy it, and tell 'em to bring it here, that I may give them the direction where to take it. Come back with the man, and I'll give you a shilling. Come back with him in less than five minutes, and I'll give you half a crown!"

The boy was off like a shot.

"I'll send it to Bob Cratchit's! He shan't know who sends it. It's twice the size of Tiny Tim. Joe Miller never made such a joke as sending it to Bob's will be!"

The hand in which he wrote the address was not a steady one; but write it he did, somehow, and went downstairs to open the street door, ready for the coming of the poulterer's man.

It *was* a Turkey! He never could have stood upon his legs, that bird. He would have snapped 'em short off in a minute, like sticks of sealing wax.

Scrooge dressed himself "all in his best," and at last got out into the streets. The people were by this time pouring forth, as he had seen them with the Ghost of Christmas Present; and, walking with his hands behind him, Scrooge regarded everyone with a delighted smile. He looked so irresistibly pleasant, in a word, that three or four good-humoured fellows said, "Good morning, sir! A merry Christmas to you!" And Scrooge said often afterwards that, of all the blithe sounds he had ever heard, those were the blithest in his ears.

In the afternoon, he turned his steps toward his nephew's house.

He passed the door a dozen times, before he had the courage to knock. But he made a dash, and did it.

"Is your master at home, my dear?" said Scrooge to the girl. Nice girl! Very.

"Yes, sir."

"Where is he, my love?"

"He's in the dining room, sir, along with mistress."

"He knows me," said Scrooge, with his hand already on the dining-room lock. "I'll go in here, my dear."

"Fred!"

"Why, bless my soul!" cried Fred, "who's that?"

"It's I. Your uncle Scrooge. I have come to dinner. Will you let me in, Fred?"

Let him in! It is a mercy he didn't shake his arm off. He was at home in five minutes. Nothing could be heartier. His niece looked just the same. So did Topper when *he* came. So did the plump sister when *she* came. So did everyone when *they* came. Wonderful party, wonderful games, wonderful unanimity, and happiness!

". . . in his ears, blithe sounds."

But he was early at the office next morning. Oh, he was early there. If he could only be there first, and catch Bob Cratchit coming late! That was the thing he had set his heart upon.

And he did it. The clock struck nine. No Bob. A quarter past. No Bob. Bob was full eighteen minutes and a half behind his time. Scrooge sat with his door wide open, that he might see him come into the tank.

Bob's hat was off before he opened the door; his comforter too. He was on the stool in a jiffy; driving away with his pen, as if he were trying to overtake nine o'clock.

"Hallo!" growled Scrooge, in his accustomed voice, as near as he could possibly feign it. "What do you mean by coming here to my office at this time of the day?"

"I am very sorry, sir. I *am* behind my time."

"You are? Yes. I think you are. Step this way if you please."

"It's only once a year, sir. It shall not be repeated. I was making rather merry yesterday, sir."

"Now, I'll tell you what, my friend. I am not going to stand this sort of thing any longer. And therefore," Scrooge continued, leaping from his stool, and giving Bob such a dig in the waistcoat that he staggered back into the tank again—"and therefore I am about to raise your salary!"

Bob trembled, and got a little nearer to the ruler.

"A merry Christmas, Bob!" said Scrooge, with an earnestness that could not be mistaken, as he clapped him on the back. "A merrier Christmas, Bob, my good fellow, than I have given you for many a year! I'll raise your salary, and endeavour to assist your struggling family, and we will discuss your affairs this very afternoon, over a Christmas bowl of smoking bishop. Make up the fires, and buy a second coal-scuttle before you dot another *i*, Bob!!"

Scrooge was better than his word. He did it all, and infinitely more; and to Tiny Tim, who did *not* die, he was a second father. He became as good a friend, as good a master, and as good a man as the good old city knew, or any other good old city, town, or borough in the good old world. Some people laughed to see the alteration in him; but his heart laughed, and that was enough.

He had no further intercourse with Spirits, but lived in that respect upon the Total Abstinence Principle ever afterwards; and it was always said of him that he knew how to keep Christmas well, if any man alive possessed the knowledge. May that be truly said of us, and all of us! And so, as Tiny Tim observed, God Bless Us, Every One!

Hans Christian Andersen
The Fir Tree

Out in the forest stood a pretty little Fir Tree. It had a good place; it could have sunlight, air there was in plenty, and all around grew many larger comrades—pines as well as firs. But the little Fir Tree wished ardently to become greater. It did not care for the warm sun and the fresh air; it took no notice of the peasant children, who went about talking together, when they had come out to look for strawberries and raspberries. Often they came with a whole potful, or had strung berries on a straw; then they would sit down by the little Fir Tree and say, "How pretty and small that one is!" and the Fir Tree did not like to hear that at all.

Next year he had grown a great joint, and the following year he was longer still, for in fir trees one can always tell by the number of rings they have how many years they have been growing.

"Oh, if I were only as great a tree as the other!" sighed the little Fir, "then I would spread my branches far around, and look out from my crown into the wide world. The birds would then build nests in my boughs, and when the wind blew I could nod just as grandly as the others yonder."

It took no pleasure in the sunshine, in the birds, and in the red clouds that went sailing over him morning and evening.

When it was winter, and the snow lay all around, white and sparkling, a hare would often come jumping along, and spring right over the little Fir Tree. Oh! this made him so angry. But two winters went by, and when the third came the little Tree had grown so tall that the hare was obliged to run around it.

"Oh! to grow, to grow, and become old; that's the only fine thing in the world," thought the Tree.

In the autumn woodcutters always came and felled a few of the largest trees; that was done this year too, and the little Fir Tree, that was now quite well grown, shuddered with fear, for the great stately trees fell to the ground with a crash, and their branches were cut off, so that the trees looked quite naked, long, and slender—they could hardly be recognized. But then they were laid upon wagons, and horses dragged them away out of the wood. Where were they going? What destiny awaited them in the unknown world that lies beyond the forest?

In the spring, when the Swallows and the Stork came, the Tree asked them, "Do you know where they were taken? Did you not meet them?"

The Swallows knew nothing about it, but the Stork looked thoughtful, nodded his head, and said:

"Yes, I think so. I met many new ships when I flew out of Egypt; on this ships were stately masts; I fancy these were the trees. They smelled like fir. I can assure you they're stately—very stately."

"Oh that I were only big enough to go over the sea! What kind of thing is this sea, and how does it look?"

"It would take too long to explain all that," said the Stork, and he went away.

"Rejoice in thy youth," said the Sunbeams; "rejoice in thy fresh growth, and in the young life that is within thee."

And the wind kissed the Tree, and the dew wept tears upon it; but the Fir Tree did not understand that.

When Christmastime approached, quite young trees were felled, sometimes trees which were neither so old nor so large as this Fir Tree, that never rested, but always wanted to go away. These young trees, which were always the most beautiful, kept all their branches; they were put upon wagons, and horses dragged them away out of the wood.

"Where are they all going?" asked the Fir Tree. "They are not greater than I—indeed, one of them was much smaller. Why do they keep all their branches? Whither are they taken?"

"We know that! We know that!" chirped the Sparrows. "Yonder in the town we looked in at the windows. We know where they go. Oh! they are dressed up in the greatest pomp and splendor that can be imagined. We have looked in at the windows, and have perceived that they are planted in the middle of a warm room, and adorned with the most beautiful things—gilt apples, honey cakes, playthings, and many hundred candles."

"And then?" asked the Fir Tree, and trembled through all its branches. "And then? What happens then?"

"Why, we have not seen anything more. But it was

Christmas is the time of the nose.
The clean frost of the forest, the sharp green
of cedar and fir scent the joyous season.

From the forests, from roadside stands, on car tops, on backs, in little red wagons, the tree reaches out with branches of happiness.

incomparable, all the warm brightness and the beauty."

"Perhaps I may be destined to tread this glorious path one day!" cried the Fir Tree, rejoicingly. "That is even better than traveling across the sea. How painfully I long for it! If it were only Christmas now! Now I am great and grown up, like the rest who were led away last year. Oh, if I were only on the carriage! If I were only in the warm room, among all the pomp and splendor! And then? Yes, then something even better will come, something far more charming, or else why should they adorn me so? There must be something grander, something greater still to come; but what? Oh! I'm suffering, I'm longing! I don't know myself what is the matter with me!"

"Rejoice in us," said Air and Sunshine. "Rejoice in thy fresh youth here in the woodland."

But the Fir Tree did not rejoice at all, but it grew and grew; winter and summer it stood there, green, dark green. The people who saw it said, "That's a handsome

tree!" and at Christmastime it was felled before any one of the others. The ax cut deep into its marrow, and the tree fell to the ground with a sigh; it felt a pain, a sensation of faintness, and could not think at all of happiness, for it was sad at parting from its home, from the place where it had grown up; it knew that it should never again see the dear old companions, the little bushes and flowers all around—perhaps not even the birds. The parting was not at all agreeable.

The Tree only came to itself when it was unloaded in a yard, with other trees, and heard a man say:

"This one is famous; we want only this one!"

Now two servants came in gay liveries, and carried the Fir Tree into a large, beautiful saloon. All around the walls were hung pictures, and by the great stove stood large Chinese vases with lions on the covers; there were rocking chairs, silken sofas, great tables covered with picture books, and toys worth a hundred times a hun-

Christmas trees are a beautiful importation from Germany.
The custom of having them is now widespread, even in Puritan New England.
What a forest of brilliantly bedecked evergreen would be visible
were all the firs that are to be laden and lighted this year brought together;
and what a story that forest would tell of busy hands, and buzzing consultations;
of secrets it was hard to keep; of restless expectations and wistful looks;
of the joy of givers and the gladness of receivers;
of, in a word, the merry sympathy of warm affection.

THE SATURDAY EVENING POST, DECEMBER 28, 1867

Against the dark boughs the candles glow with the hopes and promises of the new year. Even the most cynical men still resolve to change.

dred dollars, at least the children said so. And the Fir Tree was put into a great tub filled with sand; but no one could see that it was a tub, for it was hung round with green cloth, and stood on a large, many-colored carpet. Oh, how the Tree trembled! What was to happen now? The servants, and the young ladies also, decked it out. On one branch they hung little nets, cut out of colored paper; every net was filled with sweetmeats; golden apples and walnuts hung down, as if they grew there, and more than a hundred little candles, red, white, and blue, were fastened to the different boughs. Dolls that looked exactly like real people—the tree had never seen such before—swung among the foliage, and high on the summit of the Tree was fixed a tinsel star. It was splendid, particularly splendid.

"This evening," said all, "this evening it will shine."

"Oh," thought the Tree, "that it were evening already! Oh, that the lights may be soon lit up! When may that be done? I wonder if trees will come out of the forest to look at me? Will the sparrows fly against the panes? Shall I grow fast here, and stand adorned in summer and winter?"

Yes, he did not guess badly. But he had a complete backache from mere longing, and the backache is just as bad for a Tree as the headache for a person.

At last the candles were lighted. What a brilliance, what splendor! The Tree trembled so in all its branches that one of the candles set fire to a green twig, and it was scorched.

"Heaven preserve us!" cried the young ladies; and they hastily put the fire out.

Now the Tree might not even tremble. Oh, that was terrible! It was so afraid of setting fire to some of its ornaments and it was quite bewildered with all the brilliance. And now the folding doors were thrown open, and a number of children rushed in as if they would have overturned the whole Tree; the older people followed more deliberately. The little ones stood quite silent, but only for a minute; then they shouted till the room rang: they danced gleefully round the Tree, and one present after another was plucked from it.

"What are they about?" thought the Tree. "What's going to be done? What wonderful things happen next?"

And the candles burned down to the twigs, and as they burned down they were extinguished, and then the children received permission to plunder the Tree. Oh! they rushed in upon it, so that every branch cracked again: if it had not been fastened by the top and by the golden star to the ceiling, it would have fallen down.

The children danced about with their pretty toys. No one looked at the Tree except one old man, who came up and peeped among the branches, but only to see if a fig or an apple had not been forgotten.

"A story! A story!" shouted the children; and they drew a little fat man toward the tree; and he sat down just beneath it—"for then we shall be in the green wood," said he, "and the tree may have the advantage of listening to my tale. But I can only tell one. Will you hear the story of Ivede-Avede, or of Klumpey-Dumpey, who fell downstairs, and still was raised up to honor and married the Princess?"

"Ivede-Avede!" cried some, "Klumpey-Dumpey!" cried others, and there was a great crying and shouting. Only the Fir Tree was quite silent, and thought, "Shall I not be in it? Shall I have nothing to do in it?" But he had been in the evening's amusement, and had done what was required of him.

And the fat man told about Klumpey-Dumpey who fell downstairs, and yet was raised to honor and married the Princess. And the children clapped their hands, and cried, "Tell another! tell another!" for they wanted to hear about Ivede-Avede; but they only got the story of Klumpey-Dumpey. The Fir Tree stood quite silent and thoughtful; never had the birds in the wood told such a story as that. Klumpey-Dumpey fell downstairs, and yet came to honor and married the Princess!

"Yes, so it happens in the world!" thought the Fir Tree, and believed it must be true, because that was such a nice man who told it. "Well, who can know? Perhaps I shall fall downstairs, too, and marry a Princess!" And it looked forward with pleasure to being adorned again, the next evening, with candles and toys, gold and fruit. "Tomorrow I shall not tremble," it thought.

"I will rejoice in all my splendor. Tomorrow I shall

48

One thing is certain, fate would never bestow a fire upon this engine company at this particular moment.

hear the story of Klumpey-Dumpey again, and perhaps that of Ivede-Avede, too."

And the Tree stood all night quiet and thoughtful.

In the morning the servants and the chambermaid came in.

"Now my splendor will begin afresh," thought the Tree. But they dragged him out of the room, and upstairs to the garret, and here they put him in a dark corner where no daylight shone.

"What's the meaning of this?" thought the Tree. "What am I to do here? What is to happen?"

And he leaned against the wall, and thought, and

thought. And he had time enough, for days and nights went by and nobody came up; and when at length someone came, it was only to put some great boxes in a corner. Now the Tree stood quite hidden away, and the supposition is that it was quite forgotten.

"Now it's winter outside," thought the Tree. "The earth is hard and covered with snow, and people cannot plant me; therefore I suppose I'm to be sheltered here until spring comes. How considerate that is! How good people are! If it were only not so dark here, and so terribly solitary!—not even a little hare? That was pretty out there in the wood, when the snow lay thick and the

Christmas is a group effort in small towns across the country, a pouring forth of community spirit.

hare sprang past; yes, even when he jumped over me; but then I did not like it. It is terribly lonely up here!"

"Peep! peep!" said a little Mouse, and crept forward, and then came another little one. They smelled at the Fir Tree, and then slipped among the branches.

"It's horribly cold," said the two little Mice, "or else it would be comfortable here. Don't you think so, you old Fir Tree?"

"I'm not old at all," said the Fir Tree. "There are many much older than I."

"Where do you come from?" asked the Mice. "And what do you know?" They were dreadfully inquisitive.

"Tell us about the most beautiful spot on earth. Have you been there? Have you been in the storeroom, where cheeses lie on the shelves, and hams hang from the ceiling, where one dances on tallow candles, and goes in thin and comes out fat?"

"I don't know that," replied the Tree; "but I know the wood, where the sun shines and the birds sing."

And then it told all about its youth.

And the little Mice had never heard anything of the kind; and they listened and said:

"What a number of things you have seen! How happy you must have been!"

51

"I?" replied the Fir Tree; and it thought about what it had told. "Yes, those were really quite happy times." But then he told of the Christmas Eve when he had been hung with sweetmeats and candles.

"Oh!" said the little Mice, "how happy you have been, you old Fir Tree!"

"I'm not old at all," said the Tree. "I only came out of the wood this winter. I'm only rather backward in my growth."

"What splendid stories you can tell!" said the little Mice.

And next night they came with four other little Mice, to hear what the Tree had to relate; and the more it said, the more clearly did it remember everything, and thought, "Those were quite merry days! But they may come again. Klumpey-Dumpey fell downstairs, and yet he married the Princess. Perhaps I may marry a Princess too!" And the Fir Tree thought of a pretty little Birch Tree that grew out in the forest; and for the Fir Tree, that Birch was a real Princess.

"Who's Klumpey-Dumpey?" asked the little Mice.

And then the Fir Tree told the whole story. It could remember every single word; and the little Mice were ready to leap to the very top of the tree with pleasure. Next night a great many more Mice came, and on Sunday two Rats even appeared; but these thought the story was not pretty, and the little Mice were sorry for that, for now they also did not like it so much as before.

"Do you know only one story?" asked the Rats.

"Only that one," replied the Tree. "I heard that on the happiest evening of my life; I did not think then how happy I was."

"That's a very miserable story. Don't you know any about bacon and tallow candles—a storeroom story?"

"No," said the Tree.

"Then we'd rather not hear you," said the Rats.

And they went back to their own people. The little Mice at last stayed away also; and then the Tree sighed and said:

"It was very nice when they sat round me, the merry little Mice, and listened when I spoke to them. Now that's past too. But I shall remember to be pleased when they come to take me out of this dark, tiresome place."

But when did that happen? Why, it was one morning that people came and rummaged in the garret: the boxes were put away, and the Tree brought out; they certainly threw him rather roughly on the floor, but a servant dragged him away at once to the stairs, where the daylight shone.

"Now life is beginning again!" thought the Tree.

It felt the fresh air and the first sunbeams, and now it was out in the courtyard. Everything passed so quickly that the Tree quite forgot to look at itself, there was so much to look at all round. The courtyard was close to a garden, and here everything was blooming; the roses hung fresh and fragrant over the little paling, the linden trees were in blossom, and the swallows cried, "Quinze-wit! quinze-wit! my husband's come!" But it was not the Fir Tree that they meant.

"Now I shall live!" said the Tree, rejoicingly, and spread its branches far out; but, alas! they were all withered and yellow; and it lay in the corner among nettles and weeds. The tinsel star was still upon it, and shone in the bright sunshine.

In the courtyard a couple of the merry children were playing who had danced round the tree at Christmastime, and had rejoiced over it. One of the youngest ran up and tore off the golden star.

"Look what is sticking to the ugly old fir tree!" said the child, and he trod upon the branches till they cracked again under his boots.

And the Tree looked at all the blooming flowers and the splendor of the garden, and then looked at itself, and wished it had remained in the dark corner of the garret; it thought of its fresh youth in the wood, of the merry Christmas Eve, and of the little Mice which had listened so pleasantly to the story of Klumpey-Dumpey.

"Past! past!" said the old Tree. "Had I but rejoiced when I could have done so! Past! Past!"

And the servant came and chopped the Tree into little pieces; a whole bundle lay there; it blazed brightly under the great brewing copper, and it sighed deeply, and each sigh was like a little shot; and the children who were at play there ran up and seated themselves at the fire, looked into it, and cried, "Puff! puff!" But at each explosion, which was a deep sigh, the Tree thought of a summer day in the woods, or of a winter night there, when the stars beamed; he thought of Christmas Eve and of Klumpey Dumpey, the only story he had ever heard or knew how to tell; and then the Tree was burned.

The boys played in the garden, and the youngest had on his breast a golden star, which the Tree had worn on its happiest evening. Now that was past, and the Tree's life was past, and the story is past too: past! past!—and that's the way with all stories.

The memory of Christmas is as sweet as the thirst for it; the respite from school, master and books, is manna to live on.

O. Henry

The Gift of the Magi

One dollar and eighty-seven cents. That was all. And sixty cents was in pennies. Pennies saved one and two at a time by bulldozing the grocer and the vegetable man and the butcher until one's cheeks burned with the silent imputation of parsimony that such close dealing implied. Three times Della counted it. One dollar and eighty-seven cents. And the next day would be Christmas.

There was clearly nothing to do but flop down on the shabby little couch and howl. So Della did it. Which instigates the moral reflection that life is made up of sobs, sniffles and smiles, with sniffles predominating.

While the mistress of the home is gradually subsiding from the first stage to the second, take a look at the home. A furnished flat at $8.00 per week. It did not exactly beggar description, but it certainly had that word on the lookout for the mendicancy squad.

In the vestibule below was a letter box into which no letter would go, and an electric button from which no mortal finger could coax a ring. Also appertaining thereunto was a card bearing the name "Mr. James Dillingham Young."

The "Dillingham" had been flung to the breeze during a former period of prosperity when its possessor was being paid $30 per week. Now, when the income was shrunk to $20, the letters of "Dillingham" looked blurred, as though they were thinking seriously of contracting to a modest and unassuming D. But whenever Mr. James Dillingham Young came home and reached his flat above he was called "Jim" and greatly hugged by Mrs. James Dillingham Young, already introduced to you as Della. Which is all very good.

Della finished her cry and attended to her cheeks with the powder rag. She stood by the window and looked out dully at a gray cat walking a gray fence in a gray backyard. Tomorrow would be Christmas Day, and she had only $1.87 with which to buy Jim a present. She had been saving every penny she could for months, with this result. Twenty dollars a week doesn't go far. Expenses had been greater than she had calculated. They always are. Only $1.87 to buy a present for Jim. Her Jim. Many a happy hour she had spent planning for something nice for him. Something fine and rare and sterling—something just a little bit near to being worthy of the honor of being owned by James Dillingham Young.

There was a pier-glass between the windows of the room. Perhaps you have seen a pier-glass in an $8.00 flat. A very thin and very agile person may, by observing his reflection in a rapid sequence of longitudinal strips, obtain a fairly accurate conception of his looks. Della, being slender, had mastered the art.

Suddenly she whirled from the window and stood before the glass. Her eyes were shining brilliantly, but her face had lost its color within twenty seconds. Rapidly she pulled down her hair and let it fall to its full length.

Now, there were two possessions of the James Dillingham Youngs in which they both took a mighty pride. One was Jim's gold watch that had been his father's and his grandfather's. The other was Della's hair. Had the Queen of Sheba lived in the flat across the airshaft, Della would have let her hair hang out the window some day to dry just to depreciate Her Majesty's jewels and gifts. Had King Solomon been the janitor, with all his treasures piled up in the basement, Jim would have pulled out his watch every time he passed, just to see him pluck at his beard from envy.

So now Della's beautiful hair fell about her, rippling and shining like a cascade of brown waters. It reached

The holiday mood was a sentimental one, in the early 1900's.

The beautiful tresses, thick and shining, were the crown of Della's happiness, a happiness based on the happiness they gave her Jim.

55

below her knee and made itself almost a garment for her. And then she did it up again nervously and quickly. Once she faltered for a minute and stood still while a tear or two splashed on the worn red carpet.

On went her old brown jacket; on went her old brown hat.

With a whirl of skirts and with the brilliant sparkle still in her eyes, she fluttered out the door and down the stairs to the street.

Where she stopped the sign read: "Mme. Sofronie. Hair Goods of All Kinds."

One flight up Della ran, and collected herself, panting. Madame, large, too white, chilly, hardly looked the "Sofronie."

"Will you buy my hair?" asked Della.

"I buy hair," said Madame. "Take yer hat off and let's have a sight at the looks of it."

Down rippled the brown cascade.

"Twenty dollars," said Madame, lifting the mass with a practiced hand.

"Give it to me quick," said Della.

Oh, and the next two hours tripped by on rosy wings. Forget the hashed metaphor. She was ransacking the stores for Jim's present.

She found it at last. It surely had been made for Jim and no one else. There was no other like it in any of the stores, and she had turned all of them inside out. It was a platinum fob chain simple and chaste in design, properly proclaiming its value by substance alone and not by meretricious ornamentation—as all good things should do. It was even worthy of The Watch. As soon as she saw it she knew that it must be Jim's. It was like him. Quietness and value—the description applied to both. Twenty-one dollars they took from her for it, and she hurried home with the eighty-seven cents. With that chain on his watch Jim might be properly anxious about the time in any company.

Grand as the watch was, he sometimes looked at it on the sly on account of the old leather strap that he used in place of a chain.

When Della reached home her intoxication gave way a little to prudence and reason. She got out her curling irons and lighted the gas and went to work repairing the ravages made by generosity added to love. Which is always a tremendous task, dear friends—a mammoth task.

Within forty minutes her head was covered with tiny, close-lying curls that made her look wonderfully like a truant schoolboy. She looked at her reflection in the mirror long, carefully, and critically.

"If Jim doesn't kill me," she said to herself, "before he takes a second look at me, he'll say I look like a Coney Island chorus girl. But what could I do—oh! what could I do with a dollar and eighty-seven cents?"

At seven o'clock the coffee was made and the frying pan was on the back of the stove hot and ready to cook the chops.

Jim was never late. Della doubled the fob chain in her hand and sat on the corner of the table near the door that he always entered. Then she heard his step on the stair away down on the first flight, and she turned white for just a moment. She had a habit of saying little silent prayers about the simplest everyday things, and now she whispered, "Please God, make him think I am still pretty."

The door opened and Jim stepped in and closed it. He looked thin and very serious. Poor fellow, he was only twenty-two—and to be burdened with a family! He needed a new overcoat and he was without gloves.

Jim stopped inside the door, as immovable as a setter at the scent of quail. His eyes were fixed upon Della, and there was an expression in them that she could not read, and it terrified her. It was not anger, nor surprise, nor disapproval, nor horror, nor any of the sentiments that she had been prepared for.

He simply stared at her fixedly with that peculiar expression on his face.

Della wriggled off the table and went for him.

"Jim, darling," she cried, "don't look at me that way. I had my hair cut off and sold it because I couldn't have lived through Christmas without giving you a present. It'll grow out again—you won't mind, will you? I just had to do it. My hair grows awfully fast. Say 'Merry Christmas!' Jim, and let's be happy. You don't know what a nice, what a beautiful, wonderful gift I've got for you."

"You've cut off your hair?" asked Jim, laboriously, as if he had not arrived at that patent fact yet even after the hardest mental labor.

"Cut if off and sold it," said Della. "Don't you like me just as well, anyhow? I'm me without my hair, ain't I?"

Jim looked about the room curiously.

"You say your hair is gone?" he said, with an air almost of idiocy.

"You needn't look for it," said Della. "It's sold, I tell you—sold and gone, too. It's Christmas Eve, boy. Be good to me, for it went for you. Maybe the hairs of my head were numbered," she went on with a sudden serious sweetness, "but nobody could ever count my love for you. Shall I put the chops on, Jim?"

Out of his trance Jim seemed quickly to wake. He enfolded his Della. For ten seconds let us regard with discreet scrutiny some inconsequential object in the other direction.

Eight dollars a week or a million a year—what is the difference?

A mathematician or a wit would give you the wrong answer. The Magi brought valuable gifts, but that was not among them. This dark assertion will be illuminated later on.

Jim drew a package from his overcoat pocket and threw it upon the table.

"Don't make any mistake, Dell," he said, "about me. I don't think there's anything in the way of a haircut or a shave or a shampoo that could make me like my girl any less.

"But if you'll unwrap that package you may see why you had me going a while at first."

White fingers and nimble tore at the string and paper. And then an ecstatic scream of joy; and then, alas! a quick feminine change to hysterical tears and wails, necessitating the immediate employment of all the comforting powers of the lord of the flat.

For there lay The Combs—the set of combs, side and back, that Della had worshipped for long in a Broadway window.

Beautiful combs, pure tortoise shell, with jeweled rims—just the shade to wear in the beautiful vanished hair.

They were expensive combs, she knew, and her heart had simply craved and yearned over them without the least hope of possession. And now, they were hers, but the tresses that should have adorned the coveted adornments were gone.

But she hugged them to her bosom, and at length she was able to look up with dim eyes and a smile and say: "My hair grows so fast, Jim!"

And then Della leaped up like a little singed cat and cried, "Oh, oh!"

Jim had not yet seen his beautiful present. She held it out to him eagerly upon her open palm. The dull precious metal seemed to flash with a reflection of her bright and ardent spirit.

"Isn't it a dandy, Jim? I hunted all over town to find it. You'll have to look at the time a hundred times a day now. Give me your watch. I want to see how it looks on it."

Instead of obeying, Jim tumbled down on the couch and put his hands under the back of his head and smiled in an odd way.

"Dell," said he, "let's put our Christmas presents away and keep 'em a while. They're too nice to use just at present.

"I sold the watch to get the money to buy your combs. And now suppose you put the chops on."

The Magi, as you know, were wise men—wonderfully wise men—who brought gifts to the Babe in the manger. They invented the art of giving Christmas presents. Being wise, their gifts were no doubt wise ones, possibly bearing the privilege of exchange in case of duplication. And here I have lamely related to you the uneventful chronicle of two foolish children in a flat who most unwisely sacrificed for each other the greatest treasures of their house.

But in a last word to the wise of these days let it be said that of all who give gifts these two were the wisest.

Everywhere they are wisest.

They are the magi.

George Horace Lorimer

The Child Who Is King

On a time when Rupert the Good King reigned over the City in the Forests, he decreed that, throughout all his realm, there should be no sorrow nor lack of cheer on Christmas Day.

For be it known that at the Christmastime the Christ Child comes down to earth, and passes from house to house, bringing joy and peace to the poor and lowly. And always on that day sat the king among his knights, waiting in state for the coming of the Child, that he might do Him honor and reverence. And always it befell that night found him sad and silent because the Child had passed him by. For ever are the poor the first care of the Christ, and in the City in the Forests they were many.

Now it being again the eve of Christmas, the king sent his servants through the city, giving to all of his bounty, that none might be without the comfort and the cheer of the holy time. For he reasoned that, if there were no sorrow to stay the Child as He passed through the city, He would come at last to the castle. And Rupert made ready the court to receive Him, and never was braver sight seen in all Christendom.

Now there was in the king's household a jester of most excellent wit, who made much seemly diversion for his master. And he, being in the streets on Christmas Eve, playing divers merry tricks on the simple people, had chanced upon a boy making a loud outcry. For he had wandered off from the monastery where the good fathers cared for the homeless, and knew not the way thither again. Him quieted the jester with fair words, and brought him secretly to the castle, and locked him in a chamber in the tower, where none went, and there left him sleeping. For he thought to clothe him in the motley on the morrow, and thereby make a merry jest for all the little children of the court.

Full soon the midnight bells, that through the year tolled out the passing days, rang joyously, and all the East was radiant with the Star. Upon the hills the sheep in slow procession walked, and in their stalls the oxen fell upon their knees, and Heaven and Earth sang one harmonious song, praising the Child.

Right proudly in his hall sat Rupert, upon his head a crown of gold, and o'er his mail the royal robe of purple. And at his back were threescore valiant knights in shining armor clad. Through all the night they sat there, stiff and silent, and when the dawn stole down it found them waiting.

Then sang the white-robed choir a greeting to the day, and mounting up, the music woke the boy, that through the night had slept unharmed. Long lay he still and listened, and once he called aloud, but there was none to answer back. For the jester was but a light fellow, and overnight he had forgotten.

And now the boy grew frightened, and, standing up, looked out into the court. Across the way he gazed into a room where all the children of the castle stood round a noble fir, full fair with glittering toys and shining lights. To them called he: "Oh, children, come for me, that I may play around the tree"; but there was none to hear, so loud they sang their praises.

Down to the ledge a sparrow flew, and looked in wondering at the boy. "Oh, sparrow, stay with me," he cried in his sorrow and fear, "for I am all alone"; but quick the bird flew off, for everywhere were crumbs thrown out for him and waiting.

Then to the snowflakes, scurrying by, the boy called out: "Fly not so fast away, oh, snowflakes; stay here a while with me." But whirled they on the faster, for in every window there were sights to see.

And now the boy was grieved, that he alone in all the city was forgotten. But of a sudden, above the chanting of the choir, he heard a voice that called his name, and wondering, turned and saw that all the grayness of the granite walls was yellowed into gold, and in a corner stood a tree that glittered with a thousand lights. But, best of all, he saw a little child, who smiled and beckoned him with rosy fingers. And all that day they played together.

Slow dragged the day along, but to the waiting king the Child came not. But as the evening fell, he saw the Star mount up the eastern skies and hang above the tower.

"The Child is coming!" cried the King. "The Child is coming!" echoed all his knights, and every eye glanced

Compelled to mount guard, the lonely soldier knows the great stories of Christmas only through the pantomime of the revelers within.

up where beat the white star-rays upon the moss-grown stone. And as they gazed, a mist that, formless, yet was luminous with life, hid all the tower, and, floating upward to the star, it took slow shape, till all could see the hosts of Heaven bearing up the Child. And blackness followed after.

Mute stood each wondering knight, and watched the dimming star burn low and flicker out. Nor spake the king; but when that bright brand faded from the sky, he turned and strode off to the tower, and all his knights clanked after. And last of all the trembling jester crawled.

Up, up and around, around and up the snaky staircase wound the king, and every step rang to his trailing steel.

Up, up and around, around and up, past narrow slits let in the stone, where breathed the air in cold and dank, and now there sounded in his ears the fearsome hooting of an owl, and round about his head the foul bats circled on unsteady wing.

Up and around, around and up, and now the king stood on the crumbling stone before the topmost room. A moment paused he there, and then his mailed hand beat the oaken door.

"Open!" he cried, "it is the king!" And far below the vaulted ceilings echoed back: "O—pen—it—is—the—king!" but from within there came no answering cry.

Then to the oak he put his straining shoulder, and sent it crashing in, and forward stepped, but half across the threshold started back.

Stretched on the floor, a tired boy lay sleeping, upon his ruddy face a smile, and in the room a hint of the radiance lingered.

Wroth was the king that one, the meanest of his serfs, had been preferred to him, and he so shamed before all his knights.

And stooping in his anger o'er the lad, he thought to break in roughly on his dreams and ask what did he there. But in between him and the boy was stretched a hand, and in it were the prints of nails. And as he looked down at that wounded hand, his pride and wrath were melted into tears, and, catching up the sleeping boy, he turned and passed down the stairs, through the assembled knights. And when he reached the empty hall, there, too, was a radiance. From that brightness a little Child came running out to meet him, and lo! it was the Christ.

Music and jest are the lot of the man in motley.

L. Frank Baum

Kidnapped Santa Claus

Santa Claus lives in the Laughing Valley, where stands the big rambling castle in which his toys are manufactured. His workmen, selected from the ryls, knooks, pixies and fairies, live with him, and everyone is as busy as can be from one year's end to another.

It is called the Laughing Valley because everything there is happy and gay. The brook chuckles to itself as it leaps rollicking between its green banks; the wind whistles merrily in the trees; the sunbeams dance lightly over the soft grass, and the violets and wild flowers look smilingly up from their green nests. To laugh one needs to be happy; to be happy one needs to be content. And throughout the Laughing Valley of Santa Claus contentment reigns supreme.

On one side is the mighty Forest of Burzee. At the other side stands the huge mountain that contains the Caves of the Daemons. And between them the Valley lies smiling and peaceful.

One would think that our good old Santa Claus, who devotes his days to making children happy, would have no enemies on all the earth; and, as a matter of fact, for a long period of time he encountered nothing but love wherever he might go.

In Laughing Valley, contentment reigns supreme.

But the Daemons who live in the mountain caves grew to hate Santa Claus very much, and all for the simple reason that he made children happy.

The Caves of the Daemons are five in number. A broad pathway leads up to the first cave, which is a finely arched cavern at the foot of the mountain, the entrance being beautifully carved and decorated. In it resides the Daemon of Selfishness. Back of this is another cavern inhabited by the Daemon of Envy. The cave of the Daemon of Hatred is next in order, and through this, one passes to the home of the Daemon of Malice—situated in a dark and fearful cave in the very heart of the mountain. I do not know what lies beyond this. Some say there are terrible pitfalls leading to death and destruction, and this may very well be true. However, from each one of the four caves mentioned there is a small, narrow tunnel leading to the fifth cave—a cozy little room occupied by the Daemon of Repentance. And as the rocky floors of these passages are well worn by the track of passing feet, I judge that many wanderers in the Caves of the Daemons have escaped through the tunnels to the abode of the Daemon of Repentance, who is said to be a pleasant sort of fellow who gladly opens for one a little door admitting you into fresh air and sunshine again.

Well, these Daemons of the Caves, thinking they had great cause to dislike old Santa Claus, held a meeting one day to discuss the matter.

"I'm really getting lonesome," said the Daemon of Selfishness. "For Santa Claus distributes so many pretty Christmas gifts to all the children that they become happy and generous, through his example, and keep away from my cave."

"I'm having the same trouble," rejoined the Daemon of Envy. "The little ones seem quite content with Santa Claus, and there are few, indeed, that I can coax to become envious."

"And that makes it bad for me!" declared the Daemon of Hatred. "For if no children pass through the caves of Selfishness and Envy, none can get to *my* cavern."

"Or to mine," added the Daemon of Malice.

"For my part," said the Daemon of Repentance, "it is easily seen that if children do not visit your caves they have no need to visit mine; so I am quite as neglected as you are."

"And all because of this person they call Santa Claus!" exclaimed the Daemon of Envy. "He is simply ruining our business, and something must be done at once."

To this they readily agreed; but what to do was another and more difficult matter to settle. They knew that Santa Claus worked all through the year at his castle in the Laughing Valley, preparing the gifts he was to distribute on Christmas Eve; and at first they resolved to try to tempt him into their caves, that they might lead him on to the terrible pitfalls that ended in destruction.

So the very next day, while Santa Claus was busily at work, surrounded by his little band of assistants, the Daemon of Selfishness came to him and said, "These toys are wonderfully bright and pretty. Why do you not keep them for yourself? It's a pity to give them to those noisy boys and fretful girls, who break and destroy them so quickly."

"Nonsense!" cried the old graybeard, his bright eyes twinkling merrily as he turned toward the tempting Daemon; "the boys and girls are never so noisy and fretful after receiving my presents, and if I can make them happy for one day in the year I am quite content."

So the Daemon went back to the others, who awaited him in their caves, and said, "I have failed, for Santa Claus is not at all selfish."

The following day the Daemon of Envy visited Santa Claus. Said he, "The toy shops are full of playthings quite as pretty as these you are making. What a shame it is that they should interfere with your business! They make toys by machinery much quicker than you can make them by hand; and they sell them for money, while you get nothing at all for your work."

But Santa Claus refused to be envious of the toy shops.

"I can supply the little ones but once a year—on Christmas Eve," he answered; "for the children are many, and I am but one. And as my work is one of love and kindness I would be ashamed to receive money for my little gifts. But throughout all the year the children

must be amused in some way, and so the toy shops are able to bring much happiness to my little friends. I like the toy shops, and am glad to see them prosper."

In spite of this second rebuff, the Daemon of Hatred thought he would try to influence Santa Claus. So the next day he entered the busy workshop and said, "Good morning, Santa! I have bad news for you."

"Then run away, like a good fellow," answered Santa Claus. "Bad news is something that should be kept secret and never told."

"You cannot escape this, however," declared the Daemon; "for in the world are a good many who do not believe in Santa Claus, and these you are bound to hate bitterly, since they have so wronged you."

"Stuff and rubbish!" cried Santa.

"And there are others who resent your making children happy and who sneer at you and call you a foolish old rattlepate! You are quite right to hate such base slanderers, and you ought to be revenged upon them for their evil words."

"But I *don't* hate 'em!" exclaimed Santa Claus, positively. "Such people do me no real harm, but merely render themselves and their children unhappy. Poor things! I'd much rather help them than injure them."

Indeed, the Daemons could not tempt old Santa Claus in any way. On the contrary, he was shrewd enough to see that their object in visiting him was to make mischief and trouble. So the Daemons abandoned honeyed words and determined to use force.

It is well known that no harm can come to Santa Claus while he is in the Laughing Valley, for the fairies, and ryls, and knooks all protect him. But on Christmas Eve he drives his reindeer out into the big world, carrying a sleigh-load of toys and pretty gifts to the children; and this was the time and the occasion when his enemies had the best chance to injure him. So the Daemons laid their plans and awaited the arrival of Christmas Eve.

The moon shone big and white in the sky, and the snow lay crisp and sparkling on the ground as Santa Claus cracked his whip and sped away out of the Valley into the great world beyond. The roomy sleigh was packed full with huge sacks of toys, and as the reindeer

The world is his province; he knows his territory better than astrologers or meteorologists, knows each child by name and age.

dashed onward our jolly old Santa laughed and whistled and sang for very joy. For in all his merry life this was the one day in the year when he was happiest—the day he lovingly bestowed the treasures of his workshop upon the little children.

It would be a busy night for him, he well knew. As he whistled and shouted and cracked his whip again, he reviewed in mind all the towns and cities and farmhouses where he was expected, and figured that he had just enough presents to go around and make every child happy. The reindeer knew exactly what was expected of them, and dashed along so swiftly that their feet scarcely seemed to touch the snow-covered ground.

Suddenly a strange thing happened: a rope shot through the moonlight and a big noose that was in the end of it settled over the arms and body of Santa Claus and drew tight. Before he could resist or even cry out he was jerked from the seat of the sleigh and tumbled head foremost into a snowbank, while the reindeer rushed onward with the load of toys and carried it quickly out of sight and sound.

Such a surprising experience confused old Santa for a moment, and when he had collected his senses he found that the wicked Daemons had pulled him from the snowdrift and bound him tightly with many coils of the stout rope. And then they carried the kidnapped Santa Claus away to their mountain, where they thrust the prisoner into a secret cave and chained him to the rocky wall so that he could not escape.

"Ha, ha!" laughed the Daemons, rubbing their hands together with cruel glee. "What will the children do now? How they will cry and scold and storm when they find there are no toys in their stockings and no gifts on their Christmas trees! And what a lot of punishment they will receive from their parents, and how they will flock to our caves of Selfishness, and Envy, and Hatred, and Malice! We have done a mighty clever thing, we Daemons of the Caves!"

Now it so chanced that on this Christmas Eve the good Santa Claus had taken with him in his sleigh Nuter the Ryl, Peter the Knook, Kilter the Pixie, and a small fairy named Wisk—his four favorite assistants. These little people he had often found very useful in helping him to distribute his gifts to the children, and when their master was so suddenly dragged from the sleigh they were all snugly tucked underneath the seat, where the sharp wind could not reach them.

The tiny immortals knew nothing of the capture of Santa Claus until some time after he had disappeared. But finally they missed his cheery voice, and as their master always sang or whistled on his journeys, the silence warned them that something was wrong.

Little Wisk stuck out his head from underneath the seat and found Santa Claus gone and no one to direct the flight of the reindeer.

"Whoa!" he called out, and the deer obediently slackened speed and came to a halt.

Peter and Nuter and Kilter all jumped upon the seat and looked back over the track made by the sleigh. But Santa Claus had been left miles and miles behind.

"What shall we do?" asked Wisk, anxiously, all the mirth and mischief banished from his wee face by this great calamity.

"We must go back at once and find our master," said Nuter the Ryl, who thought and spoke with much deliberation.

"No, no!" exclaimed Peter the Knook, who, cross and crabbed though he was, might always be depended upon in an emergency. "If we delay, or go back, there will not be time to get the toys to the children before morning; and that would grieve Santa Claus more than anything else."

"It is certain that some wicked creatures have captured him," added Kilter, thoughtfully; "and their object must be to make the children unhappy. So our first duty is to get the toys distributed as carefully as if Santa Claus were himself present. Afterward we can search for our master and easily secure his freedom."

This seemed such good and sensible advice that the others at once resolved to adopt it. So Peter the Knook called to the reindeer, and the faithful animals again sprang forward and dashed over hill and valley, through forest and plain, until they came to the houses wherein children lay sleeping and dreaming of pretty gifts they

DRAWN BY
SARAH S. STILWELL WEBER

Play is a basic instinct, like survival, continuity. The child is father of the man; the mature mind thrives on its own invention.

65

would find in their stockings on Christmas morning.

The little immortals had set themselves a difficult task; for although they had assisted Santa Claus on many of his journeys, their master had always directed and guided them and told them exactly what he wished them to do. But now they had to distribute the toys according to their own judgment, and they did not understand children as well as did old Santa. So it is no wonder they made some laughable errors.

Mamie Brown, who wanted a doll, got a drum instead; and a drum is of no use to a girl who loves dolls. And Charlie Smith, who delights to romp and play out of doors, and who wanted some new rubber boots to keep his feet dry, received a sewing box filled with colored worsteds and threads and needles, which made him so provoked that he thoughtlessly called our dear Santa Claus a fraud.

Had there been many such mistakes the Daemons would have accomplished their evil purpose and made the children unhappy. But the little friends of the absent Santa Claus labored faithfully and intelligently to carry out their master's ideas, and they made fewer errors than might be expected under such unusual circumstances.

And, although they worked as swiftly as possible, day had begun to break before the toys and other presents were all distributed; so for the first time in many years the reindeer trotted into the Laughing Valley, on their return, in broad daylight, with the brilliant sun peeping over the edge of the forest to prove they were far behind their accustomed hour.

Having put the deer in the stable, the little folk began to wonder how they might rescue their master; and they realized they must discover, first of all, what had happened to him and where he was.

So Wisk the Fairy transported himself to the bower of the Fairy Queen, which was located deep in the heart of the Forest of Burzee; and once there, it did not take him long to find out all about the naughty Daemons and how they had kidnapped the good Santa Claus to prevent his making children happy. The Fairy Queen also promised her assistance, and then, fortified by this powerful support, Wisk flew back to where Nuter and Peter and Kilter

awaited him, and the four counseled together and laid plans to rescue their master from his enemies.

It is possible that Santa Claus was not as merry as usual during the night that succeeded his capture. For although he had faith in the judgment of his little friends he could not avoid a certain amount of worry, and an anxious look would creep at times into his kind old eyes as he thought of the disappointment that might await his dear little children. And the Daemons, who guarded him by turns, one after another, did not neglect to taunt him with contemptuous words in his helpless condition.

When Christmas Day dawned the Daemon of Malice was guarding the prisoner, and his tongue was sharper than that of any of the others.

"The children are waking up, Santa!" he cried; "they are waking up to find their stockings empty! Ho, ho! How they will quarrel, and wail, and stamp their feet in anger! Our caves will be full today, old Santa! Our caves are sure to be full!"

But to this, as to other like taunts, Santa Claus answered nothing. He was much grieved by his capture, it is true; but his courage did not forsake him. And, finding that the prisoner would not reply to his jeers, the Daemon of Malice presently went away, and sent the Daemon of Repentance to take his place.

This last personage was not so disagreeable as the others. He had gentle and refined features, and his voice was soft and pleasant in tone.

"My brother Daemons do not trust me overmuch," said he, as he entered the cavern; "but it is morning, now, and the mischief is done. You cannot visit the children again for another year."

"That is true," answered Santa Claus, almost cheerfully; "Christmas Eve is past, and for the first time in centuries I have not visited my children."

"The little ones will be greatly disappointed," murmured the Daemon of Repentance, almost regretfully, "but that cannot be helped now. Their grief is likely to make the children selfish and envious and hateful, and if they come to the Caves of the Daemons today I shall lead some of them to my Cave of Repentance."

"Do you never repent, yourself?" asked Santa Claus.

The best gift is the one we ourselves should like most to have. Children in their kindness grant this gift to adults.

"Oh, yes, indeed," answered the Daemon. "I am even now repenting that I assisted in your capture. Of course it is too late to remedy the evil that has been done; but repentance, you know, can come only after an evil thought or deed, for in the beginning there is nothing to repent of."

"So I understand," said Santa Claus. "Those who avoid evil need never visit your cave."

"As a rule, that is true," replied the Daemon; "yet you, who have done no evil, are about to visit my cave at once; for to prove that I sincerely regret my share in your capture I am going to permit you to escape."

This speech greatly surprised the prisoner, until he reflected that it was just what might be expected of the Daemon of Repentance. The fellow at once busied himself untying the knots that bound Santa Claus and unlocking the chains that fastened him to the wall. Then he led the way through a long tunnel until they both emerged in the Cave of Repentance.

"I hope you will forgive me," said the Daemon, pleadingly. "I am not really a bad person, you know; and I believe I accomplish a great deal of good in the world."

With this he opened a back door that let in a flood of sunshine, and Santa Claus sniffed the fresh air gratefully.

"I bear no malice," said he to the Daemon, in a gentle voice; "and I am sure the world would be a dreary place without you. So, good morning, and a Merry Christmas to you!"

With these words he stepped out to greet the bright morning, and a moment later he was trudging along, whistling softly to himself, on his way to his home in the Laughing Valley.

Marching over the snow toward the mountain was a vast army, made up of the most curious creatures imaginable. There were numberless knooks from the forest, as rough and crooked in appearance as the gnarled branches of the trees they ministered to. And there were dainty ryls from the fields, each one bearing the emblem of the flower or plant it guarded. Behind these were many ranks of pixies, gnomes and nymphs, and in the rear a thousand beautiful fairies floating along, all in gorgeous array.

This wonderful army was led by Wisk, Peter, Nuter and Kilter, who had assembled it to rescue Santa Claus from captivity and to punish the Daemons.

But lo! coming to meet his loyal friends appeared the imposing form of Santa Claus, his white beard floating in the breeze and his bright eyes sparkling with pleasure at this proof of the love and veneration he had inspired in the hearts of the most powerful creatures in existence.

And while they clustered around him and danced with glee at his safe return, he gave them earnest thanks for their support. But Wisk, and Nuter, and Peter, and Kilter, he embraced affectionately.

"It is useless to pursue the Daemons," said Santa Claus to the army. "They have their place in the world, and can never be destroyed. But that is a great pity, nevertheless," he continued, musingly.

So the fairies, and knooks, and pixies, and ryls all escorted the good man to his castle, and there left him to talk over the events of the night with his little assistants.

Wisk had already rendered himself invisible and flown through the big world to see how the children were getting along on this bright Christmas morning; and by the time he returned, Peter had finished telling Santa Claus of how they had distributed the toys.

"We really did very well," cried the fairy, in a pleased voice; "for I found little unhappiness among the children this morning. Still, you must not get captured again, my dear master, for we might not be so fortunate another time in carrying out your ideas."

He then related the mistakes that had been made, and which he had not discovered until his tour of inspection. And Santa Claus at once sent him with rubber boots for Charlie Smith, and a doll for Mamie Brown; so that even those two disappointed ones became happy.

As for the wicked Daemons of the Caves, they were filled with anger and chagrin when they found that their clever capture of Santa Claus had come to naught. Indeed, no one on that Christmas Day appeared to be at all selfish, or envious, or hateful. And, realizing that while the children's saint had so many powerful friends it was folly to oppose him, the Daemons never again attempted to interfere with his journeys on Christmas Eve.

Toys, mirror images of our imagination, puppets of our fantasies, are ever "educational" if they make us feel secure and joyful.

Laura Ingalls Wilder

Christmas on the Prairie

The days were short and cold, the wind whistled sharply, but there was no snow. Cold rains were falling. Day after day the rain fell, pattering on the roof and pouring from the eaves.

Mary and Laura stayed close by the fire, sewing their nine-patch quilt blocks, or cutting paper dolls from scraps of wrapping paper, and hearing the wet sound of the rain. Every night was so cold that they expected to see snow next morning, but in the morning they saw only sad, wet grass.

They pressed their noses against the squares of glass in the windows that Pa had made, and they were glad they could see out. But they wished they could see snow.

Laura was anxious because Christmas was near, and Santa Claus and his reindeer could not travel without snow. Mary was afraid that, even if it snowed, Santa Claus could not find them, so far away in Indian Territory. When they asked Ma about this, she said she didn't know.

"What day is it?" they asked her, anxiously. "How many more days till Christmas?" And they counted off the days on their fingers, till there was only one more day left.

Rain was still falling that morning. There was not one crack in the gray sky. They felt almost sure there would be no Christmas. Still, they kept hoping.

Just before noon the light changed. The clouds broke and drifted apart, shining white in a clear blue sky. The sun shone, birds sang, and thousands of drops of water sparkled on the grasses. But when Ma opened the door to let in the fresh, cold air, they heard the creek roaring.

They had not thought about the creek. Now they knew they would have no Christmas, because Santa Claus could not cross that roaring creek.

Pa came in, bringing a big fat turkey. If it weighed less than twenty pounds, he said, he'd eat it, feathers and all. He asked Laura, "How's that for a Christmas dinner? Think you can manage one of those drumsticks?"

She said, yes, she could. But she was sober. Then Mary asked him if the creek was going down, and he said it was still rising.

Ma said it was too bad. She hated to think of Mr. Edwards eating his bachelor cooking all alone on Christmas day. Mr. Edwards had been asked to eat Christmas dinner with them, but Pa shook his head and said a man would risk his neck, trying to cross that creek now.

"No," he said. "That current's too strong. We'll just have to make up our minds that Edwards won't be here tomorrow."

Of course that meant that Santa Claus could not come, either.

Laura and Mary tried not to mind too much. They watched Ma dress the wild turkey, and it was a very fat turkey. They were lucky little girls, to have a good house to live in, and a warm fire to sit by, and such a turkey for their Christmas dinner. Ma said so, and it was true. Ma said it was too bad that Santa Claus couldn't come this year, but they were such good girls that he hadn't forgotten them; he would surely come next year.

Still, they were not happy.

After supper that night they washed their hands and faces, buttoned their red flannel nightgowns, tied their nightcap strings, and soberly said their prayers. They lay down in bed and pulled the covers up. It did not seem at all like Christmastime.

Pa and Ma sat silent by the fire. After a while Ma asked why Pa didn't play the fiddle, and he said, "I don't seem to have the heart to, Caroline."

After a longer while, Ma suddenly stood up.

"I'm going to hang up your stockings, girls," she said. "Maybe something will happen."

Laura's heart jumped. But then she thought again of the creek and she knew nothing could happen.

Ma took one of Mary's clean stockings and one of Laura's, and she hung them from the mantel-shelf, on either side of the fireplace. Laura and Mary watched her over the edge of their bedcovers.

"Now go to sleep," Ma said, kissing them good night. "Morning will come quicker if you're asleep."

She sat down again by the fire and Laura almost went to sleep. She woke up a little when she heard Pa say, "You've only made it worse, Caroline." And she thought she heard Ma say: "No, Charles. There's the white sugar." But perhaps she was dreaming.

The waiting is intolerable; sleep comes sometimes before Santa. Only the most perfect vision is rewarded with a sight of him.

71

Then she heard Jack growl savagely. The door latch rattled and someone said, "Ingalls! Ingalls!" Pa was stirring up the fire, and when he opened the door Laura saw that it was morning. The outdoors was gray.

"Great fishhooks, Edwards! Come in, man! What's happened?" Pa exclaimed.

Laura saw the stockings limply dangling, and she scrooged her shut eyes into the pillow. She heard Pa piling wood on the fire, and she heard Mr. Edwards say he had carried his clothes on his head when he swam the creek. His teeth rattled and his voice shivered. He would be all right, he said, as soon as he got warm.

"It was too big a risk, Edwards," Pa said. "We're glad you're here, but that was too big a risk for a Christmas dinner."

"Your little ones had to have a Christmas," Mr. Edwards replied. "No creek could stop me, after I fetched them their gifts from Independence."

Laura sat straight up in bed. "Did you see Santa Claus?" she shouted.

"I sure did," Mr. Edwards said.

"Where? When? What did he look like? What did he say? Did he really give you something for us?" Mary and Laura cried.

"Wait, wait a minute!" Mr. Edwards laughed. And Ma said she would put the presents in the stockings, as Santa Claus intended. She said they mustn't look.

Mr. Edwards came and sat on the floor by their bed, and he answered every question they asked him. They honestly tried not to look at Ma, and they didn't quite see what she was doing.

When he saw the creek rising, Mr. Edwards said, he had known that Santa Claus could not get across it. ("But you crossed it," Laura said. "Yes," Mr. Edwards replied, "but Santa Claus is too old and fat. He couldn't make it, where a long, lean razorback like me could do so.") And Mr. Edwards reasoned that if Santa Claus couldn't cross the creek, likely he would come no farther south than Independence. Why should he come forty miles across the prairie, only to be turned back? Of course he wouldn't do that!

So Mr. Edwards had walked to Independence. ("In the rain?" Mary asked. Mr. Edwards said he wore his rubber coat.) And there, coming down the street in Independence, he had met Santa Claus. ("In the daytime?" Laura asked. She hadn't thought that anyone could see Santa Claus in the daytime. No, Mr. Edwards said; it was night, but light shone out across the street from the saloons.)

Well, the first thing Santa Claus said was "Hello, Edwards!" ("Did he know you?" Mary asked, and Laura asked, "How did you know he was really Santa Claus?" Mr. Edwards said that Santa Claus knew everybody. And he had recognized Santa at once by his whiskers. Santa Claus had the longest, thickest, whitest set of whiskers west of the Mississippi.)

So Santa Claus said, "Hello, Edwards! Last time I saw you you were sleeping on a corn-shuck bed in Tennessee." And Mr. Edwards well remembered the little pair of red yarn mittens that Santa Claus had left for him that time.

Then Santa Claus said: "I understand you're living now down along the Verdigris River. Have you ever met up, down yonder, with two little young girls named Mary and Laura?"

"I surely am acquainted with them," Mr. Edwards replied.

"It rests heavy on my mind," said Santa Claus. "They are both of them sweet, pretty, good little young things, and I know they are expecting me. I surely do hate to disappoint two good little girls like them. Yet with the water up the way it is, I can't ever make it across that creek. I can figure no way whatsoever to get to their cabin this year. Edwards," Santa Claus said. "Would you do me the favor to fetch them their gifts this one time?"

"I'll do that, and with pleasure," Mr. Edwards told him.

Then Santa Claus and Mr. Edwards stepped across the street to the hitching posts where the pack mule was tied. ("Didn't he have his reindeer?" Laura asked. "You know he couldn't," Mary said. "There isn't any snow." Exactly, said Mr. Edwards. Santa Claus traveled with a pack mule in the southwest.)

And Santa Claus uncinched the pack and looked

*"How did you know he was really Santa Claus?"
Laura asked. Mr. Edwards explained he had known
Santa at once, by his whiskers.*

In the deep country the chores are endless but the good grace of the laborers is infinite, especially around December 25th.

through it, and he took out the presents for Mary and Laura.

"Oh, what are they?" Laura cried; but Mary asked, "Then what did he do?"

Then he shook hands with Mr. Edwards, and he swung up on his fine bay horse. Santa Claus rode well, for a man of his weight and build. And he tucked his long, white whiskers under his bandanna. "So long, Edwards," he said, and he rode away on the Fort Dodge trail, leading his pack mule and whistling.

Laura and Mary were silent an instant, thinking of that.

Then Ma said, "You may look now, girls."

Something was shining bright in the top of Laura's stocking. She squealed and jumped out of bed. So did Mary, but Laura beat her to the fireplace. And the shining thing was a glittering new tin cup.

Mary had one exactly like it.

These new tin cups were their very own. Now they each had a cup to drink out of. Laura jumped up and down and shouted and laughed, but Mary stood still and looked with shining eyes at her own tin cup.

Then they plunged their hands into the stockings again. And they pulled out two long, long sticks of candy. It was peppermint candy, striped red and white. They looked and looked at that beautiful candy, and Laura licked her stick, just one lick. But Mary was not so

greedy. She didn't take even one lick of her own stick.

Those stockings weren't empty yet. Mary and Laura pulled out two small packages. They unwrapped them, and each found a little heart-shaped cake. Over their delicate brown tops was sprinkled white sugar. The sparkling grains lay like tiny drifts of snow.

The cakes were too pretty to eat. Mary and Laura just looked at them. But at last Laura turned hers over, and she nibbled a tiny nibble from underneath, where it wouldn't show. And the inside of that little cake was white!

It had been made of pure white flour, and sweetened with white sugar.

Laura and Mary never would have looked in their stockings again. The cups and the cakes and the candy were almost too much. They were too happy to speak. But Ma asked if they were sure the stockings were empty.

Then they put their arms down inside them, to make sure.

And in the very toe of each stocking was a shining bright, new penny!

They had never even thought of such a thing as having a penny. Think of having a whole penny for your very own. Think of having a cup and a cake and a stick of candy *and* a penny.

There never had been such a Christmas.

Now of course, right away, Laura and Mary should have thanked Mr. Edwards for bringing those lovely presents all the way from Independence. But they had forgotten all about Mr. Edwards. They had even forgotten Santa Claus. In a minute they would have remembered, but before they did, Ma said, gently, "Aren't you going to thank Mr. Edwards?"

"Oh, thank you, Mr. Edwards! Thank you!" they said, and they meant it with all their hearts. Pa shook Mr. Edwards's hand, too, and shook it again. Pa and Ma and Mr. Edwards acted as if they were almost crying, Laura didn't know why. So she gazed again at her beautiful presents.

She looked up again when Ma gasped. And Mr. Edwards was taking sweet potatoes out of his pockets. He said they had helped to balance the package on his head when he swam across the creek. He thought Pa and Ma might like them, with the Christmas turkey.

There were nine sweet potatoes. Mr. Edwards had brought them all the way from town, too. It was just too much. Pa said so. "It's too much, Edwards," he said. They never could thank him enough.

Mary and Laura were too much excited to eat breakfast. They drank the milk from their shining new cups, but they could not swallow the rabbit stew and the cornmeal mush.

"Don't make them, Charles," Ma said. "It will soon be dinnertime."

For Christmas dinner there was the tender, juicy, roasted turkey. There were the sweet potatoes, baked in the ashes and carefully wiped so that you could eat the good skins, too. There was a loaf of salt-rising bread made from the last of the white flour.

And after all that there were stewed dried blackberries and little cakes. But these little cakes were made with brown sugar and they did not have white sugar sprinkled over their tops.

Then Pa and Ma and Mr. Edwards sat by the fire and talked about Christmastimes back in Tennessee and up north in the Big Woods. But Mary and Laura looked at their beautiful cakes and played with their pennies and drank water out of their new cups. And little by little they licked and sucked their sticks of candy, till each stick was sharp-pointed on one end.

That was a happy Christmas.

William Meade Prince painted Santa traveling by packhorse, not reindeer, in the Southwest.

Betty Smith

The Christmas Tree in Brooklyn

Christmas was a charmed time in Brooklyn. It was in the air, long before it came. The first hint of it was Mr. Morton going around the schools teaching Christmas carols, but the first sure sign was the store windows.

You have to be a child to know how wonderful is a store window filled with dolls and sleds and other toys. And this wonder came free to Francie. It was nearly as good as actually having the toys to be permitted to look at them through the glass window.

Oh, what a thrill there was for Francie when she turned a street corner and saw another store all fixed up for Christmas! Ah, the clean shining window with cotton batting sprinkled with star dust for a carpet! There were flaxen-haired dolls and others which Francie liked better who had hair the color of good coffee with lots of cream in it. Their faces were perfectly tinted and they wore clothes the like of which Francie had never seen on earth. The dolls stood upright in flimsy cardboard boxes. They stood with the help of a bit of tape passed around the neck and ankles and through holes at the back of the box. Oh, the deep blue eyes framed by thick lashes that stared straight into a little girl's heart and the perfect miniature hands extended, appealingly asking, "Please, won't *you* be my mama?" And Francie had never had a doll except a two-inch one that cost a nickel.

And the sleds! (Or, as the Williamsburg children called them, the sleighs.) There was a child's dream of heaven come true! A new sled with a flower someone had dreamed up painted on it—a deep blue flower with bright green leaves—the ebony-black painted runners, the smooth steering bar made of hard wood and gleaming varnish over all! And the names painted on them! "Rosebud!" "Magnolia!" "Snow King!" "The Flyer!" Thought Francie, "If I could only have one of those, I'd never ask God for another thing as long as I live."

There were roller skates made of shining nickel with straps of good brown leather and silvered nervous wheels, tensed for rolling, needing but a breath to start them turning, as they lay crossed one over the other, sprinkled with mica snow on a bed of cloudlike cotton.

There were other marvelous things. Francie couldn't take them all in. Her head spun and she was dizzy with the impact of all the seeing and all the making up of stories about the toys in the shop windows.

The spruce trees began coming into Francie Nolan's neighborhood the week before Christmas. Their branches were corded to make shipping easier. Vendors rented space on the curb before a store and stretched a rope from pole to pole and leaned the trees against it. All day they walked up and down this one-sided avenue of aromatic leaning trees, blowing on stiff ungloved fingers. And the air was cold and still, and full of the pine smell and the smell of tangerines which appeared in the stores only at Christmastime and the mean street was truly wonderful for a little while.

There was a cruel custom in the neighborhood. At midnight on the Eve of our dear Saviour's birth, the kids gathered where there were unsold trees. There was a saying that if you waited until then, you wouldn't have to buy a tree, that "they'd chuck 'em at you." This was literally true. The man threw each tree in turn, starting with the biggest. Kids volunteered to stand up against the throwing. If a boy didn't fall down under the impact,

There is magic in toyshop windows in December.

the tree was his. If he fell, he forfeited his chance at winning a tree. Only the roughest boys and some of the young men elected to be hit by the big trees. The others waited shrewdly until a tree came up that they could stand against. The littlest kids waited for the tiny, foot-high trees and shrieked in delight when they won one.

On the Christmas Eve when Francie was ten and her brother, Neeley, nine, Mama consented to let them go down and have their first try for a tree. Francie had picked out her tree earlier in the day. She had stood near it all afternoon and evening praying that no one would buy it. To her joy, it was still there at midnight. It was ten feet tall and its price was so high that no one could afford to buy it. Its branches were bound with new white rope and it came to a sure pure point at the top.

The man took this tree out first. Before Francie could speak up, a neighborhood bully, a boy of eighteen known as Punky Perkins, step-

The trees waited for buyers but Francie prayed no one would buy hers.

ped forward and ordered the man to chuck the tree at him. The man hated the way Punky was so confident. He looked around and asked, "Anybody else wanna take a chanct on it?"

Francie stepped forward. "Me, Mister."

A spurt of derisive laughter came from the tree man. The kids snickered. A few adults who had gathered to watch the fun guffawed. "Aw g'wan. You're too little," the tree man objected.

"Me and my brother—we're not too little together."

She pulled Neeley forward. The man looked at them—a thin girl of ten with starveling hollows in her cheeks but with the chin still baby-round. He looked at the little boy with his fair hair and round eyes—Neeley

Nolan, just nine years old, all innocence and trust.

"Two ain't fair," yelped Punky.

"Shut your lousy trap," advised the man, who held all power in that hour. "These here kids is got nerve. Stand back, the rest of youse. These kids is goin' to have a show at this tree."

The others made a wavering lane, a human funnel with Francie and her brother making the small end of it. The big man at the other end flexed his great arms to throw the great tree. He noticed how tiny the children looked at the end of the short lane. For the split part of a moment, the tree thrower went through a kind of Gethsemane.

Oh, Jesus Christ, his soul agonized, why don't I just give 'em the tree and say Merry Christmas? I can't sell it no more this year and it won't keep till next year. The kids watched him solemnly as he stood there in his moment of thought. But then, he rationalized, if I did that, all the others would expect to get 'em handed to 'em. And next year, nobody a-tall would buy a tree off of me. I ain't a big enough man to give this tree away for nothin'. No, I gotta think of myself and my own kids. He finally came to his conclusion. Oh, what the hell! Them two kids is gotta live in this world. They *got* to learn to give and to take punishment. As he threw the tree with all his strength, his heart wailed out, It's a rotten, lousy world!

Francie saw the tree leave his hands. The whole world stood still as something dark and monstrous came through the air. There was nothing but pungent darkness and something that grew and grew as it rushed at her. She staggered as the tree hit them. Neeley went to his knees but she pulled him up fiercely before he could go down. There was a mighty swishing sound as the tree settled. Everything was dark, green and prickly. Then she felt a sharp pain at the side of her head where the trunk of the tree had hit her. She felt Neeley trembling.

When some of the older boys pulled the tree away, they found Francie and her brother standing upright, hand in hand. Blood was coming from scratches on Neeley's face. He looked more like a baby than ever with his bewildered blue eyes and the fairness of his skin made more noticeable because of the clear red blood. But they were smiling. Had they not won the biggest tree in the neighborhood? Some of the boys hollered, "Hooray!" A few adults clapped. The tree man eulogized them by screaming, "And now get the hell out of here with your tree."

Such phrases could mean many things according to the tone used in saying them. So Francie smiled tremulously at the kind man. She knew that he was really saying, "God-bye—God bless you."

It wasn't easy dragging that tree home. They were handicapped by a boy who ran alongside yelping, "Free ride! All aboard!" who'd jump on and make them drag him along. But he got sick of the game eventually and went away.

In a way, it was good that it took them so long to get the tree home. It made their triumph more drawn out. Francie glowed when a lady said, "I never saw such a big tree!" The cop of their corner stopped them, examined the tree, and solemnly offered to buy it for fifteen cents if they'd deliver it to his home. Francie nearly burst with pride although she knew he was joking.

They had to call to Papa to help them get the tree up the narrow stairs. Papa came running down. His amazement at the size of the tree was flattering. He pretended to believe that it wasn't theirs. Francie had a lot of fun convincing him although she knew all the while that the whole thing was make-believe. Papa pulled in front and Francie and Neeley pushed in back and they began forcing the big tree up the two narrow flights of stairs. Papa started singing, not caring that it was rather late at night. He sang "Holy Night." The narrow walls took up

his clear sweet voice, held it for a breath and gave it back with doubled sweetness. Doors creaked open and families gathered on the landings, pleased and amazed at something unexpected being added to that moment of their lives.

Francie saw the Tynmore sisters, who gave piano lessons, standing together in their doorway, their gray hair in crimpers, and ruffled, starched nightgowns showing under the voluminous wrappers. They added their thin poignant voices to Papa's. Floss Gaddis, her mother and her brother, Henny, who was dying of consumption, stood in their doorway. Henny was crying and when Papa saw him he let the song trail off; he thought maybe it made Henny too sad.

Flossie was in a Klondike-dance-hall-girl costume waiting for an escort to take her to a masquerade ball which started soon after midnight. More to make Henny smile than anything else, Papa said, "Floss, we got no angel for the top of this Christmas tree. How about you obliging?"

Floss was all ready to make a smart-alecky reply, but there was something about the big proud tree, the beaming children and the rare goodwill of the neighbors that changed her mind. All she said was, "Gee, ain't you the kidder, Mr. Nolan."

They set the tree up in the front room after Mama had spread a sheet to protect the carpet from falling pine needles. The tree stood in a big tin bucket with broken bricks to hold it upright. When the rope was cut away, the branches spread out to fill the room. They draped over the piano and some of the chairs stood among the branches. There was no money to buy decorations or lights. But the great tree standing there was enough. The room was cold. It was a poor year, that one—too poor for them to buy the extra coal for the front-room stove. The room smelled cold and clean and aromatic.

Every day, during the week the tree stood there, Francie put on her sweater and stocking cap and went in and sat under the tree. She sat there and enjoyed the smell and the dark greenness of it.

Oh, the mystery of a great tree, a prisoner in a tin wash bucket in a tenement front room!

Norman
Rockwell

Poem from a King's Prayerbook

In the mid-sixteenth century this poem was written on the flyleaf of a prayerbook belonging to Edward VI, the frail and devout son of Henry VIII who became King of England at nine and died at sixteen. The legend it preserves gives a clue as to how the big bird, long regarded as a bringer of good fortune to the houses on which it nests, became also the bringer of babies.

THE STORK

The stork she rose on Christmas Eve
And said unto her brood,
I now must fare to Bethlehem
To view the Son of God.

She gave to each his dole of meat,
She stowed them fairly in,
And fair she flew and fast she flew
And came to Bethlehem.

The white stork is rare today, its European habitat destroyed.

Now where is He of David's line?
She asked at house and hall.
He is not here, they spake hardly,
But in the manger stall.

She found him in the manger stall
With that most Holy Maid;
The gentle stork she wept to see
The Lord so rudely laid.

Then from her panting breast she plucked
The feathers white and warm;
She strewed them in the manger bed
To keep the Lord from harm.

"Blessed be the gentle stork
Forever more," quoth He,
"For that she saw my sad estate
And showed pity.

"Full welcome shall she ever be
In hamlet and in hall,
And called henceforth the Blessed Bird
And friend of babies all."

A precocious scholar, Boy King Edward VI studied Latin, Greek.

Washington Irving

The Christmas Coach

There is nothing in England that exercises a more delightful spell over my imagination than the lingerings of the holiday customs of former times.

Of all the old festivals, however, that of Christmas awakens the strongest and most heartfelt associations. There is a tone of solemn and sacred feeling that blends with our conviviality, and lifts the spirit to a state of hallowed and elevated enjoyment. The services of the church about this season are extremely tender and inspiring. They dwell on the beautiful story of the origin of our faith, and the pastoral scenes that accompanied its announcement.

It is a beautiful arrangement that this festival, which commemorates the announcement of the religion of peace and love, has been made the season for the gathering together of family connections, and calling back the children of a family who have launched forth in life and wandered, once more to assemble about the hearth.

Norman Rockwell's son served as model for the boy pressing his nose against the coach window in this classic illustration showing travelers

In the course of a December tour in Yorkshire, I rode for some distance in one of the public coaches, on the day preceding Christmas. The coach was crowded, both inside and out, with passengers, who, by their talk, seemed principally bound to the mansions of relations and friends to eat the Christmas dinner. It was loaded also with hampers of game, and baskets and boxes of delicacies and hares hung dangling their long ears about the coachman's box—presents from distant friends for the impending feasts. I had three fine rosy-cheeked schoolboys for my fellow-passengers inside, full of the buxom health and manly spirits which I have observed in the children of this country. They were returning home for the holidays in high glee, and promising themselves a world of enjoyment. It was delightful to hear the gigantic plans of pleasure of the little rogues, and the imprac-

ticable feats they were to perform during their six weeks' emancipation from the abhorred thraldom of book, birch and pedagogue. They were full of anticipations of the meeting with the family and household, down to the very cat and dog; and of the joy they were to give their little sisters by the presents with which their pockets were crammed; but the meeting to which they seemed to look forward with the greatest impatience was with Bantam, which I found to be a pony, and, according to their talk, possessed of more virtues than any steed since the days of Bucephalus. How he could trot! how he could run! and then such leaps as he would take—there was not a hedge in the country that he could not clear.

They were under the particular guardianship of the coachman, to whom, whenever an opportunity present-ed, they addressed a host of questions, and pronounced

coming home for the holidays. It is the same scene Washington Irving described in his account of a Christmas in England around 1820.

him one of the best fellows in the whole world. Indeed, I could not but notice the more than ordinary air of bustle and importance of the coachman, who wore his hat a little on one side, and had a large bunch of Christmas greens stuck in the buttonhole of his coat. He is always a personage full of mighty care and business, and he is particularly so during this season, having so many commissions to execute in consequence of the great interchange of presents.

Perhaps the impending holiday might have given a more than usual animation to the country, for it seemed to me as if everybody was in good looks and good spirits. Game, poultry and other luxuries of the table were in brisk circulation in the villages; the grocers', butchers' and fruiterers' shops were thronged with customers. The housewives were stirring briskly about, putting their dwellings in order; and the glossy branches of holly, with their bright red berries, began to appear at the windows. The scene brought to mind an old writer's account of Christmas preparations:

"Now capons and hens, besides turkeys, geese, and ducks, with beef and mutton—must all die; for in twelve days a multitude of people will not be fed with a little. Now plums and spice, sugar and honey, square it among pies and broth. Now or never must music be in tune, for the youth must dance and sing to get them a heat, while the aged sit by the fire. The country maid leaves half her market, and must be sent again, if she forgets a pack of cards on Christmas Eve. Great is the contention of Holly and Ivy, whether master or dame wears the breeches. Dice and cards benefit the butler; and if the cook do not lack wit, he will sweetly lick his fingers."

Children, parents, merchants all conspire to make the jolly old man—here painted by N.C. Wyeth—a reality in our lives.

Clement C. Moore

A Visit from St. Nicholas

If it weren't for a dignified professor of religion, author of A Compendious Lexicon of the Hebrew Language, Santa might use handcart or packhorse, or even rocket ship, to deliver toys on Christmas Eve. The sleigh that flies, light as thistledown despite its bulky load of toys; the eight reindeer with magical, mysterious names and prancing hoofs—this marvelous mode of transportation was the inspired creation of Dr. Clement C. Moore, who in 1822 wrote a poem for the amusement of his children.

Dr. Moore was a preacher as well as a teacher, and the son of a bishop. Educated at Columbia University, he knew all there was to know about saints including the Dutch saint, Nicholas, whose name stood for generosity and gift-giving. But Dr. Moore was a warmhearted, tolerant, humorous man, and his version of Saint Nicholas owed more to the jolly traditions of the Dutch settlers of New York than to religious history. Legend has it that he started composing the verses while on a trip to market, by sleigh, to buy the Christmas turkey.

His picture of Santa Claus, jolly and plump, with the stub of his pipe in his teeth, may be a description of the Moores' Dutch handyman, Jan Duyckinck.

Once home, Dr. Moore jotted the verses down on paper, and that night, seated before the fireplace, he read them aloud to his family. Dr. and Mrs. Moore were the parents of six children.

One version of the story has it that there was a guest staying with the Moores that year, in their roomy old-fashioned home called Chelsea House (there's now a New York City skyscraper on the site). If so, she was Miss Harriet Butler, daughter of Moore's friend David Butler, who was rector of a church in Troy, New York, and she later gave a handwritten copy of the poem to the editor of the Troy Sentinel. The following Christmas the poem was printed in that newspaper, and readers were as delighted as Dr. Moore's children had been. Five years later, in 1837, the poem appeared with several others by Dr. Moore in The New York Book of Poetry, and in 1844 it appeared as a book for children, with illustrations.

Since then? No one has an accurate count of how many times the poem has appeared in print, or in how many different languages. It is a worldwide favorite, and the reindeer-drawn sleigh that flies through the nighttime sky has become a peculiarly American contribution to the lore of Christmas.

'TWAS THE NIGHT BEFORE CHRISTMAS,
  when all through the house
Not a creature was stirring, not even a mouse;
The stockings were hung by the chimney with
  care
In hopes that ST. NICHOLAS soon would be
  there;
The children were nestled all snug in their beds,
While visions of sugar-plums danced through
  their heads;
And Mamma in her 'kerchief, and I in my cap,
Had just settled our brains for a long winter's
  nap—

When out on the lawn there arose such a
  clatter,
I sprang from my bed to see what was the
  matter;
Away to the window I flew like a flash,
Tore open the shutters and threw up the sash.
The moon on the breast of the new-fallen
  snow
Gave the lustre of midday to objects below;
When, what to my wondering eyes should
  appear,
But a miniature sleigh, and eight tiny reindeer,
With a little old driver, so lively and quick,
I knew in a moment it must be SAINT NICK.
More rapid than eagles his coursers they came,
And he whistled, and shouted, and called them
  by name:

"Now, *Dasher!* now, *Dancer!* now, *Prancer* and
  Vixen!
On, *Comet!* on, *Cupid!* on, *Donder* and *Blitzen!*
To the top of the porch! to the top of the wall!
Now, dash away! dash away! dash away all!"
As dry leaves that before the wild hurricane fly,
When they meet with an obstacle, mount to the sky,

So up to the house-top the coursers they flew,
With a sleigh full of toys—and ST. NICHOLAS too!
And then, in a twinkling, I heard on the roof,
The prancing and pawing of each little hoof.
As I drew in my head, and was turning around
Down the chimney ST. NICHOLAS came with a bound.
He was dressed all in fur, from his head to his foot,
And his clothes were all tarnished with ashes and
    soot!
A bundle of toys he had flung on his back,
And he looked like a pedlar just opening his pack;

He spoke not a word, but went straight to his work,
And filled all the stockings—then turned with a jerk,
And laying his finger aside of his nose,
And giving a nod, up the chimney he rose.
He sprang to his sleigh, to his team gave a whistle,
And away they all flew, like the down off a thistle.
But I heard him exclaim, ere he drove out of sight,
"HAPPY CHRISTMAS TO ALL! AND TO ALL
    A GOOD NIGHT!"

His eyes—how they twinkled! his dimples,
    how merry!
His cheeks were like roses, his nose like a cherry!
His droll little mouth was drawn up like a bow,
And the beard of his chin was as white as the snow.
The stump of a pipe he held tight in his teeth,
And the smoke, it encircled his head like a wreath.
He had a broad face, and a little round belly,
That shook, when he laugh'd, like a bowlful of jelly.
He was chubby and plump; a right jolly old elf;
And I laughed, when I saw him, in spite of myself.
A wink of his eye, and a twist of his head,
Soon gave me to know I had nothing to dread.

Mark Twain
Susie's Letter from Santa

Lucky little Susie Clemens! She lived at 351 Farmington Avenue, Hartford, Connecticut, in the new house that was so much admired by neighbors and townspeople in the 1870's. It was trimmed with shiny red-and-black brickwork; it had three turrets, five balconies, and a forest of chimneys rising from the tile roof. Inside were nineteen large rooms and five bathrooms—in a day when few homes had even one.

Susie lived there with her famous father who wrote and lectured as Mark Twain, though his real name was Samuel Clemens. There were also two younger sisters, a beautiful but delicate mother, and the six servants it took to make

Mark with daughters Susie and Clara.

the huge house livable, but a very special relationship existed between Susie and her father. He treated her like a princess, buying her toys like a silver thimble and a Noah's Ark set that included 200 hand-carved wooden animals. Tragically, Susie died of meningitis when she was only twenty-four. Her brokenhearted father said later that it made him feel a little better to know that she died at home, in the wonderful fairy-tale house where she had spent a happy childhood.

Wonderful Christmases were part and parcel of that happy childhood. One year when she was very young Susie wrote a letter to Santa Claus and received the following letter in reply:

Palace of St. Nicholas
In the Moon
Christmas Morning

My dear Susie Clemens:

I have received and read all the letters which you and your little sister have written me by the hand of your mother and your nurses; I have also read those which you little people have written me with your own hands—for although you did not use any characters that are in grown people's alphabet, you used the characters that all children in all lands on earth and in the twinkling stars use; and as all my subjects in the moon are children and use no character but that, you will easily understand that I can read your and your baby sister's jagged and fantastic marks without any trouble at all. But I had trouble with those letters which you dictated through your mother and the nurses, for I am a foreigner and cannot read English writing well. You will find that I made no mistakes about the things which you and the baby ordered in your own letters—I went down your chimney at midnight when you were asleep and delivered them all myself—and kissed both of you, too, because you are

good children, well trained, nice mannered, and about the most obedient little people I ever saw. But in the letter which you dictated there were some words which I could not make out for certain, and one or two small orders which I could not fill because we ran out of stock. Our last lot of kitchen furniture for dolls has just gone to a very poor little child in the North Star away up in the cold country above the Big Dipper. Your mama can show you that star and you will say: "Little Snow Flake" (for that is the child's name), "I'm glad you got that furniture, for you need it more than I." That is, you must *write* that, with your own hand, and Snow Flake will write you an answer. If you only spoke it she wouldn't hear you. Make your letter light and thin, for the distance is great and the postage very heavy.

There was a word or two in your mama's letter which I couldn't be certain of. I took it to be "a trunk full of doll's clothes." Is that it? I will call at your kitchen door about nine o'clock this morning to inquire. But I must not see anybody and I must not speak to anybody but you. When the kitchen doorbell rings, George must be blindfolded and sent to open the door. Then he must go back to the dining room or the china closet and take the cook with him. You must tell George he must walk on tiptoe and not speak—otherwise he will die someday. Then you must go up to the nursery and stand on a chair or the nurse's bed and put your ear to the speaking tube that leads down to the kitchen and when I whistle through it you must speak in the tube and say, "Welcome, Santa Claus!" Then I will ask whether it was a trunk you ordered or not. If you say it was, I shall ask you what *color* you want the trunk to be. Your mama will help you to name a nice color and then you must tell me every single thing in detail which you want the trunk to contain. Then when I say "Good-bye and a merry Christmas to my little Susie Clemens," you must say "Good-bye, good old Santa Claus, I thank you very much and please tell that little Snow Flake I will look at her star to-night and she must look down here—I will be right in the west bay window; and every fine night I will look at her star and say, 'I know somebody up there and *like* her, too.' " Then you must go down into the library and make George close the doors that open into the main hall and everybody must keep still for a little while. Then while you are waiting I will go to the moon and get those things and in a few minutes I will come down the chimney that belongs to the fireplace that is in the hall—if it is a trunk you want—because I couldn't get such a large thing as a trunk down the nursery chimney, you know.

People may talk if they want, till they hear my footsteps in the hall. Then you tell them to keep quiet a little while until I go up the chimney. Maybe you will not hear my footsteps at all—so you may go now and then and peep through the dining-room doors, and by and by you will see that which you want, right under the piano in the drawing room—for I shall put it there. If I should leave any snow in the hall, you must tell George to sweep it into the fireplace, for I haven't time to do such things. George must not use a broom, but a rag—or he will die someday. You watch George and don't let him run into danger. If my boot should leave a stain on the marble, George must not holystone it away. Leave it there always in memory of my visit; and whenever you look at it or show it to anybody you must let it remind you to be a good little girl. Whenever you are naughty and somebody points to that mark which your good old Santa Claus's boot made on the marble, what will you say, little sweetheart?

Good-bye for a few minutes, till I come down and ring the kitchen doorbell.

Your loving Santa Claus
Whom people sometimes call
"The Man in the Moon"

The young place infinite faith in the mails, dreaming of a snowy Pony Express between their hearth and the frozen tip-top of the world.

Francis P. Church

Yes, Virginia, There is a Santa

*H*er whole name was Mrs. Laura Virginia O'Hanlon Douglas. She earned a master's degree from Columbia University and a doctorate from Fordham, and she had a long and distinguished career as a teacher and administrator in the New York City school system, but to millions she will always be the little girl who wrote a letter asking about Santa Claus.

"I was only a child, and my parents did everything for me that any parents could do," Mrs. Douglas told an audience of college students some forty years later. "Quite naturally I believed in Santa Claus, for he had never disappointed me. But like you, I turned to those of my own generation, and so when less fortunate little boys and girls said there wasn't any Santa Claus, I was filled with doubts. I asked my father, and he was a little evasive on the subject.

"It was a habit in our family that whenever any doubts came up as to how to pronounce a word, or some question of historical fact was in doubt, we wrote to the 'Question and Answer' column in The New York Sun. *Father would always say, "If you see it in* The Sun, *it's so," and that settled the matter.*

" 'Well, I'm just going to write to The Sun *and find out the real truth,' I said to father."*

The editorial was written by Francis Pharcellus Church, a Civil War correspondent for the The New York Times *before he joined* The Sun *as a writer specializing in theological and controversial subjects.*

Mr. Church died in 1906.

The New York Sun *died in 1950.*

Mrs. Douglas died May 13, 1971, at the age of eighty-one.

But little Virginia, her letter, and the answer she received will live forever in America's heart.

Dear Editor: I am 8 years old.

Some of my little friends say there is no Santa Claus. Papa says "If you see it in *The Sun* it's so."
Please tell me the truth; is there a Santa Claus?

Virginia O'Hanlon

Virginia, your little friends are wrong. They have been affected by the skepticism of a skeptical age. They do not believe except they see. They think that nothing can be which is not comprehensible by their little minds. All minds, Virginia, whether they be men's or children's, are little. In this great universe of ours man is a mere insect, an ant, in his intellect, as compared with the boundless world about him, as measured by the intelligence capable of grasping the whole of truth and knowledge.

Yes, Virginia, there is a Santa Claus. He exists as certainly as love and generosity and devotion exist, and you know that they abound and give to your life its highest beauty and joy. Alas! how dreary would be the world if there were no Santa Claus! It would be as dreary as if there were no Virginias. There would be no childlike faith then, no poetry, no romance to make tolerable this existence. We should have no enjoyment, except in sense and sight. The eternal light with which childhood fills the world would be extinguished.

Not believe in Santa Claus! You might as well not believe in fairies! You might get your papa to hire men to watch in all the chimneys on Christmas Eve to catch Santa Claus, but even if they did not see Santa Claus coming down, what would that prove? Nobody sees Santa Claus, but that is no sign that there is no Santa Claus. The most real things in the world are those that neither children nor men can see.

No Santa Claus! Thank God, he lives, and he lives forever. A thousand years from now, Virginia, nay, ten times ten thousand years from now, he will continue to make glad the heart of childhood.

from *The New York Sun*, September 21, 1897

People dress up like him, we sing about him, artists paint him. Someone must have seen him, else how would we know just how he looks?

91

No matter the snow, no matter the cold, errands of good cheer and friendship bring everyone out of his house at Christmastime.

Hamlin Garland

My First Christmas Tree

When I was ten years old we moved to Mitchell County, an Iowa prairie land, and there we prospered in such wise that our stockings always held toys of some sort, and even my mother's stocking occasionally sagged with a simple piece of jewelry or a new comb or brush. But the thought of a family tree remained the luxury of millionaire city dwellers; indeed it was not till my fifteenth or sixteenth year that our Sunday school rose to the extravagance of a tree, and it is of this wondrous festival that I write.

The land about us was only partly cultivated at this time, and our district schoolhouse, a bare little box, was set bleakly on the prairie; but the Burr Oak schoolhouse was not only larger but it stood beneath great oaks as well and possessed the charm of a forest background through which a stream ran silently. It was our chief social center. There of a Sunday a regular preacher held "Divine Service" with Sunday school as a sequence. At night—usually on Friday nights—the young people met in "lyceums," as we called them, to debate great questions or to "speak pieces" and read essays; and here it was that I saw my first Christmas tree.

I walked to that tree across four miles of moonlit snow. Snow? No, it was a floor of diamonds, a magical world, so beautiful that my heart still aches with the wonder of it and with the regret that it has all gone—gone with the keen eyes and the bounding pulses of the boy.

Our home at this time was a small frame house on the prairie almost directly west of the Burr Oak grove, and as it was too cold to take the horses out my brother and I, with our tall boots, our visored caps and our long woolen mufflers, started forth afoot, defiant of the cold. We left the gate on the trot, bound for a sight of the glittering unknown. The snow was deep and we moved side by side in the grooves made by the hoofs of the horses, setting our feet in the shine left by the broad shoes of the wood sleighs whose going had smoothed the way for us.

Our breaths rose like smoke in the still air. It must have been ten below zero, but that did not trouble us in those days, and at last we came in sight of the lights, in sound of the singing, the laughter, the bells of the feast.

It was a poor little building without tower or bell and

its low walls had but three windows on a side, and yet it seemed very imposing to me that night as I crossed the threshold and faced the strange people who packed it to the door. I say "strange people," for though I had seen most of them many times they all seemed somehow alien to me that night. I was an irregular attendant at Sunday school and did not expect a present; therefore I stood against the wall and gazed with open-eyed marveling at the shining pine which stood where the pulpit was wont to be. I was made to feel the more embarrassed by reason of the remark of a boy who accused me of having forgotten to comb my hair.

This was not true, but the cap I wore always matted my hair down over my brow, and then, when I lifted it off, invariably disarranged it completely. Nevertheless I felt guilty—and hot. I don't suppose my hair was artistically barbered that night—I rather guess Mother had used the shears—and I can believe that I looked the half-wild colt that I was; but there was no call for that youth to direct attention to my unavoidable shagginess.

I don't think the tree had many candles, and I don't remember that it glittered with golden apples. But it was loaded with presents, and the girls coming and going clothed in bright garments made me forget my own looks—I think they made me forget to remove my overcoat, which was a sodden thing of poor cut and worse quality. I think I must have stood agape for nearly two hours listening to the songs, noting every motion of Adoniram Burtch and Asa Walker as they directed the ceremonies and prepared the way for the great event—that is to say, for the coming of Santa Claus himself.

A furious jingling of bells, a loud voice outside, the lifting of a window, the nearer clash of bells, and the dear old Saint appeared (in the person of Stephen Bartle) clothed in a red robe, a belt of sleigh bells, and a long white beard. The children cried out, "Oh!" The girls tittered and shrieked with excitement, and the boys laughed and clapped their hands. Then "Sandy" made a little speech about being glad to see us all, but as he had many other places to visit, and as there were a great many presents to distribute, he guessed he'd have to ask some of the many pretty girls to help him. So he called

From a long way off comes a letter from a friend whose kindness time has not dimmed. You hear from him once a year, less sometimes, but thoughts and best wishes suddenly ring through the cold air with the clarity of a silver bell—yours, and the friend's. Dale Nichols painted the mail sleigh making its rounds. At right, the Christmas tree lives even though it has been cut off from the forest; candles, caught in the constellations of tinsel and angel hair, mirror the stars outside. This seen-through-a-window scene was painted by Stevan Dohanos.

upon Betty Burtch and Hattie Knapp—and I for one admired his taste, for they were the most popular maids of the school.

They came up blushing, and a little bewildered by the blaze of publicity thus blown upon them. But their native dignity asserted itself, and the distribution of the presents began. I have a notion now that the fruit upon the tree was mostly bags of popcorn and "corny copias" of candy, but as my brother and I stood there that night and saw everybody, even the rowdiest boy, getting something we felt aggrieved and rebellious. We forgot that we had come from afar—we only knew that we were being left out.

But suddenly, in the midst of our gloom, my brother's name was called, and a lovely girl with a gentle smile handed him a bag of popcorn. My heart glowed with gratitude. Somebody had thought of us; and when she came to me, saying sweetly, "Here's something for you,"

I had not words to thank her. This happened nearly forty years ago, but her smile, her outstretched hand, her sympathetic eyes are vividly before me as I write. She was sorry for the shock-headed boy who stood against the wall, and her pity made the little box of candy a casket of pearls. The fact that I swallowed the jewels on the road home does not take from the reality of my adoration.

At last I had to take my final glimpse of that wondrous tree, and I well remember the walk home. My brother and I traveled in wordless companionship. The moon was sinking toward the west, and the snow crust gleamed with a million fairy lamps. The sentinel watchdogs barked from lonely farmhouses, and the wolves answered from the ridges. Now and then sleighs passed us with lovers sitting two and two, and the bells on their horses had the remote music of romance to us whose boots drummed like clogs of wood upon the icy road.

Midnight, a country church, a patient horse, the deep and dreamless sleep of the winter solstice, as painted by Mead Schaeffer.

The President poses with his sons in 1904. He adored them; they were integral members of the Cabinet and every safari he took.

Theodore Roosevelt

The Tree in the White House Closet

Why was the Christmas tree in a closet? Because President Theodore Roosevelt had decreed there would be no tree in the White House in 1902. Not that TR was against Christmas. Far from it! The gregarious TR, his gracious wife and his lively brood celebrated the holiday with their customary gusto—as the letter indicates. There were gifts for all, games and sports, memorable meals, parties and dancing. But, in 1902, no tree.

The President was an ardent conservationist second. He was horrified to learn that young pines and spruces had been carelessly cut from some of the national forests, for sale as Christmas trees. He feared that the increasing demand for Christmas trees might ravage the woodlands he loved and valued. Always one to practice what he preached, TR announced that the first family would do without a tree.

TR reckoned without the resourceful sons who got their independence of mind from him. Archie, eight, and Quentin, five, managed to purchase and smuggle into the White House a contraband tree. A sympathetic White House carpenter helped them to erect it in a place where it would be safely out of sight till Christmas morning—inside a closet that opened off the boys' room.

There is a happy footnote to the story. Gifford Pinchot, chief of the U.S. Bureau of Forests and a close friend, managed to persuade TR that some selective cutting of young trees could actually benefit the forests, and before the next Christmas rolled around the ban on White House trees was lifted. About that same time, the U.S. government began to encourage farmers to plant and harvest Christmas trees as a cash crop. This soon provided an adequate supply for the market and pressure on the natural forests was reduced.

Theodore Roosevelt *writes to* Master James A. Garfield

White House, December 26, 1902.

Jimmikins:

. . . . Yesterday morning at a quarter of seven all the children were up and dressed and began to hammer at the door of their mother's and my room, in which their

six stockings, all bulging out with queer angles and rotundities, were hanging from the fireplace. So their mother and I got up, shut the window, lit the fire (taking down the stockings, of course), put on our wrappers and prepared to admit the children. But first there was a surprise for me, also for their good mother, for Archie had a little Christmas tree of his own, which he had

The first President to have a Christmas tree in the White House was Franklin Pierce.
The year was 1832, and the guests he invited in to see the lighted and decorated tree
were fellow members of the New York Avenue Presbyterian Church.
Larger and more widely publicized was the White House tree of 1889,
when the Benjamin Harrisons observed the holiday season with warmhearted hospitality.
It is the duty of Christians to make merry, President Harrison proclaimed;
and he is generally regarded as the Chief Executive who set the pattern
for seasonal festivity at 1600 Pennsylvania Avenue.

News stories about Roosevelt sparing the life of a cub while on a bear hunt inspired toy manufacturers to produce the "Teddy."

rigged up with the help of one of the carpenters in a big closet; and we all had to look at the tree and each of us got a present off of it. There was also one present each for Jack, the dog, Tom Quartz, the kitten, and Algonquin, the pony, whom our Archie would no more think of neglecting than I would neglect his brothers and sisters. Then all the children came into our bed and there they opened their stockings. Afterward we got dressed and took breakfast, and then all

went into the library, where each child had a table set for his bigger presents. Quentin had a perfectly delightful electric railroad, which had been rigged up for him by one of his friends, the White House electrician, who has been very good to all the children. Then Ted and I, with General Wood and Mr. Bob Ferguson, who was a lieutenant in my regiment, went for a three-hour ride; and all of us, including all the children, took lunch at the house with the children's aunt, Mrs. Captain Cowles—Archie and Quentin having their lunch at a little table with their cousin Sheffield. Late in the afternoon I played games of single stick with General Wood and also Mr. Ferguson. I am going to get your father to come on and try it soon. We have to try to hit as light as possible, but sometimes we hit hard, and today I have a bump over one eye and a swollen wrist. Then all our family and kinsfolk and the Senator and Mrs. Lodge's family and kinsfolk had our Christmas dinner at the White House, and afterward danced in the East Room, closing up with the Virginia reel.

On the morning of December 25th, in full orchestra, the world awakes. Normal two-armed children turn into octopuses as their hands become almost as full as the hearts of grandparents eager to please. What more joyous than dolls and drums, trumpets and toy soldiers?

Dylan Thomas

Conversation about Christmas

Small Boy: Years and years ago, when you were a boy . . .

Self: When there were wolves in Wales, and birds the colour of red-flannel petticoats whisked past the harp-shaped hills, when we sang and wallowed all night and day in caves that smelt like Sunday afternoons in damp front farmhouse parlours, and chased, with the jawbones of deacons, the English and the bears . . .

Small Boy: You are not so old as Mr. Beynon Number Twenty-Two who can remember when there were no motors. Years and years ago, when you were a boy . . .

Self: Oh, before the motor even, before the wheel, before the duchess-faced horse, when we rode the daft and happy hills bareback . . .

Small Boy: You're not so daft as Mrs. Griffiths up the street, who says she puts her ear under the water in the reservoir and listens to the fish talk Welsh. When you were a boy, what was Christmas like?

Self: It snowed.

Small Boy: It snowed last year, too. I made a snowman and my brother knocked it down and I knocked my brother down and then we had tea.

Self: But that was not the same snow. Our snow was not only shaken in whitewash buckets down the sky, I think it came shawling out of the ground and swam and drifted out of the arms and hands and bodies of the trees; snow grew overnight on the roofs of the houses like a pure and grandfather moss, minutely ivied the walls, and settled on the postman, opening the gate, like a dumb, numb thunderstorm of white, torn Christmas cards.

Small Boy: Were there postmen, then, too?

Self: With sprinkling eyes and wind-cherried noses, on spread, frozen feet they crunched up to the doors and mittened on them manfully. But all that the children could hear was a ringing of bells.

Small Boy: You mean that the postman went rat-a-tat-tat and the doors rang?

Self: The bells that the children could hear were inside them.

Small Boy: I hear thunder sometimes, never bells.

Self: There were church bells, too.

Small Boy: Inside them?

Self: No, no, no, in the bat-black, snow-white belfries, tugged by bishops and storks. And they rang their tidings over the bandaged town, over the frozen foam of the powder and ice-cream hills, over the crackling sea. It seemed that all the churches boomed, for joy, under my window; and the weathercocks crew for Christmas, on our fence.

Small Boy: Get back to the postmen.

Self: They were just ordinary postmen, fond of walking, and dogs, and Christmas, and the snow. They knocked on the doors with blue knuckles . . .

"These wait all upon thee; that thou mayest give them their meat in due season."

Psalms 104:27

His aching back, his dog nipped shins, his cold reddened nose belie the satisfaction he gets from delivering happiness to his constituents.

Small Boy: Ours has got a black knocker . . .

Self: And then they stood on the white welcome mat in the little, drifted porches, and clapped their hands together, and huffed and puffed, making ghosts with their breath, and jogged from foot to foot like small boys wanting to go out.

Small Boy: And then the Presents?

Self: And then the Presents, after the Christmas box. And the cold postman, with a rose on his button-nose, tingled down the teatray-slithered run of the chilly glinting hill. He went in his ice-bound boots like a man on fishmonger's slabs. He wagged his bag like a frozen camel's hump, dizzily turned the corner on one foot, and, by God, he was gone.

Small Boy: Get back to the Presents.

Self: There were the Useful Presents: engulfing mufflers of the old coach days, and mittens made for giant sloths; zebra scarves of a substance like silky gum that could be tug-o'-warred down to the galoshes; blinding tam-o'-shanters like patchwork tea-cosies, and bunny-scutted busbies and balaclavas for victims of head-shrinking tribes; from aunts who always wore wool next to the skin, there were moustached and rasping vests that made you wonder why the aunties had any skin left at all; and once I had a little crocheted nosebag from an aunt now, alas, no longer whinnying with us. And pictureless books in which small boys, though warned, with quotations, not to, *would* skate on Farmer Garge's pond, and did, and drowned; and books that told me everything about the wasp, except why.

Small Boy: Get on to the Useless Presents.

Self: On Christmas Eve I hung at the foot of my bed Bessie Bunter's black stocking, and always, I said, I would stay awake all the moonlit, snowlit night to hear the roof-alighting reindeer and see the hollied boot descend through soot. But soon the sand of the snow drifted into my eyes, and though I stared towards the fireplace and around the flickering room where the black sacklike stocking hung, I was asleep before the chimney trembled and the room was red and white with Christmas. But in the morning, though no snow melted on the bedroom floor, the stocking bulged and brimmed: press

it, it squeaked like a mouse-in-a-box; it smelt of tangerine; a furry arm lolled over, like the arm of a kangaroo out of its mother's belly; squeeze it hard in the middle, and something squelched; squeeze it again—squelch again. Look out of the frost-scribbled window: on the great loneliness of the small hill, a blackbird was silent in the snow.

Small Boy: Were there any sweets?

Self: Of course there were sweets. It was the marshmallows that squelched. Hardboileds, toffee, fudge and allsorts, crunches, cracknels, humbugs, glaciers, and marzipan and butterwelsh for the Welsh. And troops of bright tin soldiers who, if they would not fight, could always run. And Snakes-and-Families and Happy Ladders. And Easy Hobbi-Games for Little Engineers, complete with Instructions. Oh, easy for Leonardo! And a whistle to make the dogs bark to wake up the old man next door to make him beat on the wall with his stick to shake our picture off the wall. And a packet of cigarettes: you put one in your mouth and you stood at the corner of the street and you waited for hours, in vain, for an old lady to scold you for smoking a cigarette and then, with a smirk, you ate it. And, last of all, in the toe of the stocking, sixpence like a silver corn. And then downstairs for breakfast under the balloons!

Small Boy: Were there Uncles, like in our house?

Self: There are always Uncles at Christmas. The same Uncles. And on Christmas mornings, with dog-disturbing whistle and sugar fags, I would scour the swathed town for the news of the little world, and find always a dead bird by the white Bank or by the deserted swings: perhaps a robin, all but one of his fires out, and that fire still burning on his breast. Men and women wading and scooping back from church or chapel, with taproom noses and wind-smacked cheeks, all albinos, huddled their stiff black jarring feathers against the irreligious snow. Mistletoe hung from the gas in all the front parlours; there was sherry and walnuts and bottled beer and crackers by the dessertspoons; and cats in their furabouts watched the fires; and the high-heaped fires crackled and spat, all ready for the chestnuts and the mulling pokers. Some few large men sat in the front

Norman Rockwell used a favorite model, James K. Van Brunt, a man! for all three of these gossiping aunts.

parlours, without their collars, Uncles almost certainly, trying their new cigars, holding them out judiciously at arm's-length, returning them to their mouths, coughing, then holding them out again as though waiting for the explosion; and some few small aunts, not wanted in the kitchen, nor anywhere else for that matter, sat on the very edges of their chairs, poised and brittle, afraid to break, like faded cups and saucers. Not many those mornings trod the piling streets: an old man always, fawn-bowlered, yellow-gloved, and, at this time of year, with spats of snow, would take his constitutional to the white bowling-green, and back, as he would take it wet or fine on Christmas Day or Doomsday. . . .

Small Boy: Why didn't you go home for Christmas dinner?

Self: Oh, but I did, I always did. I would be slap-dashing home, the gravy smell of the dinners of others, the bird smell, the brandy, the pudding and mince, weaving up my nostrils, when out of a snow-clogged side-lane would come a boy the spit of myself, with a pink-tipped cigarette and the violet past of a black eye, cocky as a bullfinch, leering all to himself. I hated him on sight and sound, and would be about to put my dog-whistle to my lips and blow him off the face of Christmas when suddenly he, with a violent wink, put *his* whistle to *his* lips and blew so stridently, so high, so exquisitely loud, that gobbling faces, their cheeks bulged with goose, would press against their tinseled windows, the whole length of the white echoing street.

Small Boy: What did you have for Dinner?

Self: Turkey, and blazing pudding.

Small Boy: Was it nice?

Self: It was not made on earth.

Small Boy: What did you do after dinner?

Self: The Uncles sat in front of the fire, took off their collars, loosened all buttons, put their large moist hands over their watchchains, groaned a little, and slept. Mothers, aunts, and sisters scuttled to and fro, bearing tureens. The dog was sick. Auntie Beattie had to have three aspirins, but Auntie Hannah, who liked port, stood in the middle of the snowbound backyard, singing like a big-bosomed thrush. I would blow up balloons to see

how big they would blow up to; and, when they burst, which they all did, the Uncles jumped and rumbled. In the rich and heavy afternoon, the Uncles breathing like dolphins and the snow descending, I would sit in the front room, among festoons and Chinese lanterns, and nibble at dates, and try to make a model man-o'-war, following the Instructions for Little Engineers, and produce what might be mistaken for a seagoing tram. And then, at Christmas tea, the recovered Uncles would be jolly over their mince-pies; and the great iced cake loomed in the centre of the table like a marble grave. Auntie Hannah laced her tea with rum, because it was only once a year. And in the evening, there was Music. An uncle played the fiddle, a cousin sang Cherry Ripe, and another uncle sang Drake's Drum. It was very warm in the little house. Auntie Hannah, who had got on to the parsnip wine, sang a song about Rejected Love, and Bleeding Hearts, and Death, and then another in which she said that her Heart was like a Bird's Nest; and then everybody laughed again, and then I went to bed. Looking through my bedroom window, out into the moonlight and the flying, unending, smoke-coloured snow, I could see the lights in the windows of all the other houses on our hill, and hear the music rising from them up the long, steadily falling night. I turned the gas down, I got into bed. I said some words to the close and holy darkness, and then I slept.

Small Boy: But it all sounds just like an ordinary Christmas.

Self: It was.

Small Boy: But Christmas when you were a boy wasn't any different to Christmas now.

Self: It was, it was.

Small Boy: Why was Christmas different then?

Self: I mustn't tell you.

Small Boy: Why mustn't you tell me? Why is Christmas different for me?

Self: I mustn't tell you.

Small Boy: Why can't Christmas be the same for me as it was for you when you were a boy?

Self: I mustn't tell you. I mustn't tell you because it is Christmas now.

Against the white paper of time we cut our own silhouettes. Christmas is the moment we take the impression, discord or content.

105

J. W. Foley

Tommy's Letters

Appletown, December 1, 1905.

Dear Grandma:

I have often thought of you in the past year but you know how busy boys have to be to keep all the chores done and go to school. We do not get much time to write letters. But the other day I was thinking how kind you had always been to us boys and it was a shame I do not write oftener. So today I sat right down after I came from school to write you a good, long letter and let you know that I often think of you even if I do not write. The ground here is all white with snow which makes us think that it will soon be Christmas again. I suppose you do not care so much for Christmas now as you did when you were a little girl. Mamma says that after folks grow up they do not care so much for it except to make the boys and girls happy by giving them something that they want. It must be awful nice to send a sled or a pair of skates or a tool chest to a boy and then sit on Christmas day and think how happy he is. If all of us did that what a bright world it would be. I suppose though that when folks grow up they have so very many things to think about they forget to send things, when they mean to send them all the time but it slips their mind. It isn't that they can't afford it or don't want to but they don't just happen to think about it until it's Christmas day and then it is too late. And then they must feel awful sorry to think how happy it would have made some little boy if they had sent something but they didn't.

I have an idea Eddie Brooks' Grandma is going to send him a sled for Christmas. I don't know what makes me think so, but it seems to me I heard it somewhere. I guess I can make my old one do for another year. One of the runners is broke but I think I can get it fixed. It won't be very safe though.

Dear Grandma, I hope you are having a good winter and your rheumatism don't bother you very much. I often wish I was there to carry out ashes for you and do the heavy work but I have to go to school so I will grow up and be a credit to you all. You know I am named after Grandpa, which makes me all the more anxious to grow up well.

With much love from us all,

Your affectionate grandson,
Tommy

Appletown, December 1, 1905.

Dear Uncle Bill:

I guess you will be surprised when you get this letter because you don't expect any from me but I was writing to Grandma today and I thought I would write to all of our folks and let them know how I am getting along. You know boys don't write very much because they write compositions in school and that takes about all the time they have got to spare for writing. But we ought to write to our relatives once in a while because we are apt to grow up and go away and then the family will be all broke up and scattered. I know you are a bachelor and haven't got any boys to call your own and that maybe it will interest you to know that I'm getting along

Mischief disappears. In its place wings sprout, rooms tidy, slippers and pipes arrive; briefly father and mother are boss.

very well in school because I am your nephew on my mother's side.

It don't seem like over a year since you sent me my pair of skates for Christmas, does it? I wonder if you have changed very much. I have, a good deal. I am tall and my feet are bigger and the skates you sent me are hardly big enough for me now but I guess I can make them do through the winter. One of the straps is wore out but I guess I can have it fixed so it will do. It is quite dangerous to skate with old straps on, though. One of the boys slipped last week and nearly went into an air hole. His skates were too small and one of the straps broke and let him slide.

We ought to be glad of what we have, though, and not expect new skates every year when we are growing so fast.

I suppose you are too busy to think much about Christmas. I enclose you a copy of a letter I wrote to Santa Claus telling what I want. Of course I know all about who Santa Claus is, but I only send it to show you how well I am getting along in writing and spelling. I think Grandmamma is apt to send me the sled and Papa said if I would be a good boy he would get me the tool chest. So that only leaves the skates and if I don't get a new pair the old ones will do.

I hope you are having good health. I wish I could be where I could help you sometimes in your office, cleaning out the wastebasket and doing the sweeping which I would be only too glad to do if we both lived in the same town. We all send our best love to you.

Your affectionate nephew,
Tommy

Appletown, December 1, 1905.
Dear Aunt Lizzie:

Maybe you have almost forgotten about your little nephew Tommy away out here and so I thought I would drop you a few lines to let you know I am well and getting along fine and hope you are the same. I do not write letters very often because you know how it is with boys. They cannot think of many things to say and are apt to make a good many blots if they write with ink. I just happened to think that maybe I had never written to thank you for those splendid books you sent me for last Christmas and as Christmas will soon be here again I do not want to get too far behind. They were splendid books and I have read them all over and over again. I do not know of anything a boy likes better than books. It improves the mind and keeps them out of mischief and when we grow up to be men we can look back and see how the good books we got for Christmas helped to make us better. Nobody ever regrets sending a boy good books for Christmas, don't you think so?

One of the books you sent me had a sequel. It was the Red Ranger or the Mystery of the Indian Scout. The sequel is the Lost Trail or the Lives of the Gold-Hunters. We do not have it in the bookstore here. I am awful anxious to know if the Red Ranger finds the Lost Trail or not. Have you ever read the sequel? If you have I wish you would write and tell me if he finds the lost trail. I have lent the Red Ranger to some of the boys and they will all appreciate it very much if you will let us know.

If you know any good books for boys I wish you would write down their names and send them to me.

You know two or three good books will last you nearly all winter. Some parts you can read over and over again where there is a lot of excitement until they are nearly worn out. The Red Ranger was that kind and the sequel would probably be almost as good.

It is too bad we are so far away from each other. Sometimes I think how much I could help you and Uncle Jerry not having any boys of your own it would be extremely valuable to you. By chopping wood and filling the woodbox and otherwise doing chores. I could run in on the way from school and see if I couldn't do some chores for you.

I hope you and Uncle Jerry will have a Merry Christmas.

Your affectionate nephew,
Tommy

P.S.—We all send love. The Red Ranger is by the author of the Desert Chief or the Capture of the White Princess.
Tommy

The magnifying glass is only for Santa's eyes; there are good children enough everywhere and Christmas makes them even better.

Donald Culross Peattie

Gold, Frankincense and Myrrh

Beneath the fragrant Christmas tree lie piled the gifts in their gay wrappings. Eager hands reach for them, and the children seize their own with innocent greediness. But in this first glow of the holy morning, before we tear at the bright papers and ribbons, let us pause to remember the meaning of presents on Christmas Day. It is very ancient, as old as the gospel itself. A gift given at Christmastime symbolizes the love that Christians bear to one another, in the name of One who loved them all.

Wise men indeed were they that first intended this, and wise men were the first Christmas givers. Only in St. Matthew's Gospel do we read about them, and he tells it in this wise:

"Now when Jesus was born in Bethlehem of Judea in the days of Herod the king, behold, there came wise men from the east to Jerusalem, saying, Where is he that is born King of the Jews? for we have seen his star in the east, and are come to worship him."

Thus begins the second chapter of Matthew; and later the apostle adds:

"When they saw the star, they rejoiced with exceeding great joy. And when they were come into the house, they saw the young child with Mary his mother, and fell down, and worshipped him: and when they had opened their treasures, they presented unto him gifts; gold, and frankincense, and myrrh."

How strangely scented and melodiously ringing are those three names! All the distant East, all the splendor of kings, the mystery that lies in things faraway and long ago, come to us in those syllables.

Myrrh, and frankincense, and gold! Why were these things chosen? Whence did they come? And what, in actuality, are they?

They are emblems of princely generosity, costly now as in ancient times, and still surviving at many a Christian altar.

The Magi brought their best to the Newborn. They must have felt that nothing poor earth could offer to the King of Heaven would be more appropriate than gold. Well may we agree with them today, for gold is one of the noble metals. No single acid can destroy it, not will it rust away, like iron or tin. As a consequence, it is almost never found as a compound, but in free nuggets or as dust, or alloyed with such metals as mercury or silver. No one can successfully imitate or fake gold, so heavy and incorruptible is it. And it is a metal easily turned to the uses of beauty. It has been woven into fabrics at least since Biblical times (Exodus 39:2-3), for its ductility, as chemists say, is so great that a single grain of fine gold may be drawn out into a wire 1/1000 of an inch in diameter, extending for a length of about one mile.

Pure, supple, almost indestructible, gold is indeed a royal metal among all the base ones occurring in the earth's crust.

The expert hammer of a goldbeater, whose ancient art is referred to by Homer, can beat an ounce of gold into a sheet two hundred feet square, a mere shimmering film. Ordinarily, such beaten gold is made into "books" containing twenty-five leaves apiece, each three and one-quarter inches square. When pure gold becomes this thin, it will transmit light almost like glass, but dimly, letting only the green rays through. With this gold the artist gilds his statue, the bookbinder stamps the title on his fine volume.

In the ancient world into which Christianity was born, gold was far rarer than now; the golden ornaments retrieved by archaeologists from graves in Troy or Crete or Egypt were royal or noble treasures exclusively. Not every wife, then, could wear a precious little band on her fourth finger. But as gold became a medium of exchange, it traveled the world. It came to Palestine from Egyptian Nubia, which we call the northern Sudan; also from the Midianites, who wandered through what is now central Jordan, south and east of the Dead Sea. Where did the Three Wise Men get it? As we are not sure where they themselves came from, we can but guess that—if they truly were "kings of Orient," as the old carols call them—they may have brought their gold from the mines of Indian Mysore.

In any case, it was in love and reverence that the Wise Men offered to the Christ Child the most precious stuff the ancient world knew.

Since those same ancient days, also, many have be-

The commercial treasures of the Middle East honored the birth of Him whose body would in death be anointed by the same spices.

111

lieved that "incense owns a Deity nigh." No one knows who first lit incense to his God, but doubtless he who did it reasoned that, since all of us enjoy agreeable smells, God probably liked them too. So as times grew less savage and the rituals of worship more spiritualized, burning incense was substituted for the smoke of sacrificial flesh upon the altar. But that sweet reek was not common until the time of Jeremiah. After his day, it was made from an expensive and elaborate formula, containing sixteen different ingredients, with only priests allowed to concoct it. And the chief element in this holy recipe was frankincense, the second gift of the wise men to the Child.

Frankincense is a resin, from a kind of tree held so sacred of old that in southern Arabia and Ethiopia, where it grew, only a few particularly pure persons were allowed even to approach it.

Legends told that the precious trees were guarded by winged serpents. All this makes the tree sound fabulous, but it does indeed exist in Nature, and botanists have named it. It belongs to the genus *Boswellia*, and is a member of the torchwood family. This means little to most of us, unless we happen to have seen the rare elephant trees that grow in the Gila and Imperial valleys in our own far Southwest—the only members of the family native to the continental United States.

To conjure up a frankincense tree, think of a tree about fifteen feet high, with a patchy bark like a sycamore's. It is as crooked as a snake and all but leafless. The few leaves are compound, like those of an ash, and they sprout at the end of the crazy twigs. The flowers and fruit vaguely resemble a cherry's, although this tree is neither sycamore nor ash nor cherry; indeed, the scaly bark and contorted limbs remind one more of some archaic reptile than of the pleasant shady comfort that we call a tree.

To obtain the precious frankincense itself, an Arab cuts a slash in the trunk, as a Vermonter cuts a maple, and then strips off a narrow piece of bark, about five inches long, below the cut. The sap slowly oozes out and is allowed to harden for about three months. At last it is collected in lumps, to be shipped from such strange and faraway places as Berbera and Aden, near the mouth of the Red Sea, and Bombay.

These lumps are yellow or colorless, dusty-looking, with a bitter taste. But they burn with a bright white flame, and then there arises to heaven that sweet, heavy perfume of mystery the Wise Men thought pleasing to God.

This ritual of burning frankincense had been beloved of the Old Testament worshippers long before the night of the Star and the journey of the three wondering Magi toward it in the dark. But Christians did not adopt frankincense till five whole centuries after the Nativity. It is, however, approved for use in the New Testament. Today it finds a place chiefly in the Catholic Church, whose shrines are still full of its perfume. Incense today is compounded partly of the real frankincense and partly of the resin of a very different tree, the spruce fir of northern Europe.

Nowadays the source of true frankincense is not so much Arabia and Ethiopia as the island of Socotra off Africa's eastern tip—a remote, mountainous, harborless island of stones and thorny thickets, where the frankincense trees were, at least until recent times, guarded by the subjects of an Arabian sultan.

From this same distant part of the world comes the last of the gifts of the Magi, myrrh, a shrub related to frankincense, of the genus *Commiphora*. The sap of myrrh is extracted in the same way as that of frankincense, and it comes in small lumps of reddish-brown resin. But its symbolism is more somber. The word myrrh comes from the Hebrew *mar*, meaning "bitter." The ancient Egyptians used this resin in embalming, and hence its connection with solemn occasions. Was this a strange gift for an Infant King? Not for one destined to die for his people.

Such were the first of all Christmas presents, birthday presents to the little Lord of Light. They were offered in a spirit of wondering humility and love.

In all that we ourselves may give, gaily in the modern manner, may there linger too some sweet savor, some hidden glint, of the greater love that gives the celebration of Christmas its real meaning!

Christmas is the birthday of childhood; all people, no matter their ages, are invited to the celebration of this birth.

The crowds are thick, the time is short, the mind works furiously to keep pace with the purse. The list dwindles, disappears. Success!

114

Irvin S. Cobb

Christmas Gifts—Giving and Getting

To a happily married man the proper exercise of the true Christian spirit consists largely in giving your wife for Christmas the things she wants most and having her give you the things she wants next to most. With scarcely a break the arrangement has come down to us married men from the Garden of Eden. Maybe Christmas wasn't organized then, but woman was. I am indulging in no cheap punnery when I refer to the mother of our race as the First Christmas Eve.

I picture the scene: It is nightfall of December the twenty-fourth in the year One, B.C. The lion and the lamb lie down to rest together. The time is about to come when should these two lie down together only the lion will get up in the morning, the lamb remaining down until thoroughly digested. But now the first vegetarianism epidemic is in vogue and there are no meat-eaters. Our original grandparents also seek repose upon the grassy lea. It is by deliberate intent that the lady in the case has lured her guileless helpmate to a spot where the heaviest laden apple tree in the orchard—and the only one in the entire collection bearing a sign reading "All Persons Are Prohibited From Picking Fruit off This Tree"—spreads its sheltering boughs. There is a purpose in the woman's seeming fancy. She knows exactly what she is about. But Adam, the poor slob, suspects nothing. That is the first woman he has ever met. He is, as the saying goes, easy. He prepares to stretch himself beneath the leafy canopy. He aims to drift right off to sleep. He has put in a hard day, loafing round and killing time. Work hasn't been created into the world yet, and the poor, bored wretch is all fagged out from doing nothing. Eve speaks.

"Adam," she says, "tomorrow will be Christmas in the Garden. Let us hang up our fig leaves—Santa Claus might bring us something."

"Where do you get that Santa Claus stuff?" responds Adam, not unkindly, mind you, but in a spirit of gentle raillery. "I'm a grown man," says Adam.

"Are you, really?" she asks. There is a hidden meaning in her bantering reply, but it goes over his head. "Anyhow, dearie, let's hang up our fig leaves—there can't be any harm in it. Just to humor me, now—please!"

"Oh, very well," he says, just as every subsequent husband has said under similar conditions a thousand times. "Oh, very well, have your own way. But I'm willing to risk a couple of the best city lots in this restricted residential district I can put my hand on the party who's been handing you that Santa Claus yarn, and not have to travel more than a quarter of a mile to do it either. I saw him talking with you yesterday while I was trying to teach the two Potomac shad how to swim. Eve, thank goodness I'm not jealous, and far be it from me to interfere with your friendships round the neighborhood—I guess things do get pretty lonely for you, hanging about the place all day—but if I were you I wouldn't waste much time in the company of that Snake. He's the worst he-gossip in Eden County. He'd make trouble for anybody in a holy minute if he got the chance."

Husbandlike, though, he follows her example and hangs up his fig leaf alongside of hers, upon the face of a nearby rock where a cleft in the cliff suggests a fireplace. Two minutes later he is snoring to beat the walrus, asleep in the next glade. But does the lady drop right off too? She lies down all right, after looking under the edge of the mossy bank for burglars, but she doesn't stay there.

As soon as everything is nice and quiet, up she gets. Stealthily she plucks an apple from that forbidden tree and stealthily she slips it down inside of Adam's fig leaf. After that she can hardly wait through the night for daylight to appear. When the first pink rays of the sunlight come stealing athwart the sward she is sitting up and poking Adam in the ribs.

"Oh, dearie," she cries in well-simulated surprise, "see what Santa has brought us—a lovely red apple."

And Adam falls for the deception. It is the original fall of man. Personally he doesn't care much for apples. Offhand he can think of a dozen things he likes better for breakfast. But, manlike, he humors her. He takes one bite, and then she snatches the apple away from him and eats all of it—slowly and distinctly.

You see it now, don't you—the true inwardness of the Christmas gift-giving habit as between married couples? She has gone through the form of giving him for Christmas the very thing that she wanted all along.

The Twelve Days of Christmas

On the first day of Christmas my true love sent to me
A partridge in a pear tree.

On the second day of Christmas my true love sent to me
Two turtle doves and a partridge in a pear tree.

On the third day of Christmas my true love sent to me
Three French hens,
Two turtle doves and a partridge in a pear tree.

On the fourth day of Christmas my true love sent to me
Four cawing birds, three French hens
Two turtle doves and a partridge in a pear tree.

On the fifth day of Christmas my true love sent to me
Five gold rings!
Four cawing birds, three French hens,
Two turtle doves and a partridge in a pear tree.

On the sixth day of Christmas my true love sent to me
Six geese a-laying,
Five gold rings!
Four cawing birds, three French hens,
Two turtle doves and a partridge in a pear tree.

On the seventh day of Christmas my true love sent to me
Seven swans a-swimming, six geese a-laying,
Five gold rings!
Four cawing birds, three French hens,
Two turtle doves and a partridge in a pear tree.

On the eighth day of Christmas my true love sent to me
Eight maids a-milking,
Seven swans a-swimming, six geese a-laying,
Five gold rings!

Four cawing birds, three French hens,
Two turtle doves and a partridge in a pear tree.

On the ninth day of Christmas my true love sent to me
Nine ladies dancing, eight maids a-milking,
Seven swans a-swimming, six geese a-laying,
Five gold rings!
Four cawing birds, three French hens,
Two turtle doves and a partridge in a pear tree.

On the tenth day of Christmas my true love sent to me
Ten lords a-leaping,
Nine ladies dancing, eight maids a-milking,
Seven swans a-swimming, six geese a-laying,
Five gold rings!
Four cawing birds, three French hens,
Two turtle doves and a partridge in a pear tree.

On the eleventh day of Christmas my true love sent to me
Eleven pipers piping, ten lords a-leaping,
Nine ladies dancing, eight maids a-milking,
Seven swans a-swimming, six geese a-laying,
Five gold rings!
Four cawing birds, three French hens,
Two turtle doves and a partridge in a pear tree.

On the twelfth day of Christmas my true love sent to me
Twelve drummers drumming,
Eleven pipers piping, ten lords a-leaping,
Nine ladies dancing, eight maids a-milking,
Seven swans a-swimming, six geese a-laying,
Five gold rings!
Four cawing birds, three French hens,
Two turtle doves,
And a partridge in a pear tree!

CELEBRATION

The Feast of Christmas

No one has in recent times written more lovingly of the glories of good eating than advertising executive Silas Spitzer. Writer and gourmet cook by avocation, he served as food editor for The Saturday Evening Post's *sister publication*, Holiday. *The following* selections are excerpted from articles he wrote for Christmas issues of Holiday *in the 1950's. The recipes are from New England food expert Charlotte Turgeon's collection of traditional American foods, reprinted from* The Saturday Evening Post All-American Cookbook.

The Christmas dinner of my youth was the longest, most lavish repast of the year. It took several days to prepare, needed extra help in the kitchen, and was so elaborate that it always strained the family's finances. It began with a crunching of salted nuts and a munching of celery at about two o'clock, and drifted, without coming to any definite conclusion, into a sort of contented stupor as the late afternoon shaded into twilight.

Even on ordinary occasions we were a tribe noted for our uninhibited appetites. But on Christmas, our number supplemented by relatives and close friends, we sat down to a table so heavily laden that it can only be described as medieval. If turkey or goose were the major element of this unbuttoned orgy, it was always a bird of monumental proportions, the largest the local market could supply. If roast beef held the place of honor, it was seven ribs thick, and loomed in its platter like Gibraltar.

Gravy was served in depth, homemade bread in huge, sweet-smelling loaves. Quantities of vegetables and minor accompaniments were handed around in overflowing bowls and tureens. In the largest of these vessels was a snowy pile of whipped potatoes, with rivulets of yellow butter running down its sides from a large chunk melting in a cavity at its peak. Another fixture was our mother's wonderful red cabbage, spicy with caraway seeds, rich with goose or chicken fat and piquant with the tart-sweet taste of green apples and sugar.

From year to year, there were few surprises in this most traditional of holiday menus, except on those last few occasions when the family still assembled in force. At these later gatherings, I seem to recall several new dishes of a spectacular modern sort, introduced by the eldest sister, who had suddenly become aware of the fascinations of fashionable living as reported in the glossy periodicals of that day. With her own fair hands, she prepared and served orange-flavored sweet potatoes buried under a froth of toasted marshmallow, odd-tasting artichokes with a thick yellow sauce that was slightly curdled, and a complicated dessert involving ladyfingers, jelly, whipped cream and candied violets.

These innovations, however, were consumed with curiosity rather than gusto, and were tolerated mainly to keep the family peace. For the greater part, our Christmas dinner progressed happily through the old familiar edibles and was crowned not only by mince pie and apple pie but by a sleek jet-black plum pudding that looked like an old-fashioned anarchist's bomb, and was just about as heavy. During the final languid hour, while the grownups smoked cigars and sipped muscatel or brandy, the younger element snapped frilly favors which blossomed into frivolous paper hats.

Many Americans no longer eat on such a formidable scale, but in spite of the present generation's daintier appetites, our native Christmas food and customs still largely follow the traditions established by our English forebears. In England's earlier times there were feasting and pageantry so magnificent that even Hollywood, in its gaudiest moments, has never quite succeeded in capturing their grandeur. For hundreds of years the great moment of these banquets was the joyous entrance of the cavalcade which brought in the boar's head garlanded with rosemary and bay, a lemon or a rosy apple clenched between its bristling tusks. It was carried aloft on a great platter to the sound of harps and the singing of carols. I had always conceived of the boar's head as having only symbolical significance, but I learned from recent reading that it was also a dish relished for its own sake. In its preparation, the head itself was boned and the inside coated with minced pig's liver, chopped apples, onion, sage and rosemary. It was then solidly stuff-

Strong, fast, ferocious, the boar was favorite quarry of Norman kings, who punished unprivileged killing of the beast by death.

119

ed with sausage meat, ox tongue, truffles, mushrooms, pistachio nuts and spices, moistened liberally with apple brandy and then boiled in a cloth for the better part of a day.

A hundred four roasted peacocks were served at one famous feudal feast, borne in single file by a procession of a hundred four servants, with an escort of candle bearers, minstrels and baying hounds. Each peacock had been stuffed with spices and wild herbs, its beak gilded, and its tail feathers replaced and fanned out to their full spread of opulent color. Less spectacular, but perhaps more satisfying in a gustatory sense, was a celebrated pie that once graced the banquet of an English nobleman. Under its mountainous crust it was laden with geese, rabbits, wild ducks, woodcocks, snipe, partridges, curlews, pigeons and blackbirds, and was brought to the guests on a cart that was specially built to carry it.

A poet of Elizabeth's time, boasting of country Christmases, writes of "their thirty-pound butter'd eggs, their pies of carps' tongues, their pheasants drenched with ambergris, the carcasses of three fat wethers bruised for gravy, to make sauce for a single peacock." As may be imagined, it took floods of drink to wash down these unctuous and heavily flavored courses—a circumstance that did nothing to hamper the boisterousness of the occasion.

Peacock, curlew, partridge, blackbird . . . These exotic birds may have been spectacular but they were surely less tender and flavorsome than the modern American turkey that is specially bred and carefully nurtured to grace the holiday table.

AMERICAN ROAST TURKEY WITH OYSTER STUFFING

12- to 14-pound turkey

Stuffing:
1 cup chopped celery
1 cup chopped onion
8 tablespoons butter
8 cups day-old soft bread crumbs

½ teaspoon powdered sage
½ teaspoon powdered thyme
½ teaspoon nutmeg
3 tablespoons chopped parsley
2 teaspoons salt
¼ teaspoon pepper
2 eggs, slightly beaten
1 pint oysters
1 teaspoon lemon juice

Gravy:
¾ cup fat
¾ cup flour
6 cups liquid
Parsley

If possible, buy a fresh turkey. If you are using the frozen variety thaw it completely before stuffing. Wipe the bird inside and out with a damp towel. Cut the neck off as close to the body as possible without cutting the skin. Cut off the wing tips. Rub a little salt and pepper into both the neck and body cavities. Keep the turkey in a cool place while preparing the stuffing.

Stuffing: Cook the chopped celery and onion in butter just until tender. Combine all the ingredients for the stuffing in a large bowl and toss well with a salad fork and spoon until thoroughly blended. The oysters should be left whole if very small, otherwise cut them in large pieces. Add any oyster liquor to the stuffing. Cool the stuffing before packing it loosely into the turkey cavities. Close both openings by sewing them up with kitchen thread or inserting small skewers and lacing the openings.

The Giblets: Place the wing tips, neck, heart and gizzard in 3 cups of water. Add ½ teaspoon salt, a small onion, a stalk of celery with leaves cut up, 1 small bay leaf and a small pinch of powdered thyme. Cover and simmer for 2 hours or cook in a pressure cooker for 15 to 20 minutes at 10-pound pressure. Set aside for use in making gravy.

Extravagantly fueled on brandy or rum, with calories and conscience disregarded, the great pudding is the crown of the feast day.

1 teaspoon baking soda
1 teaspoon salt
½ teaspoon nutmeg
1 teaspoon cinnamon
¼ teaspoon mace
1 cup soft bread crumbs
½ cup brandy

Combine suet, brown sugar, milk and eggs. Mix fruits and almonds with ¼ cup of the flour. Sift remaining flour with soda, salt and spices. Add fruits, crumbs and flour-and-spice mixture to suet mixture. Mix well. Turn into well-greased 1-quart covered pudding mold. Steam 3 hours. (*Steaming directions*: Use steamer or deep covered kettle. In using kettle, place filled and covered mold on trivet or wire rack in kettle. Pour in boiling water to ½ depth of mold. Place cover on kettle and steam, replenishing the boiling water when necessary to keep the proper level of ½ depth of mold.) Turn out on hot platter, heat brandy in small saucepan, pour over pudding, light brandy and bring pudding to the table flaming. Serve with hard sauce.

HARD SAUCE

½ cup butter; dash of salt
2 cups sifted confectioners' sugar
Brandy if desired

Soften butter; beat in sugar until light and fluffy. Add brandy to taste, beating it in thoroughly. To serve, spoon over thin slices of pudding.

Sweetmeats and Sugarplums

FRUITCAKE BARS

1 can (6 ounces) frozen concentrated orange juice,
   thawed, undiluted
½ cup and 2/3 cup packed light brown sugar,
   divided
1 cup raisins
1 package (8 ounces) pitted dates, chopped
1 jar (1 pound) mixed candied fruit, finely chopped
½ cup soft butter or margarine
4 eggs
1 cup unsifted all-purpose flour
1/8 teaspoon baking soda
½ teaspoon cinnamon
½ teaspoon nutmeg
¼ teaspoon allspice
¼ teaspoon cloves
1 cup chopped nuts

In medium saucepan combine undiluted concentrated orange juice and ½ cup brown sugar. Stir over low heat until mixture comes to a boil. Add raisins and dates, bring to a boil again. Remove from heat, stir in mixed candied fruit and set aside.

In large bowl cream butter and remaining 2/3 cup brown sugar. Beat in eggs, one at a time. Blend in flour, baking soda, cinnamon, nutmeg, allspice and cloves. Stir in nuts and fruit mixture. Turn into 2 waxed paper-lined 15-by-10-by-1-inch baking pans. Bake in 300-degree oven 35 to 40 minutes, or until cake tester inserted in center comes out clean.

When cool, frost with orange glaze (see recipe below). Cut into 3-by-1-inch bars. Garnish with halved candied cherries. Makes about 100 bars.

ORANGE GLAZE

1½ cups sifted confectioners' sugar
¼ cup orange juice
1 tablespoon soft butter or margarine

In small bowl mix all ingredients until smooth.

WALNUT KISSES

3 egg whites
1/8 teaspoon salt
2 cups sifted confectioners' sugar
¾ teaspoon vanilla
¼ teaspoon almond extract
2 teaspoons water
1 cup chopped walnuts

Preheat the oven to 225 degrees F. Use Teflon-coated baking sheets or line metal baking sheets with brown paper.

Beat the egg whites and salt until stiff but still moist. Add the sugar slowly and alternately with a mixture of the extracts and water which is added drop by drop. When very thick and glossy fold in the nutmeats.

Drop by half-teaspoonfuls onto the baking sheet. Bake 40 to 45 minutes. Remove from the pan while hot. Makes 40 to 50 small cookies.

GINGERBREAD BOYS AND GIRLS

½ cup butter
½ cup margarine
1½ cups sugar
1 egg
2 tablespoons dark corn syrup
4 teaspoons grated orange rind
3 cups all-purpose unbleached flour
2 teaspoons soda
2 teaspoons cinnamon
1 teaspoon ginger
½ teaspoon nutmeg
½ teaspoon cloves
½ teaspoon salt

Blend the butter and margarine and gradually beat in the sugar until light and fluffy. Add the egg and beat until smooth.

Add the corn syrup and orange peel and mix.

Sift all the dry ingredients and stir into the butter

mixture. Form the dough into a ball and wrap it in wax paper. Chill in the refrigerator.

Preheat the oven to 375 degrees F. Roll out the dough on a lightly floured surface to a thickness of ¼ inch. Cut with a gingerbread-boy cutter. To differentiate between the sexes, cut out small triangular pieces and put on the sides of some of the heads to look like hair ribbons.

Place on ungreased baking sheets 1 inch apart. Bake 8 to 10 minutes. Allow to stand 2 minutes on the pans before transferring to a wire rack to cool. Makes 18 to 24, depending on size.

CANDIED ORANGE SLICES

6 oranges
Water
1½ cups packed dark brown sugar
2 cups water
Granulated sugar

Place oranges in large saucepan or kettle. Cover with water. Cover and bring to a boil over medium heat. Reduce heat and simmer 40 minutes, or until peel is tender. Drain and cool.

Cut oranges into 3/8-inch crosswise slices and cut slices in half; place in bowl. In medium saucepan mix together brown sugar and water. Stir over low heat until sugar dissolves and mixture comes to a boil. Boil, stirring frequently, for 20 minutes or until thick and syrupy. Pour over orange slices. Cover and refrigerate overnight.

Remove orange slices from syrup and roll in granulated sugar; place on rack to dry overnight. Roll in sugar again just before packing in gift boxes. Makes 6 cups.

POPCORN BALLS

2/3 cup granulated sugar
½ cup water
3 tablespoons white corn syrup
1/8 teaspoon salt
1 teaspoon vanilla
½ teaspoon vinegar

Prepare about 6 cups of popped corn, allowing a little extra if there are helpers who will eat some while waiting for the syrup to cook.

To prepare syrup, combine sugar, water and corn syrup in a large aluminum saucepan. Stir until sugar is dissolved, then cook without stirring until the firm ball stage is reached (248 degrees F on a candy thermometer). Add salt, vanilla and vinegar and continue cooking until a little syrup dropped into cold water forms brittle threads (firm crack stage, or 290 degrees F). Pour syrup over popped corn in a large mixing bowl.

As soon as it is cool enough to handle, spread butter on your hands and use them to mix thoroughly and shape into balls.

CANDIED APPLES

10 to 12 medium red apples
10 to 12 wooden sticks (skewers)
2 cups sugar
1 cup light corn syrup
½ cup water
2 teaspoons cinnamon
Red food coloring (about ½ teaspoon)

Wash and dry apples. Insert stick in stem end of each.

Combine other ingredients. Heat slowly, stirring constantly until sugar dissolves. Bring to a boil and boil rapidly to the soft-crack stage (280 degrees on a candy thermometer).

Remove from heat. As soon as bubbling stops, begin dipping apples. Tilt pan and swirl apples through, letting surplus syrup drip off. Place on greased cookie sheet to cool, spaced well apart so apples will not touch.

If syrup becomes too thick, reheat slightly over low heat. For last few apples, stand apple in saucepan and spoon remaining syrup up and over it.

Three to five minutes after dipping, shift apples on the cookie sheet to prevent sticking. When cool, wrap individually in waxed paper or plastic.

Tied with bright yarn or ribbon, the popcorn balls can serve as tree ornaments.

O Little Town of Bethlehem

Phillips Brooks

Lewis H. Redner

Christmas sing merrilie

The deeply philosophical words of "O Little Town of Bethlehem" were written by a Boston minister and theologian, Phillips Brooks.

God Rest Ye Merry, Gentlemen

1. God rest ye mer - ry, gen - tle - men, Let noth - ing you dis - may, For
2. From God, our Heav - en - ly Fa - ther, A bless - ed an - gel came, And
3. The shep - herds at these ti - dings Re - joic - ed much in mind, And

Je - sus Christ, our Sa - vi - our, Was born up - on this day: To
un - to cer - tain shep - herds Brought ti - dings of the same: How
left their flocks a - feed - ing In tem - pest, storm and wind, And

save us all from Sa - tan's pow'r, When we were gone a - stray:
that in Beth - le - hem was born The Son of God by name: O ——
went to Beth - le - hem straight way, The Bless - ed Babe to find:

ti - dings of com - fort and joy, Com - fort and joy, O ti - dings of com - fort and joy.

Traditional English Melody

Traditional English Words

God rest ye merrie Gentlemen

The form of this London melody, popular in English towns in the eighteenth century, was influenced by street ballads and round singing.

Silent Night

1. Si - lent night, Ho - ly night, All is calm, all is bright.
2. Si - lent night, Ho - ly night, Shep - herds quake at the sight.
3. Si - lent night, Ho - ly night, Son of God, love's pure light.

'Round yon Vir - gin Moth - er and Child Ho - ly In - fant so ten - der and mild,
Glo - ries stream from heav - en a - far, Heav'n-ly hosts sing Al - le - lu - ia;
Ra - diant beams from Thy ho - ly face, With the dawn of re - deem - ing grace,

Sleep in heav - en - ly peace,___ Sleep in heav - en - ly peace.___
Christ the Sa - vior is born,___ Christ the Sa - vior is born.___
Je - sus, Lord, at Thy birth,___ Je - sus, Lord, at Thy birth.___

Joseph Mohr   *Franz Gruber*

Holy Night

The music of the world's best loved Christmas carol was written by Franz Gruber, an Austrian church organist, in 1818.

O Come, All Ye Faithful

1. O come all ye faith - ful, Joy - ful and tri - um - phant, O
2. Sing, choirs of an - gels, Sing in ex - ul - ta - tion,
3. Yea, Lord, we greet Thee, Born this hap - py morn - ing;

come ye, O come ye to Beth - le - hem, Come and be - hold Him
Sing, all ye cit - i - zens of heav'n a - bove: Glo - ry to God
Je - sus, to Thee be glo - ry giv'n, Word of the Fa - ther

born the King of an - gels;
In the high - est; } O come let us a - dore Him, O
now in flesh ap - pear - ing;

come let us a - dore Him, O come let us a - dore Him, Christ the Lord.

English translation, Rev. Frederick Oakeley

Latin Hymn, Attributed to John Reading

"Adeste Fideles" is a Latin hymn to be sung with dignity and voices in unison. The tempo lends itself well to processions.

Things To Do

Maybe getting ready for Christmas is the very best part of the holiday season.

Children know. Long after they have forgotten gifts received they may remember red-and-green paper chains carried home from kindergarten, the desk blotter laboriously assembled for father at Cub Scout meetings, the lopsided pincushion made for mother.

What is the magic of the handmade gift or decoration?

It comes from the heart—witness the bloodstains from pricked finger and hammered thumb.

It's one of a kind. Individually planned for a special person or a special place in the home. Assembled with happy anticipation and loving thoughts as well as tape and glue.

The projects suggested on these pages are not ones you can begin the day before Christmas. You will need to start these early—and you should have children to help you, because children are far better at finding acorns and bird's nests, seed pods and pine cones, than grown-ups are.

Decorate a Pioneer-Style Tree

When the main house at Conner Prairie Pioneer Settlement was built in 1823 it was the only brick residence in Central Indiana and the finest homestead for miles around. Today the spacious two-story home near Noblesville is the centerpiece of a "living museum" complex where visitors see costumed men and women working at tasks that were commonplace in pioneer days but are almost forgotten today.

Conner Prairie is closed in winter except for two weekends just before Christmas, when it is lit by candles and decorated as it might have been for a holiday season in the 1830's. There's a punchbowl, fruit and fancy cookies in the dining room; bread and pies are being made in the kitchen. The brightest quilts and embroidered coverlets are displayed on four-posters in bedrooms that are fragrant with pomander balls and tiny nosegays of dried flowers. Tradition has it these were gifts for holiday guests to take home with them.

In the spacious living room, where tiny-paned windows with ruffled curtains overlook the White River, stands a Christmas tree thought to be like the very first ones seen in the Midwest.

The tree itself is a red cedar, slender and prickly and quite different from the horizontal-branching firs and spruces we use for Christmas trees today. The red cedar is the only evergreen native to central Indiana, so it would have been the only kind available to the pioneers.

The ornaments hung on the tree are all ones mentioned in old letters or diaries of the place and period—red apples, cookies, tiny cornhusk dolls, and Bible verses printed on scraps of parchment and hung from the tree's twigs with bits of bright yarn. There are strings of popcorn but no cranberries, as cranberries don't grow wild in Indiana and the pioneers wouldn't have had them. Instead there are red and orange rose-hips. Bits of sheep's-wool are laid on the branches, to look like snow.

Recently a research historian reported finding a mention of another kind of tree ornament—a tiny basket made of half an eggshell with a bit of ribbon glued to it for a handle, filled with nutmeats and small bits of candy. Might such baskets have hung on the tree as gifts for visiting children, as the spice balls and nosegays were gifts for the ladies who came to call? No one is sure, but the ladies who serve as guides and hostesses at Conner Prairie are saving washed and dried eggshell halves which they will hang on next year's pioneer Christmas tree.

THINGS TO HANG ON YOUR TREE

The tree decorated at home for family and friends need not follow the rules of historical authenticity so closely as the Conner Prairie tree, which is displayed in a museum setting and sponsored by an educational institution.

Volunteer hostesses and their young helpers dress the part of pioneers to ready Conner Prairie for Christmas visitors. On the prickly cedar tree go cookies and popcorn, gingerbread boys and girls (see recipe on page 130) and cornhusk dolls. Cornhusks are easy to work with if they are moistened with water to which a few drops of glycerine have been added, to keep them soft and pliable. One easy way to make a cornhusk doll is to start with a wooden clothespin. Fold the husks around it and tie with yarn or raffia at the doll's neck, waist, and wrists.

At home, you can use a nursery-grown spruce or any other kind of tree you like. You can string cranberries, even if they don't grow wild in your part of the country. You can design your own ornaments and make them from a variety of materials, so long as you keep to the spirit of pioneer days.

Apples, popcorn and cranberries: Apples are quite heavy, so choose the smaller sizes and provide a sturdy hanger. One way: run stiff wire down through the core and twist the end around a cinnamon stick to keep it from pulling out. Later you can eat the apples and use the cinnamon sticks to stir mugs of hot cider.

To make garlands, use the largest needles you have and the heavy thread marked "Button and Carpet." Try to buy a brand of popcorn that turns out large and fluffy, and aim the needle through the largest and most solid segment. Very often the popcorn breaks apart as the needle goes through (in that case, the stringer gets to eat the fragments.) Children may find it easier and more satisfying to string cranberries and merely *eat* popcorn. You can string popcorn and cranberries separately, or combine them.

After Christmas, hang the garlands outdoors for the birds to enjoy.

COOKIES—TO EAT OR TO LOOK AT:

If cookies are to hang on the tree as ornaments, they should have holes made in them before they are baked. You can run narrow ribbon or yarn through the hole (after the cookie cools) but an easier way is to hang the cookie from a clean pipe cleaner bent into S-shape. To make inedible cookies that can be saved from year to year, mix 2 cups of flour and 1 cup of salt with enough water to make a stiff dough. Roll, cut with fancy cutters, make hole for hanging, and bake 2 hours in a slow oven (250 degrees F). Decorate with paint or with glued-on seeds. Store wrapped in tissue paper, in a dry, airy place.

If you like needlework, cut traditional cookie shapes (bell, star, angel, reindeer) from felt, two at a time. No seam allowance is needed. Overcast along the edges with matching thread, stuffing a little cotton inside before sewing the last side. Trim with stitched-on or glued-on rickrack, ribbon and bits of contrasting felt.

Make a "Tree" of Weeds and Flowers

Lois Douglas starts thinking about Christmas in June. That's when she begins drying roses, daisies and other flowers that will reappear later in the Christmas decorations she makes. Her big harvest comes in September and October, when she drives out in the country to gather roadside weeds: teasel, goldenrod, ironweed. She gets bearded wheat and cornhusks from farmers; she brings moss and grapevines from the woods. Mrs. Douglas has even found a way to use hedge apples, the pimply, green, strong-smelling fruits regarded as a nuisance by everyone else who finds them along the roadside.

To dry and preserve these natural materials Mrs. Douglas uses a variety of techniques. Some flowers are dried in a microwave oven, others are buried in silica gel or sand. Some—like the big blossoms of hydrangea and snowball bush—are simply left where they grow, to dry on their own stems until harvest time. Weeds are generally tied in bunches and hung head down from the garage rafters. Leaves are placed like bouquets in vases of glycerine-and-water solution for several weeks, a method of preservation that leaves them leathery but supple. The hedge apples are sliced and then dried all day in a very slow oven—the result, cup-shaped and fluted, looks like a big poppy blossom.

"There are a lot of good books on drying flowers," Mrs. Douglas says. "If you're interested, read one or two, then start experimenting. You have to learn to use the plant materials available in your part of the country, and get the kind of effect you like. So try different methods, and see how things turn out."

Many natural materials have interesting textures or shapes but are dull brown or gray. Mrs. Douglas tints these, because she likes a variety of soft colors to work with. She has a special fondness for shades of pink, lavender and purples ("Purple is the color of the church season of Advent, leading up to the birth of Christ, so it's appropriate for the decorations you display during the weeks before Christmas."), but she also uses blue, yellow and gold.

"The dark green of pine branches can be a cold color; the bright red so often used with it can be harsh," Mrs. Douglas says. "Too, people get tired of red and green at Christmas. Why not pink, purple, gold, soft green? These are colors of life and joy, and surely life and joy *is* the message of Christmas."

TINTING DRIED PLANT MATERIALS

There are two methods for coloring dried plant materials; you can use either spray paint or liquid dye (RIT is the brand generally available).

When painting, Mrs. Douglas never uses just one can of spray paint. She buys a number of different shades of different colors. She spreads the dry weeds or leaves on a plastic dropcloth on the garage floor, then starts experimenting. A little of one color, then a little of another produces a softer, more interesting effect than one color alone.

Cornhusks and hydrangea blossoms can be successfully tinted by dipping them in liquid dye and then hanging them on the clothesline to drip-dry. Some dark materials can be successfully bleached in a Chlorox solution and then tinted a light or bright color with dye.

MAKING A DRIED PLANT "TREE"

The pastel-colored "tree" displayed on Mrs. Douglas's coffee table is made of tinted plant materials mounted on a yard-high cone of wire mesh. She also makes a five-foot "tree" for her home, and she has helped to make two fifteen-foot-tall ones for decorating the sanctuary of the North Methodist Church in Indianapolis.

To make the table-size one, buy 36-inch wire mesh from a hardware store. This comes with ¼- or ½-inch holes in it; she likes the ¼-inch kind best. Mark first, then cut with a tin-snips 4 triangular sections, each 15 inches wide at the base and 36 inches tall.

Shape each triangle by rolling it a little, then put them

Every year Lois Douglas helps to decorate her church with dried flowers and other plant materials. At right: A fifteen-foot-tall tree stands at the altar, with a life-size papier-mâché Madonna for visual accent. The small pictures show grapevine garlands and sunburst arrangements of tinted weeds that decorate side walls of the sanctuary. Below, left: Priscilla Douglas, following her mother's directions, completes a thirty-six-inch tree for her Chicago apartment.

together so as to form a cone. Overlap the cut edges and fasten them together with short bits of wire. The resulting frame need not be neat, as it will be entirely covered.

When the frame is ready, place it in the middle of a plastic dropcloth or old bedsheet and start applying your dried, tinted plant materials. Flowers with stems are easiest to attach—just tuck their stems into the holes in the wire mesh. Other materials—such as the dried hedge apple slices and cornhusk pompons—need to be wired in place.

The trick is to mix colors and textures tastefully as you cover the "tree" frame. Helpful hints: Use very fine-textured, lacy materials in bunches, so they don't disappear. Use large materials—like the cornhusk bows and hydrangea blossoms—singly and spaced well apart. The colors will harmonize if they are all soft rather than harsh colors.

"Use your imagination," she suggests. "There are no hard and fast rules to follow, and no two decorations will ever be alike."

Make Pomander Balls

These spicy balls can serve as decorations that scent the whole house for Christmas. They are also nice gifts that children can make for aunts and grandmothers who will find that a pomander ball hung in the closet will keep things sweet-smelling for a year or longer.

Start making pomander balls at least six weeks before Christmas to allow time for them to dry completely before they are used as decorations or gifts.

You will need medium-sized oranges, a great many whole cloves, powdered orris root, ground cinnamon, and a steel knitting needle or something similar to pierce the orange rind. Begin by sticking cloves in the orange

The pomander ball's sweet, spicy scent will linger like a memory of Christmas cheer.

until it is entirely covered. Children enjoy this task, which is sweet-smelling and not too demanding, as the cloves need not be set in rows or any pattern.

Mix together equal parts of orris root and cinnamon and roll the balls in this powder until they are well coated. (Use cinnamon alone if orris root is not available.) Then wrap loosely in tissue paper and leave in a warm, dry place. Inspect from time to time—if the balls are drying too fast they may shrivel, and if too slowly they may mildew. When dry, shake off the surplus powder and trim with ribbons.

Apples, pears, or lemons may be used to make pomander balls of slightly different shapes and sizes.

Make a Woodland Wreath

"My wreath is the product of many hours of work and many sore fingers," says Judy Horn of Dayton, Ohio. "There are no shortcuts. Each nut and pine cone must first be attached to a length of wire, then the wire must be securely fastened to the wreath frame. All this takes

time, but the result is a sturdy wreath that will last a lifetime, and one that looks so nice you'll want to leave it up year-round."

Only a few tools are needed: a good pair of pliers with wire-cutter, a drill (hand or electric) with a small bit, and some kind of vise or clamp to hold nuts while you drill holes through them.

Buy a wire wreath frame from a craft shop or florists' supply house (the wreath shown was constructed on an eighteen-inch frame). You will also need a spool of No. 24 wire, florists' tape, and clear acrylic spray.

Pine cones come in many different sizes and they fall from the trees at different seasons (some in early spring). They should be collected when they fall, as they turn dark and brittle if left on the ground. Try to collect a number of middle-sized cones of the same size and type, for edging the wreath.

Wash cones with the garden hose to remove dust and insects. Store in wooden crates or mesh bags, in a dry place where air can circulate through them.

Collect nuts, acorns and buckeyes in autumn. Spread them on old cookie tins and bake them (20 minutes at 300 degrees F) to kill any insects or larvae they might contain. Preserve some nuts in their hulls, and some extra pieces of hull, for variety. Other seeds and pods may be used, if they are sturdy and a good color—

About 100 pine cones and 100 nuts go into making the woodland wreath, shown completed and as construction is begun.

dried peach pits and the prickly seed pods from sweet-gum trees are suitable. Crack some nuts in half and pick out the nutmeats, as the inside of the shell has an interesting pattern. If walnuts and hickory nuts can't be found in the woods where you live, substitute pecans or English walnuts from the supermarket.

Store these materials in mesh bags hung from the rafters, with a few mothballs in each bag to discourage insects or rodents, until you assemble the wreath.

Begin by wrapping all parts of the wire frame with

florists' tape. This helps to keep the wired-on cones from slipping around. Then place the frame on a table and arrange cones around both the inner and outer edges, keeping the cones as uniform as possible, smaller ones in the inner circle and larger ones outside. When you know how many cones are needed, cut a ten-inch length of wire for each one. Wind one end of each wire around a cone, near the base, and twist to fasten securely.

When all cones are wired, attach one to the outer edge. Work the cone wire through the frame, from outside to inside, and pull hard, so the base of the cone is firmly seated against the wreath frame. Use pliers to pull wire tight, wind it several times around the inner ring of the wreath frame, then clip off excess wire. Attach several more the same way, pushing the cones close together as you work, then attach one to the inner edge. Work the wire through the frame from inside to outside, pull tight, and fasten wire around the outer ring of the frame between two of the cones already attached. Continue in this way, adding a few outer cones and then one or two inner ones, until both rings are tightly filled.

"Now it's time to do the actual designing of the wreath," Mrs. Horn says. "This is when you need a variety of cones, large and small, some right side up and some upside down. Cut some in two for a different look. Break part of the petals out of some, to get a loose, flowerlike effect."

When she begins the designing, Mrs. Horn works in threes. Attach wires to three large, uniform cones and place them equal distances apart on the central part of the frame—they form a triangle on the circle. Then attach wires near the tips of three or more large cones and attach them, upside down, equal distances between the first three to form a second triangle. The next units added might be half-cones, then cones with part of the petals broken away, then small cones wired together in clusters, but always three at a time, forming triangles. Each time work the cone's wire through the frame, front to back, pull it tight and then wind it several times around a part of the frame.

When the wreath has been loosely filled in this way, begin to add nuts, acorns and buckeyes. Drill a hole through each one, near the base, run one end of a short piece of wire through the hole, and twist to fasten securely. Wire some nuts together in clusters of three. When complete, the nuts and pine cones should be crowded so close together that none can shift.

Lay the completed wreath on newspapers, outdoors, and spray thoroughly with acrylic spray so that all surfaces are coated.

Decorate With Fragrant Herbs

Legend has it that the blossoms of rosemary were white, until the first Christmas. When Mary and Joseph were on their way to Bethlehem they stopped to rest at a place where this fragrant herb grew alongside the road. When Mary rose to go on, the flowers that had been covered by her cloak were blue, like her cloak, and they are blue today.

Our-Lady's-bedstraw gets its name from another legend that says this herb was growing near the stable in Bethlehem and that its sweet-smelling, springy stems were brought in to make a comfortable bed for Mother and Child.

Still another Christmas legend tells how the herb juniper saved the life of the Christ Child when the Holy Family was fleeing from Bethlehem with King Herod's soldiers in hot pursuit. Juniper shrubs bent aside to let Mary, Joseph and the Child pass, and then thrust out their prickly and unruly branches to stop the soldiers.

So use sprigs of rosemary, bedstraw and juniper in your Christmas decorations—the delicate fragrance they bring into the house will be authentically Christmasy!

The word "herb" means any plant that is useful to man, but we usually think of herbs as plants that are scented. Frankincense and myrrh are herbs that grow to tree size.

Over the years many different herbs have been used as medicines, as cleaning aids, for seasoning foods, and for providing pleasant smells to hide unpleasant ones—that was very important in ancient times, when there was never enough soap or hot water to keep things clean.

The sage that flavors the turkey stuffing, the ginger that goes into gingerbread men, cinnamon, peppermint, vanilla—all the things that smell so good in the kitchen at Christmastime—are herbs that grow in one part of the world or another.

Our-Lady's-bedstraw grows along roadsides and in waste places, in many parts of the United States. Rosemary is found in old-fashioned flower gardens, especially in the South. Juniper is a low-growing evergreen planted as an ornamental shrub. Any herb book will teach you how to identify these and many other herbs, and how to start an herb garden where you can grow your own supply of fragrant plants.

People generally harvest their herbs in late summer or fall by cutting the stems, tying them in bunches, and hanging them head down from rafters of garage or attic, where they will give off a pleasant scent while drying. Gather grasses, weeds and some flowers, also, to add variety to your decorations. Old-fashioned strawflowers, coxcomb and baby's breath are good for the purpose. You may also want to save some clusters of berries and seed pods.

Then, when it is time to get ready for Christmas, you can create wreaths or bouquets for each room in the

Barbara and Alan White make the wreath and the arrangement in an antique deed box shown below, using herbs and old-fashioned flowers from their own garden along with a few roadside weeds. In the barn where their herbs hang drying, the Whites decorate a tree with real candles, red apples, candy canes and bows made from cornhusks.

house, using the herbs for fragrance and the other plant materials for visual accents. You will need only ring-shaped wreath forms, florists' wire, and a supply of the Oasis foam blocks used for flower arranging—all available at craft shops or florists' supply houses.

Since the dry herbs do not need to be in water, a wide variety of containers can be used for bouquets. You can use antique or modern baskets, boxes, or the wooden lugs in which some fruits and vegetables are packed, as well as bowls and vases.

To begin, cut a block of foam to fit down in the bottom of the container you plan to use. If the surface of the block is visible—as in the open box—cover the foam with moss. Place a few large flowers or seed pods first by poking their stems into the foam, then many fine, lacy

plant materials around them to fill all the space. If the stems are firm and stiff, no special techniques are needed. If the stems are weak and keep breaking, wrap florists' wire around each stem, to strengthen it, and push the wire end into the foam block.

The box shown is an antique deed case, covered with leather. A stick has been placed at the back, to make sure the lid doesn't come down and smash the plant materials, which include the Christmas herbs plus roadside weeds and strawflowers. Three tiny birds are posed around a nest-shaped arrangement of dry grasses—you can use a real bird's nest in the arrangement if you find one that is neat and attractive. (Collect the nest in autumn, after the birds have left it and before winter winds damage it.)

Acknowledgments

Illustrations on pages 14, 15, 30, 31, 43, and 54 reproduced from greeting cards in the collection of The Hallmark Corporation, Kansas City, Missouri.

Illustrations on pages 86 and 87 were painted by Jessie Wilcox Smith for *A Visit From St. Nicholas* by Clement C. Moore. Copyright © 1912 by Houghton Mifflin Company. Reproduced by permission of the publisher.

Songs on pages 132, 134, 136 and 138 arranged by Karl Schulte. Copyright © 1938; copyright renewed 1968 by Western Publishing Company, Inc. Reprinted by permission.

Dried flower arrangements on page 147 by Barbara and Alan White of The Herb Barn, Westfield, Indiana.

TEXT CREDITS

"What Was the Star of Bethlehem?" by Arthur C. Clarke first appeared in *Holiday Magazine*. Copyright © 1954 The Curtis Publishing Company. Reprinted by permission of the author and the author's agents, Scott Meredith Literary Agency, Inc., 845 Third Avenue, New York, N.Y. 10022.

"Susie's Letter From Santa" is from *My Father—Mark Twain* by Clara Clemens. Copyright © 1931 by Clara Clemens Gabrilowitsch renewed 1959 by Clara Clemens Samossoud. Reprinted by permission of Harper & Row, Publishers, Inc.

"Angels" is from *Angels: God's Secret Agents* by Billy Graham. Copyright © 1975 by Billy Graham. Reprinted by permission of the publisher, Doubleday and Company, Inc.

"The Gift of the Magi" is from *The Four Million* by O. Henry. Copyright © 1907 by Doubleday, Page & Company. Reprinted by permission of Doubleday and Company, Inc.

"Winter Wonder" by Donald Culross Peattie first appeared in *Holiday Magazine*. Copyright © 1946 The Curtis Publishing Company. "Gold, Frankincense and Myrrh" by Donald Culross Peattie first appeared in *Good Housekeeping* Magazine. Copyright © 1955 The Hearst Corporation. Both selections reprinted by permission of the author's estate and its agent, James Brown Associates, Inc., 22 East 60th Street, New York, N.Y. 10022.

"Christmas in Brooklyn" is from *A Tree Grows in Brooklyn* by Betty Smith. Copyright © 1943, 1947 by Betty Smith. Reprinted by permission of Harper & Row, Publishers, Inc.

"Conversation About Christmas" by Dylan Thomas. Copyright © 1954 by New Directions Publishing Corporation. Reprinted by permission of New Directions Publishing Corporation.

"Christmas on the Prairie" is from *Little House on the Prairie* by Laura Ingalls Wilder. Text copyright © 1935 by Laura Ingalls Wilder. Copyright renewed 1963 by Roger L. MacBride. Reprinted by permission of Harper & Row, Publishers, Inc.

PICTURE SOURCES

Pages 2,3—The Adoration of the Magi by Fra Lippo Lippi and Fra Angelico. The National Gallery, Washington. Page 7—The Adoration of the Magi by Hieronymus Bosch. The Metropolitan Museum of Art, New York. Kennedy Fund, 1912. Pages 8, 9—The Nativity with Donors and Patron Saints by Gerard David (central panel, detail: angels in upper left). The Metropolitan Museum of Art, New York. Pages 76,77—Brown Brothers, Sterling, Pennsylvania. Page 80—Portrait of Edward VI by Hans Holbein the Younger. The Metropolitan Museum of Art, New York. Collection of Jules S. Bache. Page 88—The Mark Twain Memorial, Hartford, Connecticut. Page 90—Wide World Photos, New York. Page 96, The Theodore Roosevelt Collection, Harvard College Library, Cambridge, Massachusetts.

Illustrations not otherwise credited are from the pages of *The Saturday Evening Post, Country Gentleman*, and *Child Life* magazines, and are the copyrighted property of The Curtis Publishing Company or The Saturday Evening Post Company.

Volume Two

THE SATURDAY EVENING POST

Christmas Stories

A Carol of Gifts

By Richard Burton

The gift of the Christmastide!
  A time of right good cheer,
When the door swings open wide
  And the fire leaps blithe and clear.
    Where once walked folly and fear,
      Ring the shouts of the young at play:
    And indoor mirth makes joy on earth
      And a spirit of holiday.

The gift of the loving heart,
  When the kindred ties of home
Draw close the far apart,
  Make mates of those who roam:
    Be they tossed on the ocean foam
      Or dwelling in strange, sad lands,
    In soul they meet and fondly greet
      Through the gift of the clasped hands. (1903)

*One touch of Christmas
makes the whole world kin.*

Volume Two

Contents

CHRISTMAS BEHIND THE SCENES

René Bache

Letters to Santa Claus

The faith of childhood in Santa Claus and his gifts makes a good deal of business for the Post-Office Department during the Christmas season.

Little boys and girls know only two ways of communicating with the jolly Christmas god—by the chimney and by mail. A letter, dropped into the fireplace just before bedtime, may be expected to reach him. The smoke, when the fire is lighted, will carry it up the flue; or, if it is not safely conveyed in that fashion, Kriss Kringle will come for it. In fact, a mere list of toys and other articles desired, when similarly deposited, will accomplish the purpose in view.

But these are days when postal facilities are employed much more generally and widely than was the case fifteen or twenty years ago, and the channel of communication with Santa Claus by chimney has been to a great extent abandoned, the everyday mails being preferred on account of their greater promptness and sureness of delivery. Hence it comes about that, at Christmastide each year, thousands of missives addressed by children to their patron saint are dropped into post-boxes all over the country.

They are directed in a great variety of ways— sometimes simply to the "Arctic Regions," but oftener to a more definite locality, such as "Ice Land," "Snow Land" or "The North Pole." Occasionally a European capital, such as London or Paris, is mentioned as the address of the saint, and in such a case the missive is duly forwarded— to be returned to the United States, a month or two later, with the words "Not Found" officially stamped upon it. If mailed without a postage-stamp it goes just the same, because the charge for carrying a letter to a foreign country is collectable at the other end, if not paid in advance.

Such letters, strange as it may seem, sometimes travel about all over the continent of Europe in pursuit of "Mr. Kriss Kringle," being forwarded from place to place by postal officials who seem to entertain no suspicion of their true character.

Eventually, of course, they are returned to this country, where they find their final haven in the foreign division of the Dead Letter Office in Washington. It is an interesting fact, worth mentioning in this connection, that French, German and even English children are frequently imbued with the notion that Santa Claus resides in America, and address their Christmas petitions accordingly.

The Hartz Mountains, in Germany, where such quantities of toys are made, are understood by many children to be the good saint's headquarters. Last Christmas a small Quaker girl in Philadelphia addressed in obedience to this notion her letter, which, in winding up a series of requests, said: "I will not ask thee, dear Santa, for a live baby, for I am sure that either my grandmother or my aunt means to give me one. And I know thee is so busy."

Another little girl wrote from Baltimore to Kriss Kringle at the "North Pole," asking for a pony and cart, and explained that though her Papa had no stable, there would be room for the pony in the playroom closet. Somehow the missive got as far as New York, but was sent thence to Washington with the inscription "No such post office in this State" stamped on the envelope. Technically, "Santa Claus letters," as they are called, come under the head of "fictitious" mail matter, and those which are directed to such impossible places as "Snow Land" or "Arctic Regions" are so marked at the local post offices and forwarded to the Dead Letter Office.

It is held by the Post-Office Department that such children's letters are entitled to the same privacy and respectful treatment as ordinary first-class mail enjoys. When they reach the Dead Letter Office they go through the regular course of procedure, being opened, examined for valuable contents—once in a while small sums of money are found in them—and returned to the senders in case (as often happens) their addresses are appended. If they lack stamps, for missives of the kind are liable to be dropped into the postbox "on faith" and without prepayment, the writers, if practible, are notified. The letters whose senders cannot be reached are burned.

"I would like a woolly dog," wrote one boy last Christmas. "I would like an alive one. I have a woolly dog on wheels, and he barks. I do not care for the alive one unless he can bark, too."

This is an example of the kind of letter that is dictated by the child to a sympathizing parent, who takes it down verbatim, addresses it to the North Pole, or to Peking, China, and shows the youngster how to drop it into the mailbox on the nearest corner. When, on Christmas Day, the woolly dog makes his appearance, it is obvious that the communication must have been received by Santa, and no further questions are asked.

Most Santa Claus letters are dictated in this way, but many children prefer, and are encouraged, as soon as they have acquired the art of printing words, to forward their petitions in autograph. Done in large angular letters, last Christmas, was the confidential missive of a small Washington girl, who wrote:

Please bring me a doll, and some candy. I like candy. Dear Santa Claus, bring me some green candy. 2410 G Street. That is all.

Now, why should this little girl have preferred green candy? Was it because she had found green sweetmeats more toothsome, or (as seems more likely) because she admired the color?

Here is another, from a small boy:

My dear Santa Claus: I hope you will come to my house, and don't forget. I want a drum, a bote, an engin, and a story book. And a trumpet. Yours truly, Stephen Fink, 709 24th st., N.W.

There is no art more difficult for a child to grasp than that of epistolary composition. Hence it comes about that nearly all Santa Claus letters are written with more or less help from the grown-ups. But there are occasional exceptions, of which the following is seemingly an example:

Deer Santy Claws: Maggy nex dor had two dollys last Crismus, and i had nun. I cride all day. She don't nede enny dollys this crismus. So don't giv her enny, and giv me two.

Now, is that not just like a child? Really, when one comes to think of it, children are very interesting, anthropologically considered. They are many thousands of years older than we are. We adults are of to-day, but they, in their nuances of thought and expression, represent the infancy of the human race, ages before the first civilization dawned on the earth!

It is a curious fact, noticed in the Dead Letter Office, that the children of the rich write comparatively few letters to Santa Claus. And the reason why is not far to seek. It is not that they have less faith in the myth but because they have no anxieties as to the gratification of their wants. They know that, when Christmas comes, they are sure to get whatever they desire, and it is not worth their while to bother with petitions.

When the writer was himself a little boy he was told that the chimneys of the houses of the poor were so narrow that Santa Claus could not make his way down them, and so he carried his toys and other gifts elsewhere. It was a pathetic, picturesque way of expressing the idea of the *res angusta domi* which forbids many of the best blessings of life to those who cannot afford to buy them.

Just before Christmas of last year there came to the War Department in Washington, from the Dead Letter Office, a letter from a soldier's little boy, addressed to "Santa Claus, Alaska." It was "returned for better direction," and read:

I would like you to send me, if you please, good Santa Claus, one steam car, one little red wagon, one stocking full of candy. Much Oblige. Your little friend, Daniel Le May, Jr.

The hearts of the bureau officials, toughened by official hard knocks and the influence of unsympathetic red tape, were melted by this childish appeal, and a collection was promptly taken up, the sum obtained being sufficient to purchase a locomotive and train, a miniature automobile and several pounds of fairly digestible confectionery. These were at once shipped to Master Daniel Le May, with a letter bearing a huge seal and ribbons, and stamped "Palace of Santa Claus, Alaska." It read:

My little Friend: My last train of reindeer, skimming over the cold snows and ice of my far-away home, brought me a big bushel-bag of letters from my little friends, and among them I found yours. After lighting my pipe and telling my man to close all the doors of my palace so as to keep out the cold winds, I made him get out of my factory some things for you; and, after having them packed, I told him to harness my two fleetest reindeer, Blitzen and Vixen, to my sled, and take them to the post office for you. I hope you will get them in time for Christmas. With my best wishes for a merry Christmas, I sign myself, your friend,

Santa Claus.

Done at the Palace of Santa Claus, this Christmas, A.D. 1902, under seal.

On more than one occasion the clerks at the Dead Letter Office in Washington have put their pennies together to buy gifts for children whose chimneys (as suggested by pathetic letters at Christmastide) were too narrow to let in good old Kriss Kringle.

"Please bring me a dolly," writes one scrap of femininity. "And please, Mr. Santa, brig it up the steem-heeter, and not down the chimny, so she won't get her hair burned."

A small boy writes: "Dear Saint Nicholas: I love you next to God. So, please, if God don't mind, bring me a billygote."

Goats are evidently in great demand at Christmastime. Another boy writes: "I want my billy goat to have horns, so he can but, and a tale, so I can pull it."

Equally characteristic is a Christmas petition from a youngster who has an aquarium. He writes: "Please, Mr. Santa Claus, giv me a bull-frogg. I want one that can sing."

A little girl says: "I would like some munny for myself to spend. The munny you gave me last Christmas Mamma put in the bank. I want the munny to buy candy."

Another writes: "I am a little colored girl. I want a white doll-baby, with gold hair, and eyes that shut. And a red dress, please."

Santa Claus' Christmas correspondence is full of humor and pathos. From whatever sources it emanates, the mansions of the rich or the most untidy slum, it is the literature of an innocence as yet unspoiled by the world. (1903)

Edgar S. Nash

The Origin of Christmas Customs

There are a few things in existence to-day which have not been changed or moulded in the hands of Progress. One by one legends and customs have been disproved and overthrown, yet none has dared attack the legends and the customs sacred to Christmas-tide. Here and there a savant has tried to prove that December 25th does not mark the birthday of Christ. Men and women read, smile, pass on.

The time of year corresponding to our Christmas-tide has always been a period of rejoicing. It marks the winter solstice. The days begin to lengthen, and the sun no longer journeys away from earth, but enters upon his return. It is a promise of renewed light and warmth, of the approach of the summer days, and men hailed these signs with every expression of gladness.

In Rome the Saturnalia, or feast of Saturn, fell at about the same time as our Christmas, and it marked the greatest festival of the Roman year. The city abandoned itself to gayety. Unbounded license held sway; universal mirth was the order of the day; friends feasted friends, and foes were reconciled. There were no slaves, no masters; all social distinctions were laid aside. Work was stopped throughout the city, and no war was ever entered upon at this time.

The tree as the emblem of life also figured conspicuously in the earlier religions. In Egypt the palm tree put forth a new shoot each month, and at the time of the winter solstice it was the custom among the Egyptians to decorate the houses with a branch of palm bearing twelve shoots. In Rome the fir tree was regarded with veneration; during the Saturnalian festivities, halls and houses were hung with evergreen boughs.

In England, in the days of the Druids, the houses were decked with evergreens in order that the sylvan spirits might repair to their grateful shelter and remain protected from the nipping frost and the icy winter winds.

Farther to the north the wild Teuton tribes worshiped their god in wooded places, and they looked upon the fir tree as his sacred emblem. The period corresponding to the Roman Saturnalia was the festival of Thor. This festival, like the Roman feast, was given over to the most barbaric pleasures and the wildest forms of enjoyment. Among these peoples the festivity was known as Yule-tide.

When Christianity spread abroad, men knew that in the story of Christ's nativity was realized what they in their blindness had striven to typify. So they adapted the old customs of their ancestors to the new order of things.

Among Northern European tribes a great fir tree was set up in each household at Christmas-tide. At its base were placed representations of Adam and Eve; in the branches coiled the Serpent, and on the top-most bough gleamed a candle, symbolizing that Light of the World through whom alone was victory over the Serpent possible. Later in history the tree was more profusely decorated with gaudy knick-knacks, all of which were at first symbolical. But the children were not allowed to see the tree till Christmas morning.

To account for its appearance there, the parents used to tell the children a Chaldean legend. Years ago it was the custom for every Saxon household to burn the Yule log on Christmas Eve. This was a great, knarled root or tree-trunk, cut the day before Christmas and brought into the hall on Christmas Eve with great ceremony, and accompanied with music. Each member of the household would sing a Yule song, standing on the centre of the log.

Then an attempt was made to drive the Yule log into the great hall as if it were a stubborn horse. The cry was given that the "dun" refused to move, and the whole company was summoned. All took a hand, and, loudly shouting, dragged it to the great fireplace. It was lighted with the charred remnant of the former year's log, which had been carefully preserved for this occasion, and which was supposed to insure the house against ill luck.

The children were told that during the night the Yule log gave birth to the Christmas tree which they found in the hall on Christmas morning loaded with gifts.

The Christmas tree was introduced into England by Prince Albert, consort of Queen Victoria. From the palace the custom spread, until now the Christmas tree is a necessary feature of an English Christmas.

In Germany and other European countries it was believed by the children that the tree glittering with candles and bright baubles, and the gifts found beneath the tree, were the work of jolly old Saint Nicholas, Sant Nicholaus, or Santa Claus, as we know him. This kindly saint was no legendary character. He lived about 300 A. D., and was a noted Bishop of Asia Minor. He was looked upon as the patron saint of generosity because of his liberality.

Three daughters of a poor nobleman could not marry as advantageously as they should because their father could give them no dowry. But one night one of the daughters found in her room a purse, shaped like a stocking, filled with gold, evidently thrown in the window by some one from without. The next night the second daughter found a purse

in her room, and on the third night the father caught Saint Nicholas in the act of throwing the third purse in the window.

From that story originated the custom of hanging up the stockings on Christmas Eve. Thereafter the young girls at the convent schools would hang their stockings on the door of the Mother Superior's room on Saint Nicholas night. On the following morning they would be found filled with gifts and dainties, and a little hint from Saint Nicholas as to the appearance and character of their future husbands.

Carolers making "a joyful noise unto the Lord"—a special part of the Christmas season.

Saint Nicholas is the patron saint of Russia, and his festival used to be celebrated earlier in December than the 25th, but now his name is synonymous with Christmas festivities. In parts of Europe he is known as "Pelsnichol," or Nicholas with the fur, because he is supposed to be clad in furs from head to foot.

The idea of Saint Nicholas traveling in a sleigh which was drawn by reindeer originated in the cold Northern countries. The reindeer were the swiftest animals known, and they must needs fly like the wind to carry Saint Nick the rounds of the world in one night.

In certain parts of Germany it was commonly held that on Christmas Eve the Christ-child—Criss Kindlein, or Kriss Kringle—visited earth, and, as He passed over the houses, dropped gifts through the roof for the deserving and the good.

But aside from the customs which relate to gifts and the spirit of giving at Christmas-tide, there are several observances which are indissolubly linked with this time.

Christmas is never really Christmas without the holly wreath and the mistletoe. Christians venerated the holly, or holy tree, because to them the little thorny leaves and red berries made in a wreath typified the crown of thorns and the bloody drops. Doubtless they introduced this solemn reminder at the joyous festival in order not to forget the sacredness of the occasion in the general festivities.

The mistle bush, mistletod—or mistletoe, as we know it—owes its use as a festal decoration to pagan times. According to the Scandinavian legend, Baldur, the most beloved of all the gods, had a premonition that death impended. Thereupon, his mother, Frigga, besought everything that was begotten of earth, air, fire or water to swear not to harm her son.

But in her request she overlooked the insignificant little mistletoe. Loki, the god of destruction, disguised as an old woman, visited Frigga, and, learning of her oversight, hurried back to where the gods were assembled. There they were amusing themselves by hurling all manner of missiles at Baldur, and all were turned aside. But Loki, with an arrow made of mistletoe, pierced Baldur's heart.

In reparation, the mistletoe was given to Frigga to do as she saw fit, provided it touched not earth. And she, to show that she bore no ill, hung it up, and every one who passed under it received a kiss as a token that, instead of hatred and jealousy, the mistletoe now stood for love and forgiveness.

Among the Celtic nations the mistletoe was an object of veneration, and at the festival of the winter solstice the Prince of the Druids himself cut a bough of it. The people were assembled, and then were led to the woods by the priests, who drove in advance of the company two snow-white bullocks. When the oak tree was found which bore the mistletoe, the plant was cut with a golden sickle, and the bullocks sacrificed.

At present it is the custom for the young men to carry out the doctrine taught by the Scandinavian myth and print a smacking kiss on the lips of any maiden thoughtless enough to stand beneath the suspended mistletoe bough. But for every such kiss one of the white berries of the mistletoe must be removed, and when all the berries have been kissed away the spell is broken.

Almost as important as the gift giving and gift receiving on Christmas Day is the feast of dainties spread on that festal occasion. But even the Christmas dinner has its origin in the dim, distant past. Feasts were always the accompaniment of any festival. In Egypt, at the winter solstice, every family killed and ate a goose as a religious observance.

In the hieroglyphic language of the Egyptian, the figure of a goose was the word "child." The people had noticed that the goose was remarkable for the way in which it protected its young, hence it was looked upon as the symbol of great love—that love which is willing to sacrifice itself for the object of its affection. This trait was also believed to belong to the god they worshiped, so the Egyptians celebrated this festival by killing and eating a goose.

We preserve the custom of eating fowl on this day, but the toothsome turkey has more generally supplanted the goose. The plum pudding as a dish in the Christmas feast has its meaning. The number and richness of its ingredients represented the rich gifts the Kings laid at the feet of the child Jesus.

In earlier days the mince pie, then a great pastry dish, filled with forced meat and fruits, was made box-shaped, to typify the manger in which the Child had lain.

The celebration of Christmas-tide is as old as the human race, and many of the customs have lost their origin in the hazy past. We preserve and hand down these customs because we respect their age. But pagan customs have survived in our Christian festival, not so much because of their age, as because it was necessary at the start to preserve them.

When Christianity was in its infancy, men who embraced it refused to give up the old festivals, so in view of the great end to be

obtained, the leaders of the early church allowed these customs and festivities to stand, but sought to put into them some Christian significance and meaning.

But to such strict sectarians as the Puritans and the Quakers in England the Christmas festivities appeared to be little better than pagan orgies. These worthy people thoroughly discountenanced the festival, and when the Quakers and Puritans came to found a State in the New World, they made rigid rules against any such form of festivity.

The Dutch colonists, however, were enthusiastic in their observance of Christmastide, and, though far from home, they celebrated the happy time in the old way. From the Dutch colonists in America spread the Christmas cheer, and the frowns and resolutions of the staid Puritan and Quaker colonists availed nothing against the infectious spirit of Christmas cheer and good-will which the Dutch brought into the new country. (1898)

Paul Gallico

Silent Night

But on the night of December 23 in the year 1818, in the little Austrian village of Oberndorf by Salzburg, on the banks of the frozen River Salzach, a mouse did stir.

He not only stirred; he invaded the organ loft of the church of St. Nicholas. There, because he was a cold, hungry mouse, he perpetrated a deed and initiated a chain of events that were to resound to the farthest corners of the earth.

It was the following morning, crisp, cold and clear, that an important gentleman in a black frock coat and stock let himself into the church of St. Nicholas and sat down at the organ.

His name was Franz Gruber, and he was a dark-haired, pleasant-faced man 31 years of age, with a longish nose, cleft chin and friendly eyes. The world never heard of him, but in the small ponds of the neighboring villages of Oberndorf and Arnsdorf he was a very large frog indeed. For in Arnsdorf he was the schoolmaster and in Oberndorf he was the organist of the church.

Now he flicked his long coattails out of the way, adjusted the organ bench, trod the pedals and pressed the keys. But no music issued from the pipes—only a soft, breathy sigh.

Before Herr Gruber had time to investigate this unhappy phenomenon he heard a sound by the door and turned to see his friend, Joseph Mohr, himself a musician and utility priest, who had been sent to Oberndorf on temporary basis until a permanent pastor could be found. Gruber cried, "*Grüss Gott,* Joseph. What has happened?"

The young priest—he was then 26, with merry eyes and a gay air—raised his arms in a helpless gesture and beckoned for his friend to follow.

He took Gruber to the loft behind the keyboard, where the leather bellows supplied the wind for the instrument, and pointed to the hole in the worn fabric of the leather. "I discovered it this morning. A mouse must have gnawed it, and at the first tread the whole thing gave way."

Gruber inspected the damage. A Christmas Eve Mass without music was unthinkable. He cried, "*Donnerwetter!* Here is a fine fix. What is to be done?"

"Well," Father Mohr said somewhat shyly, "I have written a little poem." He coughed and corrected himself. "Actually some words for a song."

The schoolteacher smiled at his friend and said, "I'll wager you have. You were always more of a poet than priest. I can't imagine why you ever chose the cloth."

Father Mohr replied with some asperity, "It isn't *that* kind of song."

Herr Gruber smiled again at the vehemence of his friend, for it was known that Father Mohr did enjoy *that* kind of song, the kind of song you sang with the peasants and rough rivermen when the new wine flowed and the zithers twanged. This was what caused grumbling among the more pious parishioners and brought frowns to the brows of the church fathers.

It was no wonder, Gruber thought, that his young friend was a bit wild. His mother had been a poor seamstress of Salzburg, abandoned by her husband, and she had no one to sponsor her infant boy Joseph or his baptism. Eventually it was the public hangman who agreed to stand up for the child. Later one of the monsignors had the boy educated and inducted into holy orders.

Gruber glanced down at the poem and read the first stanzas. A strange chill ran down his spine. It was indeed not *that* kind of song. It seemed to lay its hand upon his heart and speak to him gently, simply and movingly. Gruber was stirred by the words as he had never been before. Already he was beginning to listen to distant music waiting to be born.

Father Mohr said almost apologetically, "I only thought, since there is not a tone to be had from

the organ, that you might be able to arrange something for our guitars with perhaps a simple chorus for the children."

Gruber said, "Yes, yes, perhaps we could. Let me have it; I will take it and see what I can do."

All through the hour-long trudge homeward through to Arnsdorf, Gruber was composing. He passed three Christmas mummers in the guise of the Three Kings and didn't even see them. Words and music were already beginning to blend.

Silent night, holy night;
All is calm, all is bright.

Like deaf Beethoven he was hearing all of the notes inside himself.

Holy Infant so tender and mild,
Sleep in heavenly peace.

The chorus he would write for the children's voices rang through his brain.

He sat at his spinet in his simple room with its

scrubbed light pine floor, porcelain stove, few pieces of furniture of painted pine, and crucifix on the wall. The words unlocked melodies, and the music flowed forth.

That afternoon there were collected in the priest's study, beneath the wreaths and garlands of evergreen, 12 little boys and girls, scrubbed and shining in their warm woolen stockings, jackets and pinafores. The two men strummed their guitars and rehearsed their charges.

"So, now, Hannes, Eva, Peterli, you sing like this—'ta, ta, ta, ta, ta, ta, ta!' And you, Gretel, Liesel and Johann, you sing, 'da di, da di da, da.'"

The two men looked at one another with satisfaction. A little rough. A bit of trouble in the third section, but it could be easily remedied. It was going to work.

Christmas Eve! There was a crust on the snow. Beneath, it was so dry that it crunched and squeaked under the heavy boots of the church-goers. Their cheery "*Grüss Gotts*" rang through the still night. The air was sharp and crystal-clear and hurt the nostrils when inhaled. The stars seemed to hang from the sky and glitter like Christmas-tree ornaments.

Bells pealed from the tall, whitewashed tower of St. Nicholas' church. Within, hundreds of tapers and candles reflected from the golden plates and chalices, softening the stiff, Gothic-carved Madonnas and endowing them, for all their woodenness, with gentle grace. The church was decorated with pine boughs, evergreen and holly berries. The congregation sat on the hard benches, the men in their lumpy woolen garments, the women in bright aprons and shawls.

There was a rustle of surprise as the 12 children, with Mohr and Gruber carrying their guitars, appeared before the altar. The sour-mouthed pious noticed with disfavor the gay streamers of red and green hanging from the necks of the instruments. Ribbons of the same colors were woven into the corn-colored plaits of the little girls and tied to the boys' stockings.

Gruber nodded. The strings vibrated, and the tenor of Father Mohr and the basso of schoolmaster Gruber filled the church.

Thus the Christmas hymn "Silent Night" was heard for the first time—and the next day it was forgotten. No single, solitary soul of that congregration, least of all the minor poet and the minor musician who had put it together, could guess what would happen—that it was to sweep the world. No one dreamed that genius had burned for a few hours in two simple men who never would be heard from again, and that through the magic of their collaboration on a Christmas Eve in an Austrian village something deathless had been born.

It was an accident that saved the masterpiece from oblivion. The master organ repairer, Karl Mauracher, who came up from the Zillertal that spring to repair the damaged bellows, asked what they had done without music at Christmas.

Gruber told him. "It was just a trifle," he said. "I wouldn't even know where to lay my hands on it. Mohr is not here any longer. Wait. . .if it were anywhere it would be——"

There was a small cupboard at the rear of the church, and there, crumpled and dusty amidst old papers and records, he found the song.

The organ repairer's lips moved as he read the score, and a deep humming of the melody came from his massive chest. "It has something," he said softly. "Do you mind," he asked, "if I take this with me?"

Gruber laughed, pleased that their little effort had this belated moment of approval. "By all means have it for no one will have any further use for it once you have mended our organ."

Herr Mauracher shouldered his bag of tools and leather patches and departed. Franz Gruber forgot the incident. And in this manner the words and music of "Silent Night" journeyed to the lovely Zillertal Valley, thus beginning its never-ending encirclement of the world.

The song spread from Austria to Germany as folk music. Only in later years were Mohr and Gruber acknowledged the creators, though not a penny did they ever earn. It crossed borders; it went to sea with German emigrants.

Mohr and Gruber died as poor as they were born. But Gruber's old guitar still sings for him, for it was preserved and handed down in the family. Now each Christmas Eve it is brought to Oberndorf and the children's chorus gathers around the Christmas trees in the snow before the memorial chapel which stands on the site of the old St. Nicholas church, erected to the memory of the two men. There once more it sounds forth the background melody of one of the most famous, best-loved songs in the world. (1962)

Nat B. Read, Jr.

How to be Santa Claus

"Ho! Ho! Ho!" So they've asked you to play Santa and you said you would! Well, listen, you jolly old elf, you, there's a lot more to being Santa than going "Ho! Ho! Ho!" As a matter of fact, you shouldn't even go "Ho! Ho! Ho!" at all. It scares the little kids!

Playing Santa is one of the greatest thrills this side of the North Pole. It'll make you laugh—and cry—and give you moments you'll treasure for all the Christmases to come. But if you're going to step like Clark Kent into a change of clothes that makes you all-knowing and all-powerful, you'd better do a bit of boning up on *how to Santa*.

Whatever you do, don't make a mistake that most rookie Santas blunder into while playing their first season suited up: Don't refer to "Mom and Dad" with a child you don't know. Maybe the kid doesn't have a Mom or doesn't have a Dad ... or doesn't have either one. How do you get around that one? Simple: Always refer to "the folks" and you can't go wrong.

And even more basic than that, remember the surrogate Santa's cardinal role. It's the golden, unbreakable, iron-clad law of Santa-ing: *Don't promise anything*. Whatever else you might not remember, don't forget for the twinkling of an eye the consequences of Santa *himself* promising something that the child might not get. Tell the child you'll "see what you can do," or "see if the elves have made enough to go around," or simply "I'll surprise you!"

Don't ask a child what his or her name is. Santa's supposed to know that. (Say "young fellow" or "young lady.") But do act as if you recognize them and are glad to see them again. One of the safest openers is "My, how you've grown since last year!" It's a safe line since every child has grown in a year's time, but most children are genuinely awed that Santa recognizes them so quickly and remembers them from Christmas Past.

Another safe line of conversation is to encourage some development in the coming months. You ask them to be more helpful in keeping their rooms straight and in finishing their dinners during the coming year. Almost all children have room for improvement in those areas, and they always marvel at Santa's knowledge about their deficiencies.

If you see calluses on their thumbs, ask them not to suck their thumbs so much. Or you might ask them if they know their address or telephone number. If they don't know it, ask them to learn it for you. Children should know both as young as possible, so you're being a good teacher as well as a sly Santa.

After a few dozen kids, you'll begin to recognize the different attitudes the various age groups hold about Santa and the different challenges they present. The 1½- to 2½-year-olds are perhaps the most difficult. They face the prospect of meeting Santa with screaming terror or petrified silence. Don't touch a child unless it's obvious he or she appears comfortable with body contact. That's true of children of all ages, but especially the very youngest. If the young child balks, ask the parent to accompany him or her to the throne. You'll need to spend a little more time with children of this age generally to let them warm up a bit to such a foreign idea as red-suited, great-bearded Santa Claus.

Perhaps the most fun of all comes with the talkative 2½- to 3½-year-olds. They're old enough to have a trace of logic but not old enough to keep that logic untangled. They're the age group that teamed up with Art Linkletter to say the darndest things. You won't need much advice about handling this group; just allow them plenty of room for creative thinking.

The oldest of Santa's client groups (ages four to six) represents the biggest intellectual challenge. These postgraduate preschoolers are in the twilight years of their St. Nicholas fantasy. They're just on the verge of challenging the myth, or they're in the existential midst of Santa doubt, or they've recently crossed the bar into the huge fraternity which is in on the Big Secret. Whichever of these three stages they happen to be in, they're busily researching their budding intellect for the most penetrating and the most troublesome questions and tests of your Santahood.

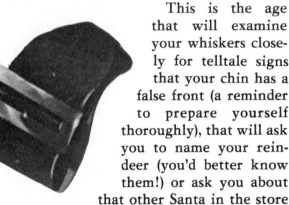

This is the age that will examine your whiskers closely for telltale signs that your chin has a false front (a reminder to prepare yourself thoroughly), that will ask you to name your reindeer (you'd better know them!) or ask you about that other Santa in the store down the street ("One of us is just a helper; can you figure out which one?").

Or another common question is "Where are your reindeer?" Don't make the common novice Santa mistake of telling him they're in the parking lot, because sure as the hair on your chinney-chin-chin, he'll circle the building to check. So what's your answer? *I left them on the roof!* (It's logical and he'll just have to take your word for it. There's no way he can check out *that* line!)

Perhaps typical of this age's thinking is the San Francisco lad who wanted $500 in cold, hard cash. "Why so much?" Santa pressed. The lad replied that after this year he wouldn't be believing in Santa Claus anymore and he'd be needing the cash to buy his own Christmas gifts from now on.

Expect the best of children, but prepare for the worst! Beard-yankers are perhaps the worst. Watch closely to make sure they don't give your false hair a tug, but if they do, don't forget to yell "Ouch!" Santas have been jabbed with forks (to see if they are real) and kicked and hit (because they didn't bring the right things last year). Santas have frequently gotten their beards caught in children's hooks, zippers and buttonholes and one unwatchful Santa even had his beard ignited by a fiendish kid's lighter.

If you've never played Santa before, you're in for a surprise when you begin hearing the repetitious litany of Christmas gift requests from the child of today's society. You'll hear very few requests for ponies, bats and balls, model railroads, toy airplanes and other generic toys. Instead you'll hear a replay of the top toy companies' television advertising appeals. Children will ask for very specific brand-name toys. They'll want the Six Million Dollar Man, Baby Alive, Evel Knievel toys, Tenderlove dolls, Hush Little Baby Doll, Baby Baby Doll, Tuesday Taylor Doll, Wake Up Thumbelina, Don't Cry Baby, G.I. Joe and Stretch Armstrong. Today's child is recorded feedback of what has been programmed into its "want" bank by Saturday morning Madison Avenue mastery every week.

Occasionally, though, a bit of creative thought still breaks through the solid wall of television commercial replays. Like last year's California child who asked for a Kentucky Fried Chicken franchise. Or the lad who asked Santa last year for "a whole bunch of racehorses—real ones!" Perhaps the most optimistic child to petition Santa last year was one who asked simply for "all the money in the world."

Several years ago a child in Massachusetts asked Santa for a bird that couldn't fly. "Why a bird that can't fly?" Santa asked. "Because the bird you gave me last year flew away!" the tyke replied.

One of Santa's most puzzling questions last year came from an El Cajon, California, youngster who wanted all of last year's presents back. "What happened to them?" Santa wanted to know. "The duck took them!" was all the explanation Santa got, leaving him to ponder the mystery the rest of his life. One child wanted an Evel Knievel motorcycle, but made it clear he didn't want just the toy version. He wanted the real full-sized machine!

One of Santa's young patrons a few years ago asked him for a wedding gown, "so that I can marry my daddy," but a surprising number each year ask for new daddies or mommies in place of the ones they're mad at this year. One

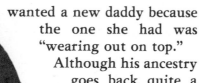

wanted a new daddy because the one she had was "wearing out on top."

Although his ancestry goes back quite a few centuries, Santa Claus is as American as Barbie Doll and the Six Million Dollar Man. It was only around the turn of the century that his image was clearly focused into the precise Santa that we know today. Before that, different people had different ideas. He was like the Easter Bunny today. Each artist pictures a slightly different rabbit: some fat, some thin, some with clothes of one sort of another, and some without. Santa Claus came in a variety of versions, too, until the emerging magazines of the late 1800s and early 1900s began to settle on a unanimous version of Santa Claus. The version they settled on was that of cartoonist Thomas Nast, widely circulated in *Harper's Weekly*.

Thomas Nast's Santa Claus drawings brought together a little bit of the Dutch *Sancte Klaas*, the Bavarian Pelz-Nicol, and the colonists' St. Nicholas and decided once and for all that Santa would be obese, would wear a red suit trimmed in white fur, would wear a stocking cap and black boots.

St. Nicholas was the patron saint of New York in the days of the early colony. (Some cynics say he still was up until the city went broke a couple of years ago!) St. Nicholas was not the same as our Santa Claus at all. St. Nick wore white instead of red. St. Nick was the patron saint of the sea while Santa Claus (if he is patron saint of anything other than profits) is patron saint of the air. St. Nick rode a white horse; Santa rides a red sleigh. St. Nick brought only sweets; Santa brings you anything within your credit range.

St. Nicholas was the figurehead on the Dutch ship, *Goede Vrouw*, and the Dutch quickly erected a church in his honor in their new colony. The children of the colony came to believe that St. Nicholas arrived on "the Christmas ship" from Holland on December 5 (which at that time was Christmas Eve).

The St. Nicholas figure descended from a real person, the Bishop of Myra, which is a town in Lycia, halfway between Rhodes and Cyprus. That was in the fourth century. St. Nicholas was a wealthy man whose "thing" was to help those who needed help—but to remain anonymous. Then someone found out who he was (maybe an investigative reporter) and thus, when good things were done for people, St. Nicholas got the credit for doing them.

Then along came a professor named Dr. Clement Clark Moore, teacher of Biblical Languages at General Theological Seminary in New York City. Dr. Moore undoubtedly taught his seminary students much about the sacred meaning of the religious Christmas observance, but history will remember him for his hallmark of the secular Yuletide.

It was Dr. Moore who composed a bit of verse to amuse his children and ended up amusing children for a century to come. Dr. Moore's little poem began, " 'Twas the night before Christmas, when all through the house. . . ." When his poem became widely known in Dr. Moore's later years, it got coupled with Thomas Nast's drawings and together they pretty well locked Santa Claus into the form we know today.

How did the stockings get hung by tradition on the fireplace mantel? Well, it seems that one year St. Nicholas dropped his purse down the chimney, and instead of falling on the hearth as it was supposed to, it got stuck in a stocking that had been hung there to dry.

Now you are all ready . . . ready for the greatest thrill of all. Step out of the drab, humdrum life you've been living, into the magical red suit that will make you more important than the President of the United States, wiser than any university dean, more interesting than a World Series pitcher and more powerful than any inhabitant of the Pentagon . . . at least to the children who are dreaming at this very moment of having a chance to meet . . . YOU! (1977)

Robert M. Yoder

Merry Christmas in Ten Pieces

Yes, Virginia, there is a Santa Claus, and he has a home up near the North Pole, where it is colder than a bathroom floor. But don't believe that story about his having a lot of little dwarfs who put toys together for him, singing as they hammer. Nobody puts toys together, until Christmas Eve. Toys come in sixteen pieces, with one missing, and are put together by a large band of Involuntary Elves who call ourselves Santa's Press-Gang Helpers. We don't exactly sing, either, although a certain low, ominous murmur can be heard rising from a million homes on Christmas Eve. Put it this way, kid: That ain't no dwarf; that's your old man, beaten down. The luckless peon bought the toys; now he is learning that he has to finish manufacturing them, too, and by one A.M. his mood will make Scrooge seem like Sunny Ebenezer.

The first thing your frightened eye lights on, in the store, is a nice little red wagon, and you think, in your fatuous adult way, that this is just the thing to brighten the young heart. If you weren't partially paralyzed by the fear that you are shopping too late, you would realize that if the kid wants a wagon at all, it isn't this chaste little model. He would want one twice this size, with demountable tires, a ram-jet engine, electric lights, an overdrive and a windshield wiper, at $79.75. The kid next door has had one like that for two years and uses it only to haul his good toys in. Then you see the rocket-firing antiaircraft gun and realize that this is the answer. While it will not do bodily harm, and is therefore a partial bust to start with, it is a realistic-looking little number, and you buy it, at an exceedingly realistic price.

About the hour on Christmas Eve when you are in mild shock for fear the thing won't arrive, the delivery man stumbles in with a large package that can't be anything else. Will you put it under the tree that way? Or will you have it out in the open, so the child may see this splendid

sight first thing in the morning? Full of Christmas sentiment, you decide to expose the gun to full, gladsome view. So you tear off the wrapping. Here is a dial, here is a leg, here is a muzzle. You thought it would look like the store model, did you? Well, Santa has a little surprise for you. It's in pieces, and you are going to have to put it together. Merry Christmas, in at least ten pieces.

There is a sheet or folder of directions which could not get under your skin worse if they were in Spanish. They are written in the special language of directions, a mechanical gobbledegook achieved by writing the directions first in Ruthenian and then allowing the translation to curdle. A stop sign from the same mumbling pen would take 200 words. In the language of directions, "close the door" would read like this: "Grasp door-opening device with right knob-grasper and exert pressure outward until Panel A fills Aperture B. If scream is heard, other hand may be caught in opening." Along with being as turgid as possible, the directions are printed in a miniature type face known as Myopia Old Style, which is two sizes smaller than pearl and is otherwise used only to print the Declaration of Independence on souvenir pennies.

Well, lying there in pieces, the gun looks like nothing at all; it's got to be assembled. The first line you encounter in the directions says: "Using

ring grasper from Assembly Kit, grasp collector ring near tube spar tightening guide rod" . . . but, thank heaven, that goes with some other toy. Your own directions start out more simply: "Connect round opening at end of Feeder Spring A with hooked end of trigger lock restraining bar by placing round opening over hook and pressing." What'd he think you'd do—spot-weld it? (The answer, unfortunately, is that he expects more than that, but not just yet.) Now the guy begins getting esoteric.

"If retaining mechanism fails to admit trigger, horizontal opening of drum impeding stopper should be widened horizontally." He means if the damned trigger won't go into the guard, you got to cut more room, and sure enough, it won't. This is going to be the only gun in the neighborhood with a demountable (falling out) trigger, unless you fix it. If retaining mechanism fails to admit what it's supposed to retain, then it should never have left the factory, but it's too late for that kind of recrimination now. Getting a hammer from the basement, a good paring knife and a screw driver, you manage to make the trigger go where it should, with one very bad moment when you think you've split the thing.

Well, the barrel, H, slides into place nicely; maybe things are beginning to go your way. The next step is to fit Firing Platform Z on Tripod, the Tripod being made by inserting Metal-tipped Ends of Legs into Sockets, which is child's play. Now all it takes is two bolts, L and M, which you slip into place with great efficiency. They must be firmly in place, the directions say, or gun will not swivel on Platform Z; you might say, it won't swivel on any platform. A neat little bag contained the bolts, and in it you find the nut for Bolt L. But half an hour later you are still rummaging through wrapping paper in a grim search for the other nut, the crucial nut, the nut without which, as the Latins say, nothing. You may have 128 nuts of assorted sizes in a jar in the basement, but you will not have one that fits Bolt M. That is a freak size used nowhere else in the whole panoply of American industry. It is part of a shipment the toy manufacturer bought up from the Uruguayan War Assets Administration.

It is 11:45 by the time you manage to make the bolt hold with a piece of wire wrapped around it, and if the kid looks at that part, he will feel sure his toy is something the fireman repainted for the poor. Meanwhile the house has grown cold, three of the Christmas tree lights have winked at you by burning out, and your cigarette has fallen out of the ash tray and burned a six-dollar hole in the carpet. But the gun is starting to look like a weapon, and there can't be much more—only a couple of odd-looking metal pieces are left and a cardboard circle which is marked "Cosmic Ray Computer Dial."

One of the pieces of metal is easy enough to use. It's the missing plug, for lack of which the barrel has had that tendency to point to the floor like the tail of a whipped hound. The other is the crank with which the young gunner moves the barrel to keep on his target. You tackle the easiest job first—the computer is nothing more than two sections of light cardboard. "Bending

Tabs A, C, E and G," the directions say, "fit them into Slots B, D, F and H." The cardboard is a special kind which is as stiff as metal for a minute and then relaxes completely as you push, so that in twenty minutes you have four dog-eared tabs holding one crumpled dial marked with a little blood from the finger you cut trying to enlarge the slots.

Now you reach the part of the directions that tell you to fix on the telescopic sight. The diagram shows a handsome metal gadget coming to a square end, fitted into a ring fastened neatly around the end of the barrel. The only piece of metal you have left, outside of the crank, is a cotter pin. Even if you had missing part R, you still would have nothing like missing part Q which fits into it. You ransack the wrapping paper again, in what the novelists call cold fury, but with no luck. Finally, with great self-control, you smooth the wrinkled directions and read that jargon over again out loud. It is then that you come across Step 2. "In assembling Model A-100 Junior, our second-rate cheaper model for pikers, Step 1 may be disregarded." The directions continue: "No sight comes with this model. There is, however, a cotter pin. You can stick it on the barrel with adhesive tape and play like it's a sight. It ain't much, but then neither are you."

There is one final step—mounting the crank. "Slip Directional Crank 16 through Arm Y into Slot EE," the directions say. "When in position, give crank one quarter turn counterclockwise. Trigger should then fall sharply back into firing position." This is simplicity itself, and the only trouble is that if the crank goes through Arm Y, it misses Slot EE by a good quarter of an inch. The bitter thoughts that arise on Christmas Eve about the incompetent sleepwalker who bored that slot must visibly affect the temperature.

But the direction writer thought about this impasse, forehanded soul that he is. "It may be necessary, for best results"—meaning, to make the thing work at all—"to enlarge aperture in Arm Y. This can be done quickly and easily by using a 16.3 metal file without tang, a 13-oz. dinging hammer and some Australian-canoe-builders' flux." This is equipment the ordinary household would be just as likely to have as a Javanese blowgun and a guroo bird, and you know, as your thoughts profane the early Christmas air, that the only 16.3 file in the world is one resting in the manufacturer's plant 850.3 miles away across the snowy landscape. So you gouge out a new Slot EE four times the proper size, the crank falls into place, wobbling foolishly, and the task is done. If it holds together until Christmas afternoon, you will be agreeably surprised, and a glance at the clock tells you that won't be long.

Yes, Virginia, there is a Santa Claus. If there weren't, ugly mobs of maddened parents would rove the streets Christmas Day armed with bolts, pins, wheels and axles, and some toy manufacturer would end up assembled on Movable Rail A wearing Feathers B and Tar C, after a slight going-over with No. 16 emery paper and a common hydraulic half-knurled center punch. (1947)

Robert M. Yoder

A Sure Sign That Christmas is Coming

In 1939, Irving Berlin completed a sheaf of songs for a movie to be called Holiday Inn and looked them over with an expert eye. Along with being a composer and the greatest source of musical accompaniment for America's festive occasions, Berlin is a publisher. It's his business to know how a song will go. Only two of these songs looked hopeful. In Berlin's estimation, "Be Careful, It's My Heart" had a chance of becoming a hit. He expected a modest success, but no more, for a song called "I'm Dreaming of a White Christmas."

Berlin has seldom been fooled by songs. This one fooled him completely. Of all his music—gay, sentimental or patriotic—it became "definitely the most successful," he says. That means topping such stand-bys as "God Bless America," which has earned well over $100,000 for the Boy Scouts and Girl Scouts, to whom Berlin assigned the royalties. White Christmas outsells even it.

What Berlin created, without in the least suspecting it, was a musical composition akin to Old Faithful, the geyser. It's a rare song hit that survives the brief, intense popularity of its first success and becomes a "standard," played year in and year out. White Christmas enjoys the rarest status of all—that of a perennial, automatic, ever-successful hit.

Every October for ten years now, as surely as the leaves begin to fall, it begins to sell anew like a fresh hit. In a day when sheet-music sales of 300,000 are considered very good, it runs to well over 3,000,000 copies. "It's a publishing business in itself," Berlin remarks, meaning that one such song alone would keep a publisher happy.

The radio stations start playing it on Thanksgiving Day—in very cautious amounts, actually, compared to the repetition of juke boxes. From Thanksgiving until midnight Christmas Day, there isn't a minute when the song isn't in the air somewhere. It is far more widespread than snow. In Vermont, a Christmas program would sound vaguely unofficial without it, though there may be eight inches of cold reality outside to make this dream a little bit unnecessary. But they sing it just as often in Louisiana and Florida and tropical places never touched by a snowflake.

Played "to death" in 1942, the year the song appeared, White Christmas has been played to death every year since, but doesn't die. For somewhere along the line it underwent a subtle transformation: It became a custom. A Gallup poll showed that of all the traditional Christmas music, only the classic "Silent Night, Holy Night" is a greater favorite. "Jingle Bells" and a dozen famous carols and hymns had to yield to Berlin's wistful air.

"The proof that I didn't expect this," the composer says, "is in the verse." For this is not, as thousands suppose, the expression of an American soldier honing for Christmas at home. According to the verse, the song is the lament of a Northerner stuck in California, and beefing about spending Christmas under the palms. When it was written, anyone with the price of a railroad ticket or a few gallons of gasoline could easily attain a White Christmas. But by the time the song appeared in 1942, millions of Americans were overseas. So in time it came to represent the longing for an old-fashioned Christmas in a world at peace.

A seasonal, topical song is born with two strikes on it. Christmas, furthermore, is perhaps the single occasion with which popular-song writers have had the least luck. Why should this prove such a resounding exception? Berlin explains its phenomenal success by saying he had thousands of collaborators. "People read a lot of things into that song," he remarks, "that I didn't put there." (1951)

Peg Bracken

Women Want the Oddest Things for Christmas

Women, as every woman knows, are gravely misunderstood. A major misconception about them, which men seem to cherish and even foster, concerns the gifts women like. It is based on the notion that women tend to focus on the price tag instead of the present.

It is time to set the record straight, and I must try. Lately I have been asking—of enough people to crowd the aisles of the annual Christmas church bazaar, including the Potholder and Penuche departments—a simple question: What is the best present anyone ever gave you?

My poll, I am glad to be able to report, proves that women are as sentimental as anyone else, and possibly more so. Indeed, women are starry-eyed and touchingly grateful for small favors; and right now, with the holiday season again charging us like a Miura bull, I think men should know this. Not only is it an interesting fact but it also can save them money.

A difference between the sexes became re-soundingly clear long before I was done with my survey. A woman, for one thing, usually knows the answer right away. A man doesn't. A man must scratch his head and think. A woman's best present involves, nearly always, a man. But a man's best present is singularly uncluttered by romance. Dollars to dough-nuts, he'll dredge it up out of the misty, many-layered, womanless past, out of the brave bright days when he was a boy. The pup he got when he was seven. The Fire Chief bike he got when he was ten. Or the dart board with real darts that went

"Thud!" Oh, boy! You'd think his girl or his wife never gave him a thing.

Now, perhaps there are sound reasons for this. Perhaps a man becomes so bemused after twenty or thirty adult Christmases, with their accompanying welter of sport shirts and camera attachments, that nothing comes very clear any more. As every woman knows, men are practically impossible to get presents for anyhow.

And perhaps a man figures, in some obscure but practical fashion, that it all comes out of his own hide anyway. He'll pay for it when the January bills roll in. Or else he figures he's paid for it already, in the number of casserole dishes he's eaten while she squeezed the price of it out of the grocery money. Or else, if she is a money-making working girl, he has likewise paid for it through a certain lack of dependable home comforts which he might otherwise be getting.

Whatever the reason, give a man a horse he can ride, a gun he can shoot, or a dart board with darts that go "Thud!" and give it to him when he's under twelve, and he will remember it, even though he probably won't remember that you gave it to him.

But women! Well, take my good friend Virginia, one of the first persons I questioned concerning her best gift ever. "The twelfth rose," she answered promptly. "But don't tell George!"

Well, the twelfth rose, it developed, was a rose which arrived on Christmas Eve—the final one of a dozen long-stemmed beauties given to her by a former suitor named Edward, delivered by a florist one at a time. He had told her that he'd always felt that a man should propose with a dozen long-stemmed roses, but he couldn't afford them all at once.

Observe, now, that Virginia didn't marry Edward. She married George; and this is probably a good thing. There is a certain pixies-in-the-bottom-of-my-garden touch to this gambit which doesn't augur too well as husband material. And if Edward couldn't afford even a dozen roses, how in the world did he think he could afford to get married?

Nevertheless, think of the gifts with which her husband has gifted Virginia! Carloads of heavy household equipment. Bushels of books, records, gadgets. Pecks of foamy lingerie, pearl earrings, candy. And yet, what flashes meteorlike through Virginia's little mind when you ask her about her best present? The twelfth rose.

Well, of course—a critic may carp—most women have a romantic memory or two tucked away, and how is a live husband to compete with a dead corsage? For that matter, why should he?

I can answer only that some of them do, and with excellent results. The best gift of another friend of mine is the small charm for her charm bracelet which her husband Joe gave her for Christmas. It is a little silver angel, the most impossibly angelic of all angels, and on the back of it is engraved, MOST OF THE TIME. LOVE, J.

Of course, this may not sound like much to a man, but it warms Amy's heart like a bonfire. Consider, too, its valuable side effects— what we might term the fallout. As any woman will perceive instantly, it gives Amy a most gratifying lead in the area of female friendsmanship. A friend notices the angel at luncheon, say, and asks to see it. Amy, co-operating gladly, hands it over. When friend reads that message of clearly

understated devotion, it sends her home in a state bordering on shock. *Her* husband never thought of giving any thing cute like that.

Now, this isn't to say that a woman always prefers that one perfect rose, or that one trinket, to that one perfect limousine. Nor is it to say that a woman can't feel sentimental about mink—a generic term here for any lavish object—if she gets it at the right time from the right person.

Unfortunately, though, it seldom works out like this. If her husband can easily afford it, then it is just another coat from daddy. And even though he can't easily afford it, still there's no escaping the fact that there's something in it for him. The caveman dragging that fur-covered carcass home was showing the world what a mighty hunter he was.

At any rate, none of the women I asked—including four minks, two beavers, and five of unknown but quite respectable ancestry—mentioned a fur. Or a jewel. Or, for that matter, the handsomely overpriced negligee-and-nightgown arrangement which harried husbands so often pick up at 5:29 on Christmas Eve. The simple fact seems to be that Presents and Possessions are filed in quite different compartments of the female brain.

Let's consider the case of my neighbor, Mary B. She is blessed, or hobbled, depending on where you sit, by having a husband who couldn't care less what he eats. But Mary, on the other hand, thinks it mightily important. Moreover she loves to cook.

For eight years, therefore, she has been doggedly cooking beautiful food—from Soufflé d'Écrevisses Florentine to Tournedos Nicoise, not to mention sauces Mornay, Bercy and Noisette—all the while knowing that her husband would be quite as happy with plain canned beans and store-bought cookies.

Then last Christmas her husband came through with the world's most beautiful gourmet cookbook, a superb, lavish, terribly expensive affair which she had wanted for years but had never felt, in all good conscience, that she could buy. This, Mary tells me, is her best present bar none, because—as she put it—it said more than it was.

Consider, too, the best present of my cousin Charlotte. Charlotte loves antiques or, more accurately, what she calls Cute Old Things, which she finds in Funny Old Shops or in obscure corners of the Salvation Army's collection depot. She has a special fondness for old bottles, old bootjacks and chipped stone pickling crocks; her husband, who doesn't share this enthusiasm, has been heard to complain that their living room is beginning to look like somebody's basement.

Nevertheless, one Christmas he gave her a twenty-five dollar receipt from one of the more disreputable of these places and told her to go buy some more.

There it is again—the lovely and warming affirmation that seems to be part and parcel of most best presents: simply, you're an odd duck, but I love you anyway.

And right here we have the reason why giving her The Gift She'd Never Buy Herself—unless she happens to be a teenager—can be an enormous booboo. Not that this isn't highly successful if the gift is what Billy Rose once called a Five-Dollar Cake of Soap, the very best-of-breed item in a category which the lady already likes. But when you choose a category you think she *should* like—say, a good big dollop of French perfume for a lady who never touches the stuff, or stout fishing waders for a Southern Camellia, you are walking on eggshells.

You see, gentlemen, most women past the age of consent cherish a notion, deluded though it may be, that they have achieved for themselves a rather satisfactory personal style. When you give

the out-and-out country-tweeds type a mad marabou trifle, you are implying, of course, "I can see the femme fatale peeping through that tailored exterior, and here is something to bring her out."

But how do you know she doesn't consider herself a tweedy-type femme fatale anyhow? Perhaps she has spent years perfecting this; and she wants and needs that marabou object like another eyebrow. She may misread the message as "Why don't you *do* something about yourself?"

You see, here you are verging perilously close to the Insult Gift—those holly-trimmed packets of toothpaste and other unlikely gift items which bloom like poinsettias in drugstores at this time of year. The merchants' enthusiasm is commendable but misguided; and anyone who gives one of these affairs to a lady of spirit is apt to get it back, right across the chops.

A variation on the Gift She'd Never Buy Herself theme, incidentally, is the Gift Unexpected, or, Let's Give Grandma a brace of falcons. A man I know, a rather philosophical type, does this frequently, in the fond hope that he is opening windows onto new vistas.

He once gave his wife an ant farm—one of those glass-enclosed ant universes, before which you are supposed to sit, hypnotized, watching the ants go around doing whatever it is ants do. But his wife was not hypnotized. She gave the ant farm to a little boy across the street who happens to be hot for bugs.

Actually, this window-opening theory reads prettier than it works out. Most of the people you know have plenty of windows open already; they just don't have the time to look out of them.

Now, with teen-agers, as I have indicated, the Gift She'd Never Buy Herself presents no problems. In the first place, it is hard to think of one. Teen-agers will buy *anything* for themselves, given the funds, and the farther out in left field, generally speaking, the better they like it. If

your gift indicates that you have discerned the latent temptress beneath that pudgy or knobby-kneed exterior, you are a hero.

A friend of mine tells me that a lipstick, given to her at Age 12, was her best present. It was a brand widely advertised as kissproof, and although my friend never put it to the test, she says it was a glorious feeling just knowing that it was there in her school-going pocketbook, safe among her grubby handkerchiefs and her streetcar tokens.

Conversely, my friend Eloise suffered greatly in her formative years. One Christmastime her lad, of whom she had expected great things, gave her a sturdy, solemn, practical, navy-blue umbrella. To Eloise this was about as romantic a gift as a jar of peanut butter. That Christmas was curtains for him.

And I'll never forget my own traumatic experience back in my salad days—and very green salad days they were. I was going with an older, sophisticated man of eighteen, and I had stars in my eyes, but he had a gleam in his. His Christmas present to me was a bottle of French champagne, which somehow wiped the "Merry" off my Christmas like a wet sponge. I had wanted something to cherish, you see, and something that I could flaunt, ever so casually, in front of the girls. Champagne wasn't romantic; it was—well, just wicked.

The rule here would seem to be this: if you are a teen-ager's dashing, sophisticated uncle, a bottle of champagne might be a dashing, sophisticated gift. But if you are her true love—or she considers you so—she wants an Ever Thine bracelet, or an Arlene Francis-type heart.

You cannot pursue the matter of presents any distance without coming upon the subjects of toe covers and sidesaddles.

Toe covers—I don't know where they got the name—are those highly improbable widgits like left-handed *fettucine* cutters or a set of seven blue velvet bookmarks, each dedicated to a different day of the week, which provoke a really sincere "Oh, you shouldn't have!" from the recipient. They are usually rewrapped and redistributed the following Christmas, if you are certain you remember whom not to give them back to.

Only by a happy fluke does a toe cover ever turn out to be someone's best present. The only instance I know of which comes even close concerns a hand-embroidered, fluted, scalloped, starched linen liner for a breadbasket—truly a magnificent toe cover—which was given to a business girl. She had no breadbasket, of course, nor did she have a summer hat; and she needed a summer hat to wear to a wedding. So she wore this hand-embroidered, fluted, scalloped, starched linen breadbasket liner, and it was a vast success. While this doesn't make it a Best Present exactly, it's still getting remarkable mileage out of a toe cover.

Sidesaddles, too, are seldom "best presents." A sidesaddle is our family's name for that good book you give your husband because you want to read it yourself, or the croquet set which the croquet fan happily gives to a member of his immediate family for the whole family to enjoy.

These can be good presents, mind you, but not best presents. An illustration of this is the best present a friend of mine, named Constance, received from her husband, named Al.

It was their second Christmas and first baby. Al's original idea, for Connie's Christmas, was a smart nonmaternity suit, which he certainly would have enjoyed seeing her in after all those smocks. Next he thought of a decent record player, for they both wanted one. But he finally discarded both these sidesaddles in favor of a one-day-a-week baby sitter for a year.

This brought him no joy. He didn't look forward to having the lady around. But to Connie, who had heard the clank of the jail gates closing

as she regarded the diaper-and-bottle-bound vista before her, it was the absolutely best present of her life.

Thus, the best present, it seems, isn't usually laden with side benefits to the giver, although it does bring its own subtle rewards.

Indeed, what the best present isn't can be quite as instructive as what it is. Item: a woman's best present isn't usually like anyone else's.

Many a fond husband and father has come a cropper here. Wandering dazedly through a department store, with his wife and daughter on his mind and the December 25 deadline breathing hot on his neck, a man may stumble into the Christmas crop of cashmeres and solve his problems in one fell swoop. Both his women like yellow, he knows, and anyway his feet hurt. So he settles for two identical yellow cardigans.

This he should not have done, as he will learn on the first shopping day after Christmas, when he finds that one or the other of the yellow cashmeres has been magically transmuted into a red pullover or an electric skillet.

Another point that it is well to keep in mind is that her best present isn't usually the one she ordered.

The huge exception here is little girls. If a little girl wants a doll buggy, expects a doll buggy and doesn't get a doll buggy, she won't even see all the hand-smocked dresses and doll houses and Teddy bears she *does* get, and you will be scouring the town in search of an open-for-business Doll Buggy Store on Christmas morning.

But adults are different, especially female adults. One woman whom I asked said that last Christmas she had pined for, and asked for, a certain marble-topped cigarette table, which her husband gave her. But the present she truly loved, the present she shows everyone, was an unexpected one. It was a little framed picture—a color snapshot of her azaleas that he had taken,

quite unknown to her, the previous spring.

It is true, too, that some of the best presents are bittersweet. My friend Phyllis had a beloved cat named Giddy, who died in her seventeenth summer, having had a rich full life and approximately 238 children. Phyllis has received some impressive gifts in her time, but the one she remembers was the exact, lively, kitten replica of Giddy, which her husband gave her the following Christmas.

Then there is Alicia, whose best present was the watch her mother gave her when she was twelve. She had wanted a watch badly; and her mother, a woman of sentiment and tradition, had her own mother's handsome heavy gold lapel watch checked over, beautifully polished and gift-wrapped.

But Alicia's idea had been something sporty—in white gold—a wrist watch, the kind the other girls had. When she saw the heirloom she was crushed; and then, when she saw her mother's face, she was doubly so, but the moment couldn't be undone. Alicia remembers it vividly—perhaps, as she says, because she did more growing up in that moment than in all her twelve years.

A woman's best present can be any one of many things, you see, depending on who she is and where she stands, and also who is standing beside her. Another friend of mine was given a gift which is hard to forget.

She and her husband had had a warm, happy marriage; he died suddenly in September. Christmas was a bleak time for her that year; but, for the sake of her two young sons, she trimmed the traditional tree in their traditional way.

Under the tree on Christmas morning she found a special gift for herself: a fifty-cent piece, wrapped as only a ten-year-old boy would wrap it, from Doug, the elder.

You see, it had been his father's custom to give his mother, among her other gifts, a small wrapped-up check. Now that Doug was the man of the family, he was keeping, as best he could, the old traditions alive. (1959)

Author Unknown

The First Merry Christmas

An English gentleman by the name of Henry Cole once found himself in something of a predicament. Actually, it was the sort of a pinch any chap could create for himself. Christmas of 1843 was drawing nigh, and he had fallen far behind in his correspondence to friends. His impulsive solution was the first Christmas card, an idea which traveled around the world and has solved similar problems for millions of tardy correspondents ever after.

But to get back to Mr. Cole, he was quite an imaginative fellow. After his initial inspiration, he contacted an acquaintance, John Calcott Horsley of the Royal Academy, and commis-

sioned him to design some sort of a card which would reflect seasonal sentiments. He also wanted a card which could be printed in quantity and sent around to all the people to whom he owed letters. In the back of Cole's mind, no doubt, there was the recent English Postal Reform which had created penny postage. Cole's lively brain had seized the moment.

Horsley's first card, shown on this page, depicted a convivial family party in progress, the adults holding their glasses up in a toast to the recipient of the card. The side panels show two of the oldest traditions of Christmas, feeding the hungry and clothing the needy.

The greeting on the first Christmas card is as

The end of Henry Cole's correspondence problem, and the beginning of a custom: the first Christmas card.

The Christmas element was often obscure in early cards.

familiar as "Hello," and just as friendly. "A Merry Christmas and a Happy New Year to you" was the simple but heartfelt message it conveyed to the recipient.

At least 1,000 copies of the Cole-Horsley card were printed. Of that number, only a dozen are known to exist today. Two of them, including the only known unused copy, are on display; they may be seen in the Hallmark Historical Collection in Kansas City, Missouri, as may all the rare cards shown on these pages, and thousands of others.

Henry Cole's novel idea really caught on in the British empire. It was boosted considerably by the penny post which made a large-scale exchange of cards possible throughout the United

Children were popular subjects during the Victorian age.

Kingdom—upon which in those days the sun never set.

An established printer of playing cards, Goodall & Sons, issued in 1862 what is probably the first large selection of Christmas cards. Other English publishers, notably Marcus Ward and the De La Rue Company, added their own beautifully printed or engraved works to the market.

England's famous woman artist, Kate Greenaway, entered the Christmas Card competition at this point, contributing outstanding greeting-card designs to Marcus Ward. Over the years, her paintings of cute children dressed in high fashion drew many imitators.

Much can be learned of the tastes, manners and preoccupations of people of an earlier generation by a study of their Christmas cards. Their archaic notions amuse us.

The Victorians, for example, imagined their beloved children as miniature men and women and saw them as innocent and coy. This is reflected in the cards of that age. Also characteristic

The humor of a bygone era is often reflected in its cards.

of the Victorian age were a kind of gamey, masculine wit and, in contrast to this, an almost mawkish sort of sentimentality.

The most popular cards of the 1860s and 1870s showed little Christmas significance. They depicted a variety of subjects, such as children, landscapes, kittens, fairies and flowers, portraits, animals, fish and even reptiles.

Then Bostonian card-maker Louis Prang appeared on the scene. He wrought two big changes in the industry. Prang, who became known as "the father of the American Christmas card," perfected the lithographic process of multicolor printing in the 1870s, thus making possible a new level of artistic quality in Christmas cards.

Prang held contests in which artists competed with their finest works. Many of the winning pieces were of the Nativity and other religious scenes; thus Prang helped put religious significance into Christmas cards.

Nineteenth-century America was a rugged and sometimes harsh place; there was a longing for

Artwork has ranged from serious, religious topics. . .

. . .to not-so-serious, fanciful illustratons.

A single, well-designed Christmas card can convey the season's greetings and a feeling of peace on earth, as well.

fragility and beauty expressed in the Christmas cards of that era.

By 1881, Prang was already printing almost five million Christmas cards a year. As incentive, he offered prizes of as much as $4,000 to promising artists who submitted designs for his growing line of cards.

Near the turn of the century, however, Prang was forced into the background by a great influx of penny cards made in Germany. The entire Christmas-card industry from then until the World War I era was virtually monopolized by the Germans.

In the 1920s, major American greeting-card companies again emerged, and as before, their Christmas cards reflected the spirit of the times. During the Great Depression, cards spoofed being poor, and always hinted that tomorrow we'd all be better off.

Through World War II, Christmas-card Santas carried American flags, and there were "missing you" sentiments for the many servicemen who were separated from their families by the oceans. In the years that followed, the grimness of the Cold War brought about a demand for more humor in greeting cards. It was then that the studio card—with its odd Santas and dopey-looking reindeer—was born.

Nowadays, the Christmas cards received and sent each year number in the billions, their number multiplied by factors such as the affluence and mobility which disperse friends and families to far places.

Just to give you an idea, Hallmark Cards, Inc., the largest and best-known publisher of cards, prints its greetings in 21 languages and distributes them in more than 100 countries and, to keep the happy wishes rolling, turns out approximately eight million greeting cards *daily*! A staff of more than 300 artists creates more than 12,000 greeting-card designs annually.

Making his rounds on wheels in an earlier card—the jolly old elf.

The Hallmark people estimate that as many as 3,000 people, involved in up to 300 separate processes, actually combine their talents in the conception and publication of a single greeting card. Each card has to run the gauntlet of 30 testing stations before it is finally ready for the

customer: About 95 working days (and possibly more, if there are overheated discussions concerning the length of Santa Claus' beard) are needed to completely develop a greeting card from the first step to the final product.

All this emanated from the conviction of a young lad, Joyce C. Hall, in 1910, that what was needed on greeting cards—and lacking at that particular time—was a "from me to you" sentiment. It sounds almost too simple, perhaps, but that little bit of sentiment, according to recent estimates in the business press, brings in today annual sales of more than $300 million to Hallmark.

Christmas cards, those convenient conveyors of peace on earth and goodwill among men, are here to stay even though the penny post is now eight cents. (1971)

The range of characters and scenes depicting seasonal sentiments is limited only by designers' imaginations.

CHRISTMAS SCENES IN FACT AND FICTION

Mack Thomas

Hard-Rock Candy

It wasn't long after Thanksgiving until the getting ready for the Christmas Service at the Methodist Church began. First there was the swing of the Bible from Proverbs to Revelation. The rest of it happened almost automatically.

Miss Ruth started the first Sunday in December, giving out parts to the three-, four-, five-, six,- seven- and eight-year-olds in her Sunday-school class. Billy Dixon got to be Joseph in the Nativity scene. Mary Lou Gannaway got to be Virgin Mary. Pud got a rhyme that went

Little fairy snowflakes
Dancing in the flue . . .
Old Man Santy Claws
What is keeping you?

Toby got to hold up the pole with the bright star of Jerusalem because nobody else would do it. The others got thought into clusters to sing "Santy Claws Is Coming to Town" or one chorus of "Jingle Bells" because Miss Henrietta's nine-, ten-, eleven-, twelve- and thirteen-year-olds were doing "Silent Night."

Mamma and Celia got to make a red flannel fairy's costume for Pud and a pole-holder's costume for Toby. Papa got to supervise the learning of Pud's rhyme. Jenny got to drive everyone almost crazy trying to make herself able to sing "Away in a Manger" for her solo an octave too high.

Somehow everything and everyone was ready by Christmas Eve. Everyone set out about seven o'clock, coming up all the ways to Luke Street and the warm lights in the windows of Methodist Church shining through the winter dark and the winter cold.

Miss Ruth was grabbing kids as they came through the wooden front doors, getting her cast together. The grown-ups stood around in their coats feeling *different* than when they were in the churchhouse on Sunday or even Prayer Meeting Night.

Down front in the right-hand corner the fat tree that flattened two feet of its top on the ceiling was hung with all the fancy in Cottonmill. There were red ropes and green ropes of bristled paper twisted or sewn on backbones of string. There were bangles and balls, and crayoned and scissored angels, dangling at branchtips. There were pieces of colored glass shaped like lean fangs of ice that hang from eaves, and thousands of long shreds of tinfoil twisting and glittering in the light. Crisscrossing everything, binding it all, were interlocked bracelets of flourpasted pieces of red and orange and green and all other possible colors of paper.

Here and there and there in the branches were little packages, ribboned and bowed. There and there and here in the branches were cap pistols and dolls. Plain cap pistols, silvery and small, and Buck Jones pistols with pearly-looking handles. Rubber dolls you could drop and not break and dolls with clothes and hair and blinking eyes, dolls that could sleep like people.

Under the tree, waiting for Santy Claws to come at the end of the program and give them out, were flat and thick and square packages wrapped in tissue and Christmas paper. And there were long presents that had to be baseball bats, and skates and scooters and even a Red Racer wagon or two. Then there were all the plain brown-paper sacks, like the kind at Tragers' Store for carrying home groceries. The top was twisted on all of them, but everyone knew they were from the Mill and had sometimes an apple and sometimes an orange and always six pecans and a four-inch piece of wiggledy hard-rock candy.

By seven-thirty all the Cottonmill Christians and some that weren't were gathered. The place was filled with Shepherds and snaggled-toothed Angels; Shepherds with Red Goose shoes and rolled-up overalls under their flowing, bed-sheet robes, Shepherds with handles from brooms and handles from mops to make-believe were things you could sit on and twist on and throw and play swords with and poke with and ride like a witch until it was time for them to be Shepherds' staffs. All the Angels had were wings and halos, and the wings felt funny and itched; the halos slipped. One of the Angels was cross-eyed, another had freckles and a sty on his eye. Another had one wing torn loose from its harness and another had a fat split lip. One Angel nicked a Shepherd's nose with his halo and screamed and cried at the top of his four-year-old lungs when the Shepherd poked him with a staff.

Finally, Brother Cartwright stood up and held up his arms like he knew how to do and settled his half of the problem by saying, "All right, now, if you grown Brothers and Sisters will find a seat, the children have their Christmas program to give us." With that he met Miss Ruth at the piano, and said, "I'll give a prayer, then the rest is up to you."

"Now, Brother Cartwright," she said, "you know good and well that I'm not able to do all this by myself. Ardell!" she said to the cross-eyed Shepherd, "you leave Bessie's halo alone!"

"But you know I've got to see that the tree doesn't catch on fire," Brother Cartwright said to Miss Ruth.

"I've got it all written down here on this piece of paper," said Miss Ruth. "Just read out what I've got as you come to it so everyone will know what the children are doing." She made him take the paper, then turned to seeing about the music and left him standing there. After a minute he quit looking at the back of her head and glanced down at the paper.

By now all the grown-ups were more or less settled on the benches. Brother Cartwright said a prayer, saying how grateful everyone was for coming through another year of joys and hardships to another birthday of Jesus the Savior, and asking blessings on the little children who were about to take part in the program, and on everything. He saw that the Shepherds and Angels were getting restless so he said Amen and cleared his throat while he tried to figure out the instructions Miss Ruth had written on the paper.

"Now why don't we all stand and start things off this evening with the first and last verses of. . .*O Little Town of Bethlehem how still we see thee lie. . .above the deep and dreamless. . .* well, I'm sure all of you know it."

Everyone stood, and Brother Cartwright said, "Would you start us off, Miss Ruth?"

Miss Ruth played the part that matches "*the silent stars go by*," and everyone came in more or less together. Not many sang the last verse because not many knew it. When they got through it Brother Cartwright waited until everyone got settled again, then read, "Now the littlest ones in the Sunbeam Class will sing 'Jingle Bells.' "

Half the ones in Miss Ruth's class that didn't have a part in the Nativity came away from the wall beside the piano and lined up bed sheet to bed sheet in the space in front of the pulpit. Miss Ruth had to get up from the piano and straighten it out about who was to stand closest to the Christmas tree. When that was settled she went back to the piano and played the last line of the song, hunching her shoulders and elbows up and down, hoping some of the children would be watching her and get an idea of when to start singing from what she was doing. There was some trouble with *"Dashing thro' the snow in a one-horse open sleigh,"* but once they were past that line everything went about as well as she had expected.

It had to be settled all over again from year to year about the clapping, but Brother Cartwright did it when "Jingle Bells" was finished so the rest of them started. The children being clapped at stood there too long or Brother Cartwright read the next thing on the list too soon, one or the other, but everything got all snarled up when the other Sunbeamers tried to start lining up to sing "Santy Claws Is Coming to Town." Miss Ruth was worrying with a sore finger she'd just hurt, thinking about how she should have let the little ones sing "Santy Claws Is Coming" and had the older ones do the one with the hard part about the one-horse open sleigh, and so Brother Cartwright quietly came down from the pulpit, and a couple of helpful women came up from their seats and got the little Sunbeamers all out of the way. When that was finally done, Brother Cartwright felt someone might have forgotten what was going to be sung so, to be on the safe side, he read it again before he got back up in the pulpit.

"Santy Claws Is Coming" sounded fine, even to Miss Ruth and she knew music. Even the Sunbeamers that sang joined in the clapping, but there's a limit to how long two hundred people can clap at six- and seven- and eight-year-old kids, even their own, so it ended, finally, and Brother Cartwright stood up and read, "Next is Pud—I guess I ought to say Alfred, it being Christmas and all—but anyhow he's going to say us a Christmas poem, called "Little Fairy Snowflakes."

Pud edged out from the wall with the red tip of his fairy cap hanging wrong and tickling his nose, looking all sheepish and uncertain and neckless, his round cheeks and chin scrunched down into his shoulders. His eyes got big when he made it to where he was supposed to stand, and he started looking all around until he saw Papa and Mamma again sitting on the second bench. He looked at Papa and waited. Papa nodded at him, and so he started, *"Little Fairy Snowflakes dancing in the flue, Old Man Santy Claws, what is keeping you?"*

Then, before clapping could start, he looked at Papa again and Papa nodded at him again, so he went on with the rest of the poem, reciting it just like Papa had carefully taught it to him before, saying, *". . .the Vinter Vind, whi. . .I mean vistling around the corner of the house."*

Everyone in Cottonmill knew that last part wasn't in the regular poem because "Little Fairy Snowflakes" was in the program every year.

When they all started laughing with their clapping, Pud got all excited and not too sure about things but thinking it must be all right because the laughing about it sounded good and not *at* him, and he started laughing too. The ones that could looked  away from Pud to where Mamma and Papa were sitting with Celia. Papa had his arms folded across his chest, and there was a big grin on his face. Celia looked like it didn't bother her at all, but Mamma almost died.

It took a while for all that to die down, but finally it was time for the Nativity. Miss Ruth had it worked out nice. There was hay down front, between the piano and the tree, and there was a manger. Burlap was scattered around and hanging from the rail where you knelt to take Communion. A doll was in the manger, wrapped good, and there was plenty of space around it for standing close.

Miss Henrietta's class lined up behind the Communion rail and waited. Toby got to stand in the pulpit and hold up the cane pole with the wire taped to it and the light at the top for the star. The three wise men got in place, and Mary Lou Gannaway came and stood looking into the manger. She was all wrapped in a bed sheet dyed a pale shade of blue.

Jenny went over by the piano and waited while Miss Ruth took the matches she'd brought from home and lit candles and handed them out to the Angels. She got them spread around the way she wanted them, then she lit a big one on a saucer and handed it to Joseph, telling him, "Now, you be careful with that, Billy, and don't set fire to anything." Billy went over and stood by Mary Lou, beside the manger. It was getting pretty crowded but the Shepherds were left to stand where they wanted to and finally everything was ready.

Brother Cartwright went back to the fuse box on the wall just inside the door and waited until Miss Ruth got back to the piano where Jenny was waiting, then he pulled the switch and Miss Ruth played the introduction to "Away in a Manger" and Jenny came in just at the right time, singing it clean and pure and making some of the notes like she was striking glass bells. When she finished there was a hush on the whole place, then Miss Ruth hit three notes, like that, do me so, and Miss Henrietta's class came in with the words, singing, *"Si-ilent Night. . .Ho-oly Night. . .All is calm. . .All is bright. . ."* and it

 was beautiful. Some of the Angels looked in love with their candles and some of the Shepherds couldn't keep from wiggling their staffs but it was beautiful, all the candles flickering in the Angels' hands and making soft shadows in the hollows and bends of faces and everything, the lights on the tree making dim branch-shadows on the walls and the ceiling, the presents all through and underneath, the star of Bethlehem dipping and bobbing just a little, silvery blue, looking far away up there above the manger, and the harmony working right in the singing, making you want to do it when the words of the song said, *"Sleep in Heavenly Pe-e-eace. . .Slee-eep in Heaven-ly Peace."*

When it was over nobody thought about clapping. A few of the mammas got up and started hugging Shepherds and Angels, not knowing exactly why. Mary Lou Gannaway's mamma had tears in her eyes when she hugged Mary Lou. Some of the men cleared their throats and made a point of switching the way they had their legs crossed. All this couldn't have lasted over a minute because it wasn't any more than that between the end of the Nativity and the church-house doors banging open for Santy Claws. He came in just when Brother Cartwright turned on the lights, stomping down the aisle with a big sack on his back, saying, "Merrr-ry Christmas! Yo ho ho ho Merrr-ry Christmas!"

The little ones started squealing, and the bigger ones started jumping up and down and clapping their hands, yelling, "Santy Claws! Santy Claws! Ohhhh! It's Santy Claws, Mamma, it really is!" and one or two of the biggest medium ones said, "Heck!" and "Aw shoot! That ain't Santy Claws!" and some that didn't intend to stand for such awful things said, "It is *too* Santy Claws! It is!" and the doubters said, "Crazy, anybody can see it's just Homer Bates," but the faithful replied, "You're the one that's crazy, Crazy! It is too Santy Claws. . .ain't it, Mamma?" and all the time he kept coming down the aisle, saying, "Yo ho ho ho ho. . .it's old Santy! Merrr-ry Christmas! Yo ho ho ho ho!"

By the time he got down by the big tree there were so many kids pushing up around him it took Brother Cartwright's help to find a place to set the sack he swung off his back. "Now you little ones move back a little so Santy can get on with handing out the presents," said the preacher. "Come on now and get back out of Santy's way. . .that's right. . .My my! Isn't it exciting! Get on back, now."

Finally, Santy Claws had enough room for giving. He took a minute looking back and forth between the tree and the sack, making it look like he couldn't decide where to start. Even the ones that were willing to bet $50,000 to a doughnut hole that it was Homer Bates joined in the yelling for "The sack! The sack you had on your back, Santy!"

"What's that?" he said, "What's that you're wanting old Santy to do?" He held his hand to his ear rim and turned his head, pretending to do his best to make out what they were saying. "The sack!" they yelled. "Oh, Santy, the sack!"

"Ohh!" he said at last, "You've had all this time to look at the tree and now you want to see what's hid in the sack! Yo ho ho ho!" He opened the sack so his hand would go down its neck in a private way, and pulled out a tiny, shiny red purse and gave it to Emily Gregg for her Ohh and Ahh. His hand went back in the sack and pulled out a fishnet pocket of marbles. Billy Dixon that once had been Joseph said, "Boy! A whole bag of Zebras!" so then Santy gave them to him with a yo and a ho.

It went on like that. There were Yo-Yos and tops and bags of marbles, which went to the boys, and there were

patent-leathery purses and cards with a rubber ball and jacks and cards with curving yellow butterfly combs and butterfly hairclips, which went to the girls. When everyone had something from the bag, Santy Claws stuffed it under his coat and scratched his neck where the beard was beginning to itch. Then under the Christmas tree he went, making straight for one of the Red Racer wagons. He had some trouble reading the tag, or made it seem like he did, twisting his head from side to side, then his beard got caught on one of the catchy branches of the fir tree. It took some doing but he got it untangled and kept it on his face, then he went at the tag on the wagon's handle again. After a twist and a couple of squints, he said, "It looks like Pud and Toby Siler."

Toby had given it up way back in the middle of "Jingle Bells." While he was standing paralyzed, taking back the giving-up so the wagon could be his, Pud was under the tree and in the red bed and out and all over it and dragging and butting it out over barricades of presents and brown-paper bags. Toby thought, "Pud's," then Papa's voice said, "Toby, you'd better help him."

"You'd better. . .I'd better. . .I. . .mine!" ran through Toby's head, and then he thought, "OURS!" and he flew hands-first from the spring of belief to helping and touching and owning.

Finally, except for the decorations, the Christmas tree was clean as a wishbone stripped of wishes. There was nothing left but the brown-paper sacks, and a good thing, too, because by then Santy Claws was looking pretty tired. Some of the papas noticed there wasn't much ho anymore in his Yo ho, and started helping him see that every kid got his sack from the mill. Before it was through, Brother Cartwright and even Miss Ruth were lending a hand.

When it got down to the sacks that had no takers, Santy Claws stood for a minute with one in each hand, looking around. Then he said, "Well, I guess that's it," to no one in particular, and put them down. After a turn or two he found his big cloth sack and put it across his shoulder. Brother Cartwright said to him, "Here now, open that sack."

Santy Claws said, "What?" and watched the preacher put two brown-paper sacks in the cloth one. "Well, now," said Santy Claws.

And the preacher said, "That should help it carry better."

"I'm much obliged," said Santy Claws, and he went up the aisle and out of the church with one last Yo ho ho.

The preacher said, "Well," and the men said, "Well," and Miss Ruth closed the lid on the upright piano. The women said, "Oh, I hate to wake it up," and started inching coats and caps on sleeping Angels. The preacher took a step and said, "Wup!" and steadied himself and said, "Watch out for the marbles."

Widow and spinster and family by family, they went out the doors and left the warm lights in the windows of the Methodist Church. They went down Luke Street and down all the ways through the winter dark and the cold, humming hymns or hugging themselves or leading Shepherds or carrying snaggled-toothed sleeping Angels with tight hands locked on a purse or a pistol, and a piece of melting, wiggledly hard-rock candy. (1964)

Borden Deal

The Christmas Hunt

It should have been the best Christmas of them all, that year at Dog Run. It started out to be, anyway. I was so excited, watching my father talking on the telephone, that I couldn't stand still. For I was ten years old and I had never been on a quail shoot in my whole life. I wanted to go on the big Christmas Day hunt even more than I wanted that bicycle I was supposed to get. And I really needed the bicycle to cover with speed and ease the two miles I had to walk to school.

The Christmas Day hunt was always the biggest and best of the season. It was almost like a field trial; only the best hunters and the finest dogs were invited by my father. All my life I had been hearing great tales of past Christmas Day hunts. And now I knew with a great ten-year-old certainty that I was old enough to go.

My father hung up the phone and turned around, grinning. "That was Walter," he said. "There'll be ten of them this year. And Walter is bringing his new dog. If all he claims for that dog is true——"

"Papa," I said.

"Lord," my mother said. "That'll be a houseful to feed."

My father put his arm around her shoulders, hugging her. "Oh, you know you like it," he said. "They come as much for your cooking as they do for the hunting, I think."

My mother pursed her lips in the way she had, and then smiled. "Wild turkey," she said. "You think you could shoot me four or five nice fat wild turkeys?"

I wanted to jump up and down to attract attention. But that was kid stuff, a tactic for the five-year-olds, though I had to admit it was effective. But I was ten. So I said, "Papa."

My father laughed. "I think I can," he said. "I'll put in a couple of mornings trying."

"Papa," I said desperately.

"Wild turkey stuffed with wild rice," my mother said quickly, thoughtfully, in her planning voice. "Giblet gravy, mashed potatoes, maybe a nice potato salad——"

"If I don't fail on the turkeys," my father said.

"Papa!" I said.

My father turned to me. "Come on, Tom," he said. "We've got to feed those dogs."

That's the way parents are, even when you're ten years old. They can talk right on and never hear a word you say. I ran after my father as he left the kitchen, hoping for a chance to get my words in edgewise. But my father was walking fast and already the clamor of the bird dogs was rising up to cover any speech I might have in mind to make.

The dogs were standing on the wire fence in long dappled rows, their voices lifted in greeting. Even in my urgent need I had to stop and admire them. There's nothing prettier in the whole world than a good bird dog. There's a nobleness

to its head, an intelligence in its eyes, that no other animal has. Just looking at them sent a shiver down my backbone; and the thought of shooting birds over them—well, the shiver just wasn't in my backbone now, I was shaking all over.

All of the dogs except one were in the same big run. But my father kept Calypso Baby in her own regal pen. I went to her and looked into her soft brown eyes. She stood up tall on the fence, her strong body stretched to its full height. Standing like that, she was as tall as I was.

"Hello, Baby," I whispered, and she wagged her tail. "Are you gonna find me some birds this Christmas, Baby? You gonna hunt for me like you do for papa?"

She lolled her tongue, laughing at me. We were old friends. Calypso Baby was the finest bird dog in that part of the country. My father owned a number of dogs and kept and trained others for his town friends. But Calypso Baby was his personal dog, the one that he took to the field trials, the one he shot over in the big Christmas Day hunt held at Dog Run.

My father was bringing the sack of feed from the shed. I put out my hand, holding it against the wire so Calypso Baby could lick my fingers.

"This year," I whispered to her. "This year I'm going." I left Calypso Baby, went with determination toward my father. "Papa," I said, in a voice not to be denied this time.

But my father was busy opening the sack of dog food.

"Papa," I said firmly. "I want to talk to you." It was the tone and the words my father used often toward me, so much of mimicry that my father looked down at me in surprise, at last giving me his attention.

"What is it?" he said. "What do you want?"

"Papa, I'm ten years old," I said.

My father laughed. "Well, what of it?" he said. "Next year you'll be eleven. And the next year twelve."

"I'm old enough to go on the Christmas hunt," I said.

Incredibly, my father laughed. "At ten?" he said. "I'm afraid not."

I stood, stricken. "But——" I said.

"No," my father said, in the voice that meant No, and no more talking about it. He hoisted the sack of feed and took it into the wire dog pen, the bird dogs crowding around him, rearing up on him in their eagerness.

"Well, come on and help me," my father said impatiently. "I've got a lot of things to do."

Usually I enjoyed the daily feeding of the dogs. But not today; I went through the motions

Kneeling for the shot ensures steady sighting, lessens the recoil.

dumbly, silently, not paying any attention to the fine bird dogs crowding around me. I cleaned the watering troughs with my usual care, but my heart was not in it.

After the feeding was over, I scuffed stubbornly about my other tasks and then went up to my room, not even coming down when my father came home at dusk excited with the two wild turkeys he had shot. I could hear him talking to my mother in the kitchen, and the ring of their voices had already the feel of Christmas, a hunting cheer that made them brighter, livelier, than usual. But none of the cheer and the pleasure came into me, even though Christmas was almost upon us and yesterday had been the last day of school.

That night I hunted. In my dreams I was out ahead of all the other men and dogs, Calypso Baby quartering the field in her busy way, doing it so beautifully I ached inside to watch her. All the men and dogs stopped their own hunting to watch us, as though it were a field trial. When Calypso Baby pointed, I raised the twelve-gauge shotgun, moved in on her on the ready, and Calypso Baby flushed the birds in her fine, steady way. They came up in an explosive whir, and I had the gun to my shoulder, squeezing off the shot just the way I'd been told to do. Three quail dropped like stones out of the covey and I swung the gun, following a single. I brought down the single with the second barrel, and Calypso Baby was already bringing the first bird to me in her soft, unbruising mouth. I knelt to pat her for a moment, and Baby whipped her tail to tell me how fine a shot I was, how much she liked for me to be the one shooting over her today.

Soon there was another covey, and I did even better on this one, and then another and another, and nobody was hunting at all, not even my father, who was laughing and grinning at the other men, knowing this was his boy, Tom, and his dog, Calypso Baby, and just full of pride with it all. When it was over, the men crowded around and patted me on the shoulder, hefting the full game bag in admiration, and then there was my father's face close before me, saying, "I was wrong, son, when I said that a ten-year-old boy isn't old enough to go bird hunting with the best of us."

Then I was awake and my father, dressed in his hunting clothes, was shaking me, and it was morning. I looked up dazedly into his face, unable to shake off the dream, and I knew what it was I had to do. I had to show my father. Only then would he believe.

"Are you awake?" my father said. "You'll have to change the water for the dogs. I'm going to see if I can get some more turkeys this morning."

"All right," I said. "I'm awake now."

My father left. I got up and ate breakfast in the kitchen, close to the warm stove. I didn't say anything to my mother about my plans. I went out and watered the dogs as soon as the sun was up, but I didn't take the time, as I usually did, to play with them.

"Me and you are going to go hunting today," I told Calypso Baby as I changed her water. She jumped and quivered all over, knowing the word as well as I did.

I went back into the house, listening for my mother. She was upstairs, making the beds. I went into the spare room where my father kept all the hunting gear. I was trembling, remembering the dream, as I went to the gun rack and touched the cold steel of the double-barreled twelve-gauge. But I knew it would be very heavy for me. I took the single-barrel instead, though I knew that pretty near ruined my chances for a second shot unless I could reload very quickly.

I picked up a full shell bag and hung it under my left arm. I found a game bag and hung it under my right arm. The strap was too long and the bag dangled emptily to my knees, banging against me as I walked. I tied a knot in the strap so the bag would rest comfortably on my right hip. The gun was heavy in my hands as I walked into the hallway, listening for my mother. She was still upstairs.

"Mamma, I'm gone," I shouted up to her. "I'll be back in a little while." That was so she wouldn't be looking for me.

"All right," she called. "Don't wander far off. Your father will be back in an hour or two and might have something for you to do."

I hurried out of the house, straight to Calypso Baby's pen. I did not look up, afraid that my mother might be watching out of the window. That was a danger I could do nothing about, so I just ignored it. I opened the gate to Baby's pen and she came out, circling and cavorting.

"Come on, Baby," I whispered. "Find me some birds now. Find me a whole lot of birds."

We started off, circling the barn so we would not be seen from the house and going straight away in its shadow as far as we could. Beyond the pasture we crossed a cornfield, Calypso Baby arrowing straight for the patch of sedgegrass beyond. Her tail was whiplike in its thrash, her head high as she plunged toward her work, and I had to hurry to keep up. The gun was clumsy in my hands and the two bags banged against my hips. But I remembered not to run with the gun, remembered to keep the breech open until I was ready to shoot. I knew all about hunting; I just hadn't had a chance to practice what I knew.

Suiting up for the hunt denotes a coming of age.

When I came home with a bag full of fine birds my father would have to admit that I knew how to hunt, that I was old enough for the big Christmas Day hunt when all the great hunters came out from town for the biggest day of the season.

When I ducked through the barbed-wire fence Calypso Baby was waiting for me, standing a few steps into the sedgegrass, her head up watching me alertly. Her whole body quivered with her eagerness to be off. I swept my arm in the gesture I had seen my father use so many times and Calypso Baby plunged instantly into the grass. She was a fast worker, quartering back and forth with an economical use of her energy. She could cover a field in half the time it took any other dog. The first field was empty, and we passed on to the second one. Somehow Calypso Baby knew that birds were here. She steadied down, hunting slowly, more thoroughly.

Then, startling me though I had been expecting it, she froze into a point, one foot up, her tail straight back, her head flat with the line of her backbone. I froze too. I couldn't move, I couldn't even remember to breech the gun and raise it to my shoulder. I stood as still as the dog, all of my knowledge flown out of my head, and yet far back under the panic I knew that the birds weren't going to hold, they were going to rise in just a moment. Calypso Baby, surprised at my inaction, broke her point to look at me in inquiry. Her head turned toward me and she looked at me, puzzled. She asked the obvious question as plain as my father's voice: *Well, what are you going to do about these fine birds I found for you?*

I could move then. I took a step or two, fumblingly breeched the gun, raised it to my shoulder. The birds rose of their own accord in a sudden wild drum of sound. I yanked at the trigger, unconsciously bracing myself against the blast and the recoil. Nothing happened. Nothing at all happened. I tugged at the trigger wildly, furiously, but it was too late and the birds were gone.

I lowered the gun, looking down at it in bewilderment. I had forgotten to release the safety. I wanted to cry at my own stupidity, I could feel the tears standing in my eyes. This was not at all like my dream of last night, when I and the dog and the birds had all been so perfect.

Calypso Baby walked back to me and looked up into my face. I could read the puzzled contempt in her eyes. She lay down at my feet, putting her muzzle on her paws. I looked down at her, ashamed of myself and knowing that she was ashamed. She demanded perfection, just as my father did.

"It was my fault, Baby," I told her. I leaned over and patted her on the head. "You didn't do anything wrong. It was me."

I started off then, looking back at the bird dog. She did not follow me. "Come on," I told her. "Hunt."

She got up slowly and went out ahead of me again. But she worked in a puzzled manner, checking back to me frequently. She no longer had the joy, the confidence, with which she had started out.

"Come on, Baby," I tried to coax her. "Hunt, Baby. Hunt."

We crossed into another field, low grass this time, and when we found the covey there was very little time for settling myself. Calypso Baby pointed suddenly; I jerked the gun to my shoulder, remembering the safety this time, and then Calypso Baby flushed the birds. They rose up before me and I pulled the trigger, hearing the blast of the gun, feeling the shock of it into my shoulder knocking me back a step.

But not even one bird dropped like a fateful stone out of the covey. The covey had gone off low and hard on an angle to the left, and I had completely missed the shot, aiming straight ahead instead of swinging with the birds. Calypso Baby did not even attempt to point singles. She dropped her head and her tail and started away from me, going back toward the house.

I ran after her, calling her, crying now but with anger rather than hurt. Baby would never like me again, she would hold me in the indifference she felt toward any person who was not a bird hunter. She would tolerate me as she tolerated my mother, and the men who came out with shiny new hunting clothes and walked all over the land talking about how the dogs didn't hold the birds properly so you could get a decent shot.

I couldn't be one of those. I ran after the dog, calling her, until at last she suffered me to come near. I knelt, fondling her head, talking to her, begging her for another chance.

"I'll get some birds next time," I told her. "You just watch. You hear?"

Frozen in time, a dog "points" to its quarry. A job well done.

At last, reluctantly, she consented to hunt again. I followed her, my hands gripping the heavy gun, determined this time. I knew it was my last chance; she would not give me another. I could not miss this time.

We hunted for an hour before we found another covey of birds. I was tired, the gun and the frustration heavier with every step. But, holding only last night's dream in my mind, I refused to quit. At last Calypso Baby froze into a beautiful point. I could feel myself sweating; my teeth were gritted hard. I just had to bring down a bird this time.

It seemed to be perfect. I had plenty of time but I hurried anyway, just to be sure. Then the birds were rising in a tight cluster and I was pulling the trigger before I had the heavy gun lined up—and in the midst of the thundering blast I heard Calypso Baby yell with pain as the random shot tore into her hip.

I threw down the gun and ran toward her, seeing the blood streaking down her leg as she staggered away from me, whimpering. I knelt, trying to coax her to me, but she was afraid. I was crying, feeling the full weight of the disaster. I had committed the worst crime of any bird hunter; I had shot my own dog.

Calypso Baby was trying to hide in a clump of bushes. She snapped at me in her fear when I reached in after her, but I did not feel the pain in my hand. I knelt over her, looking at the shredded hip. It was a terrible wound, I could see only blood and raw flesh. I snatched off the empty hunting bag I had donned so optimistically, the shell bag, and took off my coat. I wrapped her in the coat and picked her up in my arms. She was very heavy, hurting, whining with each jolting step as I ran toward the house.

I came into the yard doubled over with the catch in my side from the running, and my legs were trembling. My father was sitting on the back porch with three wild turkeys beside him, cleaning his gun. He jumped to his feet when he saw the wounded dog, and asked, "What happened? Did some fool hunter shoot her?" he continued.

I stopped, standing before my father and holding the wounded dog; I looked into his angry face. They were the most terrible words I had ever had to say, but I told him. "I shot her, papa," I said.

My father stood very still. I did not know what would happen. I had never done anything so bad in my whole life and I could not even guess how my father would react. The only thing justified would be to wipe me off the face of the earth with one irate gesture of his hand.

I gulped, trying to move the pain in my throat out of the way of the words. "I took her out bird hunting," I said. "I wanted to show you—if I got a full bag of birds, I thought you'd let me go on the Christmas Day hunt——"

"I'll talk to you later," my father said grimly, taking the dog from me and starting into the kitchen. "Right now I've got to try to save this dog's life."

I started into the kitchen behind my father. He turned. "Where's the gun you shot her with?"

"I—left it."

"Don't leave it lying out there in the field," my father said in a stern voice.

I wanted very badly to go into the kitchen, find out that the dog would live. But I turned, instead, and went back the way I had come, walking with my head down, feeling shrunken inside myself. I had overreached; I had risen up today full of pride beyond my ability, and in the stubbornness of the pride I had been blind until the terrible accident had opened my eyes so that I could see myself clearly—too clearly. I found the gun, the two bags, where I had dropped them. I picked them up without looking at the smear of blood where Calypso had lain. I went back to the house slowly, not wanting to face it, reluctant to see the damage I had wrought.

When I came into the kitchen, my father had the dog stretched out on the kitchen table. My mother stood by his side with bandages and ointment in her hands. The wound was cleaned of the bird shot and dirt and blood. Calypso Baby whined when she saw me and I felt my heart cringe with the rejection.

My father looked at me across the dog. The anger was gone out of him, his voice was slow and searching and not to be denied. "Now I want to know why you took my gun and my dog without permission," he said.

"David," my mother said to him.

My father ignored her, kept his eyes hard on my face. I knew it wouldn't do any good to look toward my mother. This was between me and my father, and there was no refuge for me anywhere in the world. I didn't want a refuge; I knew I had to face not only my father, but myself.

"I—I wanted to go on the Christmas Day hunt," I said again. "I thought if I——" I stopped. It was all that I had to say; it seemed pretty flimsy to me now.

My father looked down at the dog. I was surprised at the lack of anger in him. I could read only sadness in his voice. "She may be ruined for hunting," he said. "Even if the wound heals good, if she doesn't lose the use of her leg, she may be gun-shy for the rest of her life. At best, I'll never be able to show her in field trials again. You understand what you've done?"

"Yes, sir," I said. I wanted to cry. But that would not help, any more than anger from my father would help.

"You see now why I said you weren't old enough?" my father said. "You've got to be trained for hunting, just like a dog is trained. Suppose other men had been out there, suppose you had shot a human being?"

"David!" my mother said.

My father turned angrily toward her. "He's got to learn!" he said. "There's too many people in this world trying to do things without learning how to do them first. I don't want my boy to be one of them."

"Papa," I said. "I'm—I'm sorry. I wouldn't have hurt Calypso Baby for anything in the world."

"I'm not going to punish you," my father said. He looked down at the dog. "This is too bad for a whipping to settle. But I want you to think about today. I don't want you to put it out of your mind. You knew that when the time came ripe for it, I intended to teach you, take you out like I'd take a puppy, and hunt with you. After a while, you could hunt by yourself. Then if you were good enough—and only if you were good enough—you could go on the Christmas Day hunt. The Christmas Day hunt is the place you come to, not the place you start out from. Do you understand?"

"Yes, sir," I said. I would have been glad to settle for a whipping. But I knew that a mere dusting of the breeches would be inadequate for my brashness, my overconfidence, for the tremendous hurt I had given not only to the fine bird dog but also to my father—and to myself, as well.

"You've got to take special care of Calypso Baby," my father said. "Maybe if you take care of her yourself while she's hurt, she'll decide to be your friend again."

I looked at the dog and I could feel the need of her confidence and trust. "Yes, sir," I said. Then I said humbly, "I hope she will be friends with me again some day."

I went toward the hall, needing to be alone in my room. I stopped at the kitchen doorway, looked back at my father and mother watching me. I had to say it in a hurry if I was going to say it at all.

"Papa," I said, the words rushing softly in my throat, threatening to gag there before I could get them out. "I—I don't think I deserve that bicycle this Christmas. I don't deserve it at all."

My father nodded his head. "All right, son," he said gravely. "This is your own punishment for yourself."

"Yes," I said, forcing the word, the loss empty inside me and yet feeling better too. I turned and ran out of the room and up the stairs.

Christmas came, but without any help from me at all. I went to bed on Christmas Eve heavy with the knowledge that tomorrow morning there would be no shiny new bicycle under the tree, there would be no Christmas Day hunt for me. I couldn't prevent myself from waking up at the usual excited time, but I made myself turn over and go back to sleep. When I did, reluctantly, go downstairs, the Christmas tree did not excite me, nor the usual gifts I received every year, the heavy sweater, the gloves, the scarf, the two new pairs of blue jeans. I just wouldn't let myself think about the bicycle.

After my father had gone outside, my mother hugged me to her in a sudden rush of affection. "He would have given you the bicycle anyway," she said. "If you hadn't told him you didn't want it."

I looked up at her. "I didn't deserve it," I said. "Maybe next year I will."

She surprised me then by holding me and crying. I heard the first car arrive outside, the voices of men excited with the promise of hunting. My mother stood up and said briskly, "Well, this is not getting that big dinner cooked," and went into the kitchen without looking back.

I went out on the front porch. It was perfect quail-hunting weather, cold but not too cold, with a smoky haze lying over the earth. The dogs knew that today was for hunting; I could hear them from around behind the house, standing on the wire fence in broad-shouldered rows, their voices yelping and calling. All except Calypso Baby. All except me.

I stood aside, watching the men arrive in their cars, my father greeting them. Their breaths hung cloudy in the air and they moved with a sharp movement to their bodies. These were the best hunters in the whole countryside, and today would be a great comradeship and competition. Any man invited on this hunt could be proud of the invitation alone.

I felt almost remote as I watched, as I went with them around the side of the house to the dogs. They all went to examine Calypso Baby, and I felt a freezing inside; but my father only said, "She got shot by accident," and did not tell the whole terrible story.

Then my father looked at his watch and said, "Let's wait a few more minutes. Walter ought to be here soon. Hate to start without him."

One of the men called, "Here he comes now," and Walter drove up in his battered car.

"Come here, son," my father said, speaking to me for the first time this morning, and I went reluctantly to his side. I was afraid it was coming now, the whole story, and all the men would look at me in the same way that Calypso Baby had after I had shot her.

My father drew me to the side of Walter's car, reached in, and brought out a basket. "You wanted a bicycle," he said. "Then you decided yourself you should wait. Because you made the decision yourself, I decided you were old enough for this."

I looked at the bird-dog puppy in the basket. All of a sudden Christmas burst inside me like a sky rocket, out of the place where I had kept it suppressed all this time.

"Papa," I said. "Papa——"

"Take him," my father said.

I reached into the basket and took out the puppy. The puppy licked my chin with his harsh warm tongue. He was long, gangly, his feet and head too big for his body—but absolutely beautiful.

My father knelt beside me, one hand on the puppy. "I told Walter to bring me the finest bird-dog puppy he could find," he said. "He's kin to Calypso Baby; he's got good blood."

"Thank you, papa," I said in a choking voice. "I—I'd rather have him than the bicycle. I'll name him Calypso Boy, I'll——"

"When this puppy is ready for birds, we'll train him," my father said. "While we train the puppy, we'll train you too. When the time comes, you can both go on the Christmas Day hunt—if you're good enough."

"We'll be good enough," I said. "Both of us will be good enough."

"I hope so," my father said. He stood up and looked at the men standing around us, all of them smiling down at me and Calypso Boy. "Let's go," he said. "Those birds are going to get tired of waiting on us."

They laughed and hollered, and the dogs moiled and sounded in the excitement as they were let out of the pen. They fanned out across the pasture, each man or two men taking a dog. I

The cycle of nature, of prey and predator, involves man and his dog at hunting time.

stood watching, holding the puppy warm in my arms. I looked at Calypso Baby, standing crippled in her pen looking longingly after the hunters. I went over and spoke to her. She whined; then for the first time since the accident she wagged her tail at me.

I looked down at the puppy in my arms. "We'll be going," I told him, as he licked at my chin. "One of these days, when you're a dog and I'm a man, we'll be right out there hunting with the best of them."

It was three years more before I got to go on my first Christmas hunt. Papa had been right, of course. In the time between I had learned a great deal myself while training Calypso Boy to hunt. With the good blood in him he turned out to be a great bird dog—second only, I guess, to Calypso Baby, who recovered well from her wound and was papa's dog the day Calypso Boy and I made our first Christmas hunt.

But of all the Christmases, before and since, I guess I remember best the one when Calypso Baby was hurt—and Calypso Boy first came to me. (1960)

M.G. Chute

Johanna's Christmas Star

Johanna Olson turned over in bed to watch her husband struggling to get his boots off. He had put a handkerchief over his flashlight to dim it.

"I ain't to sleep," said Johanna. "You can turn the lights on."

"It's past two," said the sheriff.

Johanna obediently closed both eyes, but three seconds was about as long as she could keep them closed. "Things no good?" Johanna asked.

"Pretty good." The sheriff had one boot off and was hunting down in its depth for the three layers of socks that had come off with the jerk.

"Nothing much happened here," said Johanna. She kept the excitement out of her voice by not talking above a whisper. "Only Donna May brought a letter home from school."

Sheriff Olson grunted.

"What you say?" Johanna asked hopefully.

"Pretty cold out," said the sheriff.

"Miss Bates wrote it—Donna May's teacher." Johanna raised herself on her elbow and gave up trying to keep her voice down to a whisper. "Listen, they've got it planned all of a sudden for the first grade to be in the show on Friday. There's thirty-five kids in Miss Bates' class, and the play they're going to do, it only takes nine kids. That means all the rest don't get parts." She waited for this to sink in.

Sheriff Olson put his boots under the bed.

"And she wants," said Johanna, "for Donna May to be the Fairy Princess. It's all in the letter, how she's got to be dressed up."

The sheriff took off his pants, then his hat. "Yo, you ought to get started sleeping."

Johanna closed her eyes and snuggled deep into her pillow. When John Charles Olson was finally in bed, his wife opened her eyes.

"It's got most memorizing," said Johanna almost whispering again.

It was practically the last thing she had time to say quietly. In the morning it came over her all of a sudden: the day after tomorrow was Friday.

"Listen, Donna May; you eat up every scrap of that mush! Tell daddy about how you're going to have real wings and a crown, hon."

"Listen, ma; Betty Roberts don't have to wear shoes nor most nothing; that's on account of she's s'posed to be in bed right on the stage. Ain't that funny? . . .Ma-ma, Kristi's slapping at her milk with her spoon! Ma!"

"Donna May, don't you scream like that! Gosh, hon, ain't you got no sense? Want your voice like a crow's for the show?" With one hand Johanna filled the sheriff's plate with pancakes and with the other dealt with Kristi's new trick of leaving milk in the bottom of her bowl, so she could slap at it. "A real fairy with a wand and everything, tell daddy. . . .Listen, John, I've got to have extra money on account of buying the stuff Miss Bates wrote I should buy for the costume. Maybe five dollars'll be enough."

"Look, Yo; can't you sit quiet to eat?"

"Gosh, I dunno what ma and Mabel are going to think, coming back to find Donna May's been a fairy while they was in St. Paul! We could maybe phone 'em, only they won't be at the hotel until tomorrow night, and that's too late almost. Ain't it the darndest luck they couldn't 've gone after Christmas 'stead of before?"

"Ma-ma, make Kristi stop slapping at me! Ma!"

"Donna May, you stop screaming! . . .Listen, John, what you think; I should maybe try Merske's or Mr. Slabey for gilt paint? . . . 'Scuse me, I thought you was through drinking, the way you put down your cup. You yell when you're done with your plate, will you, hon, 'cause I gotta get started with the dishes?"

With John and Donna May out of the house, Johanna raced through what was left of her dishwashing. She thought some about changing sheets on the beds, but decided against it. They would last easy over another day.

She picked Kristi up from where the kid stood at the foot of her daddy's and mother's bed, patting in the bottom of the quilt like a real little housekeeper. She'd have to leave her next door and then come back to change her own clothes for shopping. The Franzens were new people, but real nice. Their own baby was a year younger than Kristi and only just beginning to walk, but Kristi got on fine with him, and Mrs. Franzen was awfully sweet about watching her good.

Johanna explained about the shopping she had to do. "It's for Donna May's costume for the show and tomorrow is dress rehearsal. She's Fairy Princess, so she's got to be fixed up pretty fancy."

Mrs. Franzen said, "My, ain't that something!" She helped Johanna pull Kristi out of her snow suit. "I didn't know there was going to be a show Friday. Can anybody go?"

"Everybody's supposed to go! Everyone in town always goes! People come from all over everywhere to go see it!"

"Ain't that something!" Mrs. Franzen again marveled. "How much are tickets?"

"Thir——Gee, I've forgot. John and I ain't been last three years. I'll find out for sure. Well, thanks for keeping watch on Kristi. Guess I better get going, so's Donna May won't be acting Fairy Princess in her play suit." She smiled at Mrs. Franzen's appreciative giggle. "Anyhow, all the mothers ain't got my troubles. The play's only got nine parts, and there's thirty-five kids in Miss Bates' class."

It was all right to talk like that to Mrs. Franzen. It wasn't like boasting, when her Donald was years off from being ready for the first grade anyhow.

After changing her stockings and her dress, Johanna found one of the children's crayons and ripped a tiny strip off a page of the telephone book. She wrote "needles" quickly, and "crown" and, after a little thought, "cherry pie." The pie could be for John's supper. With shopping and then the sewing she had to do, she wouldn't have time hardly even to cut bread for supper.

Then she got Miss Bates' letter out of the sugar canister. The first paragraph was all about why Donna May had been chosen for the Fairy Princess. Although she knew it practically by heart, she let herself read it through again. Maybe, if John fussed too much about the pie, she would read it through to him too.

The second paragraph was polite and interesting, but it wasn't quite so easy to read. Johanna leaned against the oven while she studied it.

I'm sure, with your skill and ingenuity, you'll have no difficulty in transforming Donna May into the loveliest of little fairies. I thought just the simplest of little white dresses—perhaps her own party frock—might be made the basis for rows of wee ruffles and flounces. Make them of organdy or stiffened gauze or even of crepe paper—but your own good sense will prescribe the best and easiest method! Tiny glass beads or bits of mica could be sewed on to give the sparkle of star dust to our little fairy's costume.

Johanna read the star-dust sentence through twice, but it didn't help. Then she sat down in a chair to finish the letter.

For the wand, any little rod, gilded and star-tipped, will be perfect. As for the crown, why don't we simply paint with gilt a little cardboard? The wings, of course, must be large and truly expressive. Wire and tarlatan make lovely wings, and—who knows?—perhaps they might be made to open and close like a butterfly's by means of narrow ribbons and wires, artfully concealed. But about this, as about the whole costume, you must use your own judgment, as I know you will—so ably! Hastily and gratefully,

LOUISE BATES.

Johanna sat limp. She was dumb, that was the trouble, and Donna May was going to suffer because her mother wasn't smart like the other ladies. She kept sitting, staring at "artfully," until suddenly she thought of the library.

The idea of going to the library was a good one, even if the fire station which held the library was six blocks out of the way of the stores, because a fairy costume was one thing you really could learn about in books. The crazy business was for the place to be closed just so the librarian could spend Christmas in Grand Rapids. With the show coming on, you would have thought the officials of Purgatory Springs would have realized that the library was more important now than at any other time of the year.

Shopping took quite a bit of running around, but it was well worth it, the bargains and the advice she got. Merske's Dry Goods had the tarlatan and the crepe paper, and the hardware store had wire for the wings and an old suit box she could cut down for a crown. Johanna got gilt paint at Janisky's Variety Shop and just looked at dancing slippers. They were sure real cute, but awful expensive for a kid. Mr. Janisky thought a lot about star dust, but couldn't think of anything better than lace. Mr. Slabey at the drugstore, where Johanna finally found the paintbrushes, said waxed paper crushed-up might look like glass, but you could never be sure.

Mrs. Joseph P. Reedy was buying Danish

Crowns and wands and ruffled gowns of Fairy Princesses are always noticed. Not so their mothers.

pastry at Dvorak's Bakery when Johanna got there for the cherry pie. Mrs. Reedy was president of the Parent-Teacher Association and general manager for the show, so Johanna left Dvorak's with twenty adult tickets to sell at thirty-five cents each and the same number for children at ten cents.

Johanna had only a dollar and fifteen cents left out of the five dollars John had given her; but when she had the stuff spread out on her bed after lunch, she felt pretty calm and contented about it all. She had bought quite a lot of each thing, but it was safer that way, and when she picked up Kristi and borrowed a package of needles which she had forgotten to buy, Mrs. Franzen was pretty nearly struck dumb by all that Mrs. Olson had accomplished in about two hours' time. Mrs. Franzen even took two tickets for the show; she couldn't pay for them until Tuesday, when her husband got home off the road, but that was all right.

The rest of the day wasn't Johanna's fault. Donna May got home from school acting real smart-alecky and wouldn't stand still for fittings. She cried, too, when Johanna cut the puff sleeves off the organdy dress. Johanna wasn't feeling any too good, anyhow, about having to use Donna May's best white dress, the way sewing crepe-paper ruffles on it was making big holes where the needle went in and out.

Then John, instead of being surprised and helpful over all the troubles she had been having with the sewing, started right in with fussing. He fussed about the cherry pie being bought and he sided with Kristi when she was naughty about not liking her rice and sardines. He said he sure hoped it didn't mean there was a shortage on potatoes in the United States. And he didn't like eating on the card table, because he claimed it rocked every time he tried to take a breath. But there was nothing Johanna could do about it; the wings had to lie flat on the dining-room table as long as the wire was only pinned to the tarlatan.

After supper the tarlatan took to unraveling itself; no matter how carefully Johanna sewed, it didn't want to twist around the wire right. The sheriff had found a chair that wasn't being used for sewing materials, and he looked good and lazy just sitting there doing nothing and reading.

When an inch of tarlatan had unraveled clear around the left wing, Johanna said, "You'd think I could have some of that lamp—my gosh!"

Sheriff Olson put down his paper. "Listen, Yo; don't you go getting worn out and crabby over a lot of nothingness."

"Nothingness!" said Johanna.

She talked the matter of nothingness over at intervals until ten o'clock, when the sheriff got up and went to bed.

Weeping gently, so as not to dampen the tarlatan out of shape, she worked on the wings until midnight. Messy was how they looked.

When she got into bed, John woke up. "Done with 'em?"

The sleepy smugness in his voice got her down. "No!" His awful calmness started her weeping again. "What you think? All the help I get!"

After a long time she quieted down to just sniffling. After another long time, John put his arm across her.

"Yo, listen. You asleep, Yo?"

"No."

"Yo, that star dust you was fussing about——"

"Uh?"

"Well, how'd Christmas-tree tinsel fix up?"

"Maybe," said Johanna. She couldn't say more than that, with the mean way he'd been acting, but she held his hand between the two of hers, so he'd know how sweet she thought he was.

In the morning, almost before John and Donna May were out of the house, Johanna got to work on the crown. It cut pretty easily out of the top of the suit box, and she used Kristi's head to fit it on, holding the kid still with cookies.

The gilt paint mixed to a sort of thin gray liquid with little shiny specks floating on its surface. Johanna gave up trying to use the gilt before the cardboard was all soaked through, and had a cookie herself. She couldn't feel terribly upset, because after the sheriff's idea about using tinsel for star dust, she had got to feeling that there was an answer for everything. Even the wings looked pretty good in the daylight, she thought.

Kristi, trying to finish off her cookie with a bite of crayon, didn't get a spanking for it like she maybe should have. Yellow crayon didn't color the gray cardboard so it looked exactly like gold, but it fixed it up pretty classy all the same.

By the time it had a jewel pasted straight in its middle and was lying down on the bed next to the wings, the crown was something really lovely to look at. The jewel was made by cutting a circle out of the hem of Johanna's red crepe dress. Almost you could have looked at the crown for an hour without getting tired.

When Johanna went downtown at eleven for the tinsel and to sell tickets, she took a curtain rod from the living room with her. Maybe a Christmas-tree star could be fastened to one end of it to make a wand. After the way the other things had turned out, anything was possible.

Mr. Slabey at the drugstore didn't carry Christmas-tree tinsel and he had already bought his tickets because he had two nieces in the sixth grade's part of the show, but he was real interested in the problem of the wand. After inspecting the curtain rod with his eyes squinted half shut, he suggested maybe it could be wired with a tiny battery and flashlight, so it would be something pretty snappy looking when Donna May waved it.

It was a lovely idea; it made a lump come into Johanna's throat just thinking about it.

"It'll twinkle real cute," said Mr. Slabey. He suggested trying the radio repairman at Nord-

Even the kindest, sweetest, gentlest fairy princess sometimes has to contend with a very noisy, troublesome baby sister.

land's Insurance and Washing Machine Company to see about getting it wired right. "It's got to work good or you don't want it. . . .How about candy? Ever eat candy 'round your house, Mis' Olson?"

Johanna bought the special two pounds assorted for a dollar. It was the least she could do to thank Mr. Slabey, and Mrs. Franzen really had to have some sort of present, for the nice way she was taking care of Kristi practically all the time.

The radio repairman said he didn't like fooling around with small jobs, because they took as long as big jobs, only you couldn't ever charge what they were worth or customers raised hell. In the end he said he would have the wand ready by four o'clock, but that he wasn't guaranteeing nothing to nobody.

Fifteen cents wasn't enough even to buy the Christmas-tree tinsel, let alone paying for the curtain rod to be wired, but Johanna would almost have rather jumped down a well than have had to go to the courthouse, if jumping down the well would have got her the money.

In the courthouse, John Charles Olson dressed and looked the same as he did at home, but somehow he never was the same. It was almost like having to ask for money from a stranger.

When Johanna opened the door to the sheriff's office, there were about twenty men talking to the sheriff. Johanna backed out the two steps she had walked in. Her first feelings were to leave, but she opened the door again instead.

The man that was talking stopped talking. Johanna shut the door faster than the first time. She was halfway down the corridor when she remembered that Mrs. Franzen didn't have enough cash in her house even to pay for two tickets, let alone to lend Johanna money.

"Hi, Mrs. Olson!" Deputy Billy Christenson came running after her. They met halfway back to the office. "Sheriff's busy," said Billy. "Anything I can help at?"

She couldn't very well talk personal finances to one of John's deputies. "It's the furnace," Johanna said. "And—listen, if he could come out here just a second——It wouldn't take more'n a quarter of a second."

Billy went back into the office, and right away the sheriff came out.

Johanna tried to act calm, but it wasn't much use. "It was the candy, see? I had to buy it on account of

Mr. Slabey saying how the wand should be fixed; and anyway, with Mrs. Franzen keeping care of Kristi and——"

"Yo, Billy said how the furnace——"

"I had to tell him something, didn't I?" He kept staring at the candy box like it was part of the furnace that had blown off. "All I got is fifteen cents, and I ain't even got the tinsel or——"

"What you want, Yo?" He could easy stand there, acting superior, all the time and help he had! Johanna tried hard to get over sounding breathless.

"The tinsel maybe won't come to more'n fifty cents, but the man at Nordland's didn't know about the wand, and——"

"Listen, Yo, there's men waiting. Ten bucks see you right straight through everyt'ing?"

"Ten? Oh, gosh, yes! Maybe even I could bring back some if the wand——"

He didn't have to be so snappish about it. Donna May was as much his kid as she was hers.

The white ballet slippers at Janisky's were awfully expensive, five dollars and ninety-five cents, but Mr. Janisky said they were real French imports and practically the most elegant creations he had ever had the pleasure of stocking.

Johanna paid ninety-five cents for the Christmas-tree tinsel and promised to be back with Donna May on Friday to get the slippers fitted. She decided to wait until then before asking Mr. Janisky to buy tickets for the show, because he had all of a sudden started talking about taxes.

When she stopped to pick up Kristi, Johanna told Mrs. Franzen about the wand and gave her the candy. Mrs. Franzen was awfully excited over everything and offered to go across and help Johanna wash up her breakfast dishes. But Johanna was too ashamed of the way she had left the house to let Mrs. Franzen see it.

It was pretty unfair to Donna May, the way her mother had to keep thinking about housework when she ought all the time to be putting her mind on the costume. If it hadn't been for Mrs. Franzen being so nice with the kids, things would have been plain awful. After sewing some on the tinsel, Johanna took both kids next door.

For a wonder, the wand was finished at four o'clock. The radio repairman said it was one of the hardest jobs he had ever tackled and he wouldn't do it again for fifty dollars. He held the wand in the dark under the counter to show Johanna how it went on. Even in the half dark, you could see a real twinkle of light.

It was the loveliest thing Johanna ever saw.

It cost six dollars, but it was worth that much.

A wand showed up like everything on a fairy, and black patent-leather slippers were what kids always wore on the stage anyhow.

The radio man wouldn't buy a ticket, but Mr. Nordland himself took two after he had got Johanna to promise he could call around sometime next week, in case the sheriff might want to buy her a new washing machine.

While John and the kids ate supper, Johanna finished sewing the last row of Christmas-tree tinsel on Donna May's dress. After supper she curled Donna May's hair up on an iron. She hadn't planned curling it until Friday night, because dress rehearsals weren't really so important. But John had pretended like he thought the pale yellow crown going up so straight and Donna May's pale yellow hair going down so straight were all one piece, and had laughed about it until Johanna had to show him how nice the crown would look over curls.

It did look good, too, with the red crepe jewel in its front. And the tinsel on the dress sparkled like garlands of real stars. Even John was pretty interested and impressed when she turned out the lights so he could see how the wand twinkled. It was going to be sort of fun watching Miss

Women are always late when they've had to prepare a Fairy Princess for dress rehearsal.

Bates' expression when she first got a look at Donna May carrying a fairy's wand.

But when seven o'clock came and Donna May had to be driven to school for the rehearsal, her father had to do the driving. Johanna was still in her apron and bedroom slippers, and even John could see she was a good half hour from being ready to leave the house.

Johanna lay down on Donna May's cot after she had got Kristi to sleep. The excited way she was feeling, having Donna May's costume all finished and looking so awfully pretty, she hadn't expected to more than just be able to rest her feet. But she had been asleep three hours when the sheriff waked her.

"You home already yet?"

"It's on to eleven. Want I should go get her?"

"Eleven? Oh, gosh! No, I gotta get her. Listen, did Miss Bates say anything?"

Johanna put on her black taffeta dress with the cream-colored collar. Miss Bates had seen it once already at a P. T. A. meeting, but the new red crepe had to be fixed in the hem where the jewel for the crown had come out.

"I'll lock the car and the doors," Johanna said. "You get to bed. Kristi's sleeping real good."

It was funny, going out late to get Donna May. After a few years, Donna May would be going out almost every night. She was going to be the popular sort; you could always tell the kids that got picked to be in plays and things were the kind the boys always went for. She sure looked cute with the crown sitting on her curls as she danced around with her wings and wand.

The first graders were rehearsing in one of the classrooms. Johanna found that out from Mrs. Roberts. Mrs. Roberts acted sort of bored about having to get her Betty ready for the play. The way she talked gave Johanna a sort of depressed feeling, until she realized it was most likely sour grapes with Mrs. Roberts, because Betty had the part where she was dressed in just plain pajamas.

Donna May came running out of the classroom ahead of the other kids.

"Ma! Ma! Listen, I gotta have white shoes!"

"Sure, we'll get 'em, hon. Oh, gosh! Donna May, where's your wings? Tell mother, quick!"

"They got loose, and Miss Bates says I gotta have white shoes."

The wings were folded up over a desk at the back of the room. They looked sort of crumpled, but nothing seemed to have broken loose. Johanna picked the wand up off the floor.

"Oh, Donna May! Gee, hon, can't you be careful with your things?" But the wand worked all right; even in the lighted room you could see it flicker on just like a baby star.

"Mrs. Olson? So glad you could spare us a minute. . . .Gracious, you can hardly hear yourself think. . . .Children!"

"Donna May says you want she should wear white shoes."

"Yes, she'll have to wear white slippers—ballet preferably. And the wings must be tightened. And something else I wanted to——Oh, yes, the tinsel on her costume, it's rather—well, just a wee bit garish, don't you think? The simple little frock would seem better. And some sort of little sleeves, if you can manage. Small children do have such long arms and legs!"

"Sure, I planned——She'll be fixed real——"

"I'm sure she will!"

Johanna put Donna May to bed without making her wash. If the kid didn't get enough sleep, she'd be a plain wreck for the show, and she was naughty like anything already. Johanna couldn't even find out from her whether Miss Bates had said anything special about the wand. The way Donna May talked, you'd have thought Miss Bates hadn't even noticed it.

Sheriff Olson was asleep when his wife got into bed, but Johanna didn't dare wait until morning: "Listen, John, I need money for Donna May's—"

Sheriff Olson rolled over. "Car locked, Yo?"

"Listen, John. Miss Bates says she's gotta have them white, so I've gotta have money——"

John woke clear up. "I gave you ten bucks."

Johanna got out of bed. "The ones I gotta buy cost five dollars and ninety-five cents, and all I got left is three dollars and ninety cents." She showed him the money in her purse. "And seventy cents of it I shouldn't spend, because it's from Mr. Nordland for the tickets he bought. Anyway, Miss Bates says that she's gotta have 'em white, see?"

There was silence while she got back into bed.

"Where'd the six dollars and eighty cents go?"

"What six dollars and eighty cents?"

"Listen, Yo. Three dollars and twenty cents left from ten dollars means you spent——"

"Well, good gosh, I had to get the tinsel, didn't I? And some candy for Mrs.

Franzen for watching Kristi——"

"You had the candy 'fore you came to the office."

"Well, I know, but I only had fifteen cents left from yesterday. Listen, the way you talk——All I want is enough to make five dollars and ninety-five cents. Miss Bates says——"

"All I want is what you did with the ten."

"It wasn't ten! I've got three dollars and ninety cents left like I showed you, and only seventy cents has got to come off that. And, anyhow, you said your ownself how cute the wand looked. My gosh! Can I help it if Donna May's got to have white slippers?"

"Yesterday I gave you five bucks, and today ten, and now you want five more. What you got her fixed up in? Solid silver?"

"You ain't so funny! Listen, if you think I want my own kid to go out looking ragged in front of maybe a thousand people——Anyhow, I didn't say I wanted five dollars, I said enough so the three dollars and ninety cents I've got will make five dollars and ninety-five cents after the seventy cents is off. The trouble with you is you're plain stingy!"

"The trouble with you is you didn't eat no supper, Yo."

Two nights straight she had ended up by crying. And the way he could go off sleeping all at once

Whether it be "Fourscore and seven years ago," "Abou Ben Adhem," or "Twinkle, Twinkle, Little Star," the recitation rarely lacks critic or admirer.

like nothing was wrong, it was plain mean!

All night she seemed to be dreaming. It was mostly about a sort of basement place with long, dark halls that she was leading Donna May through to get to the play. And every time they were almost there, the hall would end in a sort of bank of green snow and Donna May wouldn't have anything on except a big pair of overshoes.

Then the lights went on with a lot of applause, and Johanna woke up.

There was sun on her nose and Kristi was lying on the bed beside her, talking to herself. The alarm clock showed fourteen minutes after nine.

Under the clock was a five-dollar bill. John was so dear. It hurt Johanna's throat even just thinking how sweet he was. Kristi began to cry with being hugged so tight and being hungry.

The housework and the beds had to wait another day to get fixed right. The wings alone took until eleven o'clock to get fastened to where they didn't droop when they were tied over the back of the kitchen chair. After that Johanna still had to get the tinsel off Donna May's dress and the sleeves back on. It was one lucky thing she had been too busy to make dolls' dresses for the kids out of the sleeves, like she had planned. But it was sad taking off the tinsel, after John had been so dear thinking it up in the first place and then getting his and Donna May's breakfast and everything.

Because of the play, Donna May got home an hour early from school, almost before Johanna had the lunch cleared away. The kid was so excited, Johanna didn't dare take her downtown to get the slippers fitted; matching an old pair would have to do. With the tickets she had left to sell, lugging Donna May around with her would just about finish the poor kid off.

Mrs. Franzen wasn't any too hopeful about getting Donna May and Kristi to take naps, because her Donald had been sleeping all morning and was acting pretty peppy, but she would sure be glad to do her best. She said it was a wonder Mrs. Olson wasn't dead on her feet. Mrs. Franzen was a nice, considerate person.

The slippers didn't take long to buy, and they had metal for tapping fixed in under the toes and real satin ribbons to lace around the ankles—worth more than five dollars and ninety-five

cents really. But Johanna fussed some about the price until Mr. Janisky had bought four tickets to the show.

After that, though, ticket selling didn't go so good. When it was half past four and she had gone down the whole of one side of the shopping street, Johanna added up how many tickets she had left. After three counts, when it still added up to twenty-one, she began to feel sort of desperate. Only just as many tickets had been printed as there were seats in the auditorium. Twenty-one tickets left unsold by Mrs. John Charles Olson, mother of the Fairy Princess, meant twenty-one vacant seats.

It was getting on toward six o'clock when Johanna got back to the Franzens'. Except for the three she was holding out for herself and John and Kristi, the tickets had all gone on exchanges.

On a few she had had to add cash to the exchanges, but she could always find uses for nails and dish mops; and when guests came, things like the cigars would come in handy if they happened to be guests that smoked cigars. And at Dvorak's Bakery she had been able to exchange three tickets for three pies.

Mrs. Franzen was all upset when Johanna got back. She had got Donna May to take a nap by promising her she could play coalman if she did. Playing coalman, Donna May had skinned her knee, and Mrs. Franzen had put iodine on it. The iodine had run down until her leg was a queer yellow, just where it would show most between the fairy's short skirt and her white socks.

A queer weak feeling came into Johanna's own knees, like she had been running too hard. She said "thank you" to Mrs. Franzen and grabbed Donna May's hand. Mrs. Franzen came running after her, carrying Kristi.

"Put her anywheres," Johanna said. "Quick, you gotta take these!" She shoved two of the pies at her. She didn't care whether Mrs. Franzen thought she was rude or crazy or what, banging the door. After the show was over, she had weeks and years she could explain things in.

John was home already and wandering about, not even dressed for the show. Johanna made him watch Kristi and set the table for bread and milk and pie while she got Donna May's hair curled. Donna May was acting like a little devil, and she couldn't even be yelled at to stand quiet and behave. You could sure feel sorry for the fellows that had to keep movie stars happy and behaving both at the same time.

"Listen, Donna May, hon; please eat like a sweet girl. . . .Daddy, you tell her she's gotta!

Honest, she won't be able to stand up even, the way she keeps pecking. . . .Please, Donna May!"

"Eat somet'ing your ownself, Yo," John said.

"I can't. I don't feel so good. Listen, Donna May; mother ain't joking none. Show daddy how a real fairy princess eats. Oh, for gosh sakes, stop monkeying with your curls!"

At 7:15, Sheriff Olson drove Donna May over to school. Johanna had planned they should all go over together and then wait until eight for the show to start, but neither she nor Kristi was dressed in time.

John was back at half past seven. He didn't seem to know if the auditorium was filling up or not, and he guessed he had left Donna May in the right classroom.

"You guess! Oh, gosh, don't just stand around; put Kristi's coat on her or something! Listen, did the wings look all right? Did they wabble any?"

"Sure, they wabbled some. That don't hurt none. The teacher was there. Where's the kid's coat, hon?"

"Miss Bates was there? Why didn't you tell me first off? Honest, the way you don't tell things, you'd have me going crazy! Listen, John, did her curls look good under the crown, did Miss Bates say? Maybe I should maybe take a couple of big safety pins along to make sure with her wings. Did Miss Bates see the stuff on her knee? Honest, wouldn't you think Mrs. Franzen would have had sense enough to——Listen, you can't go wearing that old hat!"

She was wearing her formal herself. Maybe it was too dressy, but it was better than looking like she was just ordinary audience. And if the other mothers weren't dressed up, she had de-cided she could always just sit in her coat.

At ten minutes of eight, the Olsons were out of the house. The lights next door at the Franzens' were still on; they worried Johanna a lot, because people coming in late to a show made it hard to hear the actors, but John wouldn't let her stop to hurry Mrs. Franzen along. He was probably right, but it was sure a worry.

John stopped the car in front of the main entrance and took his ticket. He told Johanna to sit center toward the front, so he could find her when he got back from parking the car. It was exciting to see all the cars parked for blocks around.

It was going to be a real big crowd. The only trouble was that most of the audience stood around in the halls, just talking, when they should have been getting sat down and quiet. If someone could ring a bell or shout, it might help.

Johanna chose three seats in the middle section about twelve rows from the front. There were some vacant seats up nearer the stage, but she felt it might look sort of conceited if she acted like she wanted to sit extra close just because she was mother to the Fairy Princess.

Mr. and Mrs. Raddusky came in on Johanna's row. Mrs. Raddusky was in black satin, so tight she looked almost larger than she really was. Mr. Raddusky was small and smiling. He smiled at Johanna and wiggled a finger at Kristi.

Mrs. Raddusky felt of her seat before settling herself down into it. "Maybe she breaks, eh? No, she don't." She talked loud and laughed a lot, just like she was in her own home and not waiting for a play to begin.

Pretty soon Mrs. Raddusky started telling Johanna about the troubles she had been having making her Frankie look like a Chinese doll. But Johanna could only keep half of her mind on what Mrs. Raddusky was saying. If the show started before John got back, she would plain die.

At ten minutes after eight, a boy in white pants came out on the stage with a big card that he put up on a sort of easel. The card said: A CHRISTMAS TALE OF LONG AGO—FOURTH GRADE. Johanna tried to

In a school auditorium filled with anxious parents, a few late arrivals are a welcome distraction.

figure in her head whether the grades would most likely go up or down from there, but she couldn't keep her mind long enough off John to reason out anything that took arithmetic.

He could probably get a seat in back even if the play started, but not knowing whether he would be seeing Donna May or not was driving her pretty nearly crazy.

People were coming in the entrances in little bunches. It was funny, when the tickets and posters all said eight sharp, that they couldn't get to their seats on time. But it was different with John, because he was out parking the car and not just standing around talking and laughing.

If the committees had had real good sense, they would have marked off a parking place right in front for the cars that had brought the actors and actresses.

Even with John safely in his seat, Johanna couldn't somehow get to breathing easily. It was maybe the crowd or the way the place was heating up.

"John—listen, John; ain't Kristi cute the way she's looking all around? John, look; is there much of a crowd still outside? You'd think somebody'd tell 'em to come in. John, you spose maybe I ought to bring Miss Bates the two safety pins I got? Were they awful wabbly?"

"Listen, Yo, sit peaceful for once, huh?"

"Look around for Mrs. Swanson. Her Marian's the Dutch doll. Ain't it funny Mrs. Franzen don't get here?" She started to get up to look for Mrs. Franzen, but the lights went out. She sat down even before John told her to.

People went right on talking. Johanna sh-h-ed a couple of dozen times, but it didn't help any. The actors were going to have trouble getting heard right if people kept on being so rude. What they needed was a real big band playing one of

Complete with wooden shoes and tulips, Marian was the spittin' image of a little Dutch girl.

Sousa's marches. A piano and violin were real pretty and fairy-like sounding together, but they weren't loud enough to get all the people to shut up.

"John, listen; did Donna May's wings wabble just when you took her blanket off her or all the time?...Kristi, you want daddy to hold you?...Then stop your wriggling!"

The curtain went up. It didn't give any more warning than the lights had, but the people quieted down some.

The stage was empty when the curtain went up, but after a while three children came on, dressed like gypsies or something. They were talking to each other, but Johanna couldn't hear them. In a while some more came on, and pretty soon one of the Nielsen kids, dressed like a king with a crown and a purple cape. But the crown was real plain; it didn't even have a small jewel in front.

All of a sudden the audience began to laugh. The Nielsen kid's crown had dropped down over one ear, and he kept trying to push it back up. Every time it fell down again, a lot more people would start in laughing. Johanna wanted to scream at them to shut up laughing at the kid.

She was an awful bad mother, letting Donna May wear wings that maybe weren't fastened tight enough. It was because she was lazy and didn't take enough trouble with her sewing. If Donna May's wings didn't come loose tonight, she would never fuss again about having to sew, or about having to do anything for anybody ever.

"Listen, John, I'm going back to——"

"Sh-h-h!"

The curtain came down. Only the lights didn't

turn on. They'd have to pretty soon. Maybe if she could powder Donna May's knee some, the yellow wouldn't show so much.

The curtain went up without any lights having come on between scenes. The stage was a sort of gray blue; you could hardly see things on it.

Mrs. Raddusky stuck her elbow into Johanna's side. "*Ja,* now come our kids pretty quick out!"

Johanna stretched up to see better. She could hardly breathe, the place was so hot. There were two children in white lying on the floor.

"Betty Roberts," Mrs. Raddusky said, "and the Martinsons' kid."

"John, John, listen; this is Donna May's! Can you see good, John?"

The two kids stood up in their white pajamas. Johanna couldn't hear them. Maybe Miss Bates was making Donna May stay out of the play because of the wings coming loose. Maybe her knee was making her sick, or she was crying with being hungry because she hadn't been made to eat enough supper.

The piano started up again and something in bright green came galloping out on the stage. Mrs. Raddusky's elbow jabbed into Johanna's stomach.

"There's my Frankie! *Ja!* There he is!"

Mrs. Raddusky started making clucking noises to herself. Frankie was jumping up and down on the stage and shouting things.

The stage wasn't so awfully light. If it didn't get brighter pretty quick, it was going to be awfully hard to see the star actors real well. The only thing was that the wand showed up better when the lights weren't too bright.

After a long time there were more children on the stage. "Donna May," Johanna said softly way under her breath, "Donna May, mother loves you, darling; you're all right."

In the morning it would all be over. School plays weren't so much anyway; just a lot of kids trying to act smart. Two hours and it would all

Some things in life can be best appreciated in silence and Donna May's theatrical debut was one of those things.

be over. Maybe in two minutes.

"Listen, John——" He was sitting still, and his breath was coming heavy and even. If Mrs. Raddusky would stop clucking, Johanna's own breath would be easier maybe.

One of the kids came forward and bowed. Then nothing happened for a long time, except that the music changed. It was light, pretty music, sounding like raindrops.

Donna May Olson skipped in to the music. Her mother didn't see her until she was almost center. She was all white and gold. You couldn't see much how she was dressed because she was moving so quick.

"'S morning!" Donna May shouted. "Stop dancing, little dollies!"

Donna May skipped straight on across the stage, until the curtains hid her.

Some children sang or danced or something, and then, after a long time, the curtain came down and the lights went on.

Johanna put her arm through her husband's.

"She wasn't so awful bad, huh?" said Johanna. She couldn't more than whisper, her throat was so dry and funny feeling. She wanted to go home now and put the kids to bed and then maybe sit with John and just not talk. Or perhaps what she wanted was to hang around after the show was over, listening to what people said.

"Not too awful bad, huh?" said Johanna.

She gave a little sigh. You just couldn't talk much about some things.

She was glad, though, that there had been such absolute beauty and perfection in it all. Even John could see now that the money had been worth it. He was wiping Kristi's nose, pretending like he wasn't feeling funny inside him like Johanna was feeling. Men were cute. Johanna touched his shoulder gently with her fingertips. A hundred dollars would have been awful cheap. Ten times as much work, trouble and money would have been awful cheap. (1937)

Jim and Allan Bosworth

The Christmas Racket

After everybody but the janitor had gone home, Johnny Greer sat at his typewriter and smoked four cigarettes without punching a key. Outside was San Francisco, softened by a thin drifting fog that blurred the street lamps. The bells of St. Patrick's chimed "Silent Night, Holy Night," but Johnny heard only the surly undertone of traffic beneath the windows, where drivers forgot that Christmas Eve is a time of good will even toward other drivers. Inside was the *Evening Gazette* city room, a long and cluttered space permeated by that odor which is popularly supposed to get into a man's blood—the smell of printer's ink.

Johnny's nostrils failed to quiver at the scent, because he was an old and disillusioned hand. Six evenings a week, tongue in cheek, he turned out a column called "A Line of Cheer From Johnny Greer." It was full of corn and platitudes and Pollyanna philosophy. Thousands who read it pictured Johnny Greer as rotund and jovial, benevolent and wise—a "right jolly old elf."

They were very wrong. He was a lean and cadaverous man, grown cynical in a profession noted for cynicism, and given to grouches. What wisdom he had was a shrewd, hard kind, learned in a hard way. The column, therefore, was intellectually dishonest. It was a living, but Johnny hated it. Tonight he could afford to dislike it more than ever. He had just come from a barroom meeting with Big Bill Carnahan, a building contractor with political aspirations. Over three highballs, Carnahan had offered Johnny the job of handling his mayoralty campaign, and there was to be further discussion that evening at Carnahan's home.

Drinks made Johnny garrulous, but a man can't be garrulous alone. He saw Dominick wheel a cleaning truck into the far end of the room and begin sweeping briskly; and he speculated idly on Dominick's way of life, and how many voters like the little man it would take to put Carnahan into office. Then he sighed and rolled paper into his typewriter.

Tomorrow's piece had to be written. A Christmas column. He could look back on seven Christmas columns, and, before that, on twice seven years on rewrite desks. Working every Christmas to grind out pap about Yuletide cheer and jolly old St. Nick. Writing salivary salutes to roast turkey, chestnut stuffing and plum pudding, and yelling, "Hey, boy! Run over to Dinty's and get me a hot dog with mustard and onions!"

He stared at the unsullied paper, and took time out to examine a stack of mail. It was mainly Christmas cards. He pitched them unopened at the nearest wastebasket. "A damned commercial racket!" he muttered, and then sat up straight. Why not? For once, why not drop the Pollyanna role, and write what he thought? The managing editor would see it in galley proofs tomorrow. If he didn't like it, he knew what he could do.

Readers conjured up a pleasant picture of columnist Johnny Greer that bore little resemblance to the man himself.

He bent over the typewriter and was oblivious of Dominick, who moved nearer industriously. The lead took shape:

'Twas the night before Christmas, and up from the pressroom came three ink-stained retches—Burp, Burp and Burp. Those succinct sentiments, translated into what a lot of solid citizens REALLY think about Christmas, would——

"Happy Christmas Eve!" a voice said.

Johnny looked up. Dominick had a thin, dark face, and eyes that reminded him of a spaniel's.

"Dominick," Johnny said, "did you ever hear of Old Scrooge?"

"No," Dominick said respectfully.

"Well, he had something. I am about to write a column advocating organization of the OSS—Old Scrooge Society. All you have to do to join is to be sick and tired of Christmas. Just admit that it is a pagan custom, fast degenerating into a com-

At the end of a long day, a columnist has time to reflect on his demanding job—providing the public with inspiration, the managing editor with copy.

mercial racket, and you're in our lodge."

Dominick did not understand all the words, but he leaned on his broom and shook his head. "Oh, no, Mr. Greer!" he said earnestly. "Christmas is a fine, good, happy time. Last year was bad, yes. But now, it's justa fine!"

"Name one good reason," Johnny said.

"I gotta work," Dominick said simply. "Last Christmas I was very sick for a long time. No work, no money. No presents." His eyes showed how bad that was, and then he smiled. "What'sa matter, Mr. Greer? You gotta good job too!"

Johnny laughed. "Dominick, you've been seeing movies. You don't realize that newspaper business is monotonous drudgery, and that only once in five or ten years does a good story—a really good story—come along. And you will be shocked to learn that the once-vaunted power of the press is no more. Look at the last election!"

"Yes," Dominick said, bewildered.

"Take my advice," said Johnny. "Don't work for a newspaper. Quit, like I'm going to do." He opened a drawer and produced a bottle that had been sent him by a press agent. "We'll drink, Dominick. Not to Christmas, which is a day I ignore, but to a new job. I'm leaving this shabby, ill-ventilated house of journalistic prostitution."

"I justa drink wine, Mr. Greer."

"This calls for stronger brew. Drink to next November and the race for mayor. Remember, the Man with the Plan is Carnahan!"

Dominick took a token taste. "He's a good man?" he asked. "He's honest?"

"Let us be frank," Johnny said. "With me to help him, Carnahan can win. How'd you like a job sweeping out City Hall?"

"I like this job," Dominick said, emptying a wastebasket. "Mr. Greer, I got a big hurry. Excusa me. Giannina, she's waiting for to see her Christmas."

"If she's your wife, Dominick, don't let her give you a necktie."

"My wife, she'sa dead," Dominick said. "Giannina, she's my little girl."

"That's different," Johnny said hastily. "Well, I have to hurry, too, so let's get to work. Here, Dominick, put this dollar into Giannina's piggy bank for me. Now, let's see. . . .If half the Christmas ties were used to garrote the people who gave them, it would be justifiable homicide. Got to put that down."

At eight o'clock sharp, the bells of St. Patrick's

chimed again. Johnny pushed back his chair and read the column. If he said so himself, it was a masterpiece of sharp, satirical wit—a surprise for thousands of readers expecting sugarplum prose. Best of all, it was the kind of stuff that makes people write letters. The managing editor was too smart not to see that.

He covered his typewriter, and heard a "Merry Christmas, Mr. Greer!" from Dominick. Johnny looked up, and saw him with his hat on, at the far end of the room. He was staggering under the awkward burden of a large sheet of plate glass.

"What's that for?" Johnny demanded, staring.

Dominick laughed happily. "It'sa Giannina's Christmas!" he said, and maneuvered the glass riskily through the door. "Gooda night!"

Johnny cleared his desk, hearing the elevator whine up to get Dominick, thinking the season was even sillier than he had dreamed. Plate glass for a child's Christmas! Then he shrugged and went for his hat and coat. He'd take a cab to Big Bill Carnahan's big house in Sea Cliff, and talk business. Then back to his bachelor apartment, and tomorrow he could sleep until the managing editor called to ask if he had gone crazy.

"Merry Christmas, Johnny," said the elevator man, who had been around a long time. "You got another column like you had last year? My wife clipped that column and sent it to a dozen folks back East."

"She won't like the one tomorrow, then," Johnny said. "I just shot Santa. Good night."

He went outside. The fog was lifting. The thin wail of a siren lifted above the mutter of traffic, coming nearer. He started across the intersection and stopped short.

A big car was angled desperately toward the street's center line, with a knot of people caught in its headlights like moths drawn to a lamp. Jigsaw fragments of shattered glass lay flat along the pavement, reflecting light in irregular pools.

By the time Johnny Greer could get into the crowd, the ambulance had rolled up. He saw a tall policeman, and a hatless, white-faced man who was talking excitedly. And then he saw Dominick, lying on his back with his crumpled hat for a pillow, his face twisted with pain.

"The glass reflected my lights, officer!" the driver was saying. "It threw my lights back at me. I thought it was another car—a car on the wrong side of the street. If he had to take that glass somewhere, why didn't he use a truck?"

"You can tell that at Harbor Station," the officer said, and shouted for the crowd to make room. Johnny went in with the hospital stewards, and showed the policeman his press card.

"He works for the *Gazette*," Johnny told him. "How bad is it?"

"A busted leg, poor fellow. A fine Christmas present."

"I'll ride to Harbor Emergency with him," Johnny said. He bent over Dominick, thinking how much worse it could have been. "Take it easy," he said. "Everything will be all right."

"No," Dominick said. He closed his eyes, and when he opened them again they were wide and tragic. "No present for Giannina. No fine, happy Christmas this time for her."

"What does she like?" asked the man who didn't believe in Christmas. "Dolls? Candy? I'll find a drugstore, Dominick——"

"It'sa no good, Mr. Greer. Giannina wants a Christmas window. For a long time I tell her she'sa going to have a window. Justa the big glass. And now it'sa broke!"

He began to cry, and Johnny knew it wasn't because of the pain. They put him in the ambulance, and Johnny sat with him. "The Christmas window," he said over and over. "It'sa broke!"

"I don't understand, Dominick," Johnny said. "You mean you promised Giannina a window like in the stores, with toys and lights?"

"Oh, no, justa the big glass. So she can see Christmas."

"Give me the address. I'll see what I can do."

"It'sa too late, Mr. Greer. The stores—they're all close. And I got no more money."

"Who was going to fix this window?"

"Me, I could fix. But now——" He closed his eyes and groaned.

They put him on a table at Harbor Emergency, and Johnny left as they gave him an anesthetic. The address on the accident report was a street number in that shabby but colorful section where Chinatown and North Beach come together. Johnny went outside, cursing himself for a softhearted fool, and called a cab. It was nearly nine; the Christmas Giannina had been promised she would see was only three hours away. . . .

The cab stopped before a dingy three-story flat. Johnny struck matches until he found the name of D. Cardoni on a mailbox; then he climbed two sets of rickety stairs and went down a dim and evil-smelling hall. Downstairs, a radio made noise. He found a door.

A gray-haired, plump woman answered his knock. She had a shawl around her head, as if ready to go out on the street, and when she saw him her wrinkled face showed disappointment.

"Oh, not Dominick!" she exclaimed.

"No," said Johnny. "He's—he's late. Are you Dominick's mother?"

She shook her head. "No. Mrs. Latta. I watch Giannina while he'sa work."

"Is that you, papa?" a child's thin voice called. "Did you bring my Christmas present?"

Johnny hesitated, and Mrs. Latta opened the door wider, bowing and fussing with her apron. He went in awkwardly, and saw a big, old-fashioned, white-enameled bed in a poorly furnished but clean room. Propped high on pillows was a tiny, thin-faced girl. She had a festive red ribbon on her black braids, and wore plain gold earrings to make her look like some diminutive gypsy, and Dominick's large eyes were hauntingly eager in her small dark face.

"I'm Johnny, Giannina," he said gravely, turning his hat in both hands. "Your papa sent me. He can't get home tonight."

She studied him a moment. "But it is Christmas Eve," she said slowly. "And he is bringing me a Christmas present. Of course he will be home!"

"Oh, of course," Johnny echoed. "But he will be late. You see——" And then she shifted in her bed, and he saw the braces. He thought, *Oh, Lord; polio*, and a feeling like shame swept over him.

Mrs. Latta turned, whispering pityingly, "For three years she not walk. Maybe never walk."

But Giannina was smiling. "I will go to sleep!" she announced with the bright faith of the very young. She lifted one thin arm and covered her eyes. "I will go to sleep, and when I wake up it will be Christmas. And papa will be here with my present. You wait and see."

"Yes, Giannina," Johnny nodded. "You go to sleep." Then he took Mrs. Latta by the arm and led her into the next room. It was unfurnished, except for a big easy chair that stood facing the wall—and suddenly things were clear to Johnny. At one time there had been two windows in the wall. Now sash and glass were gone, and ugly boards covered the space, as if alterations had been long delayed. The room was blind.

"The Christmas window?" he asked, pointing.

Mrs. Latta nodded agreement, and her wrin-

Giannina trusted in Christmas.

kled face softened. "The big glass," she said.

He understood it all but one thing, and that made him ashamed too. For nearly a year he had worked in the same place with Dominick, seeing the tragedy in the little man's eyes, and never trying to learn why it was there. Dominick's life would be like this—a blank wall of low income and doctor bills and worry. Out there, fast approaching, was Christmas; out there would be something for a child to see every day. Blue sky and sunshine and silver fog curtains. Rooftops in the rain, and clothes dancing on the line in the wind. Cars moving over the hilly streets, and other children who could walk and run.

"Look, Mrs. Latta," he said. "Dominick's leg is broken. Can you stay with Giannina, if I pay you?" He pulled a bill from his pocket.

Mrs. Latta motioned it away. "No money," she said, "It'sa Christmas."

"Johnny!" Giannina called. "I'm nearly asleep!"

That would be the bells of Old St. Mary's taking up the carols now, and it was nine o'clock. He tried to swallow a lump in his throat.

"It'll take a lot of doing," he said. "Is there a phone here?"

There wasn't, but Mrs. Latta directed him to a drugstore on the corner. When he tiptoed through the other room, Giannina was still, her lips parted slightly, and her long, dark curling eyelashes lying on her small cheeks.

He sat in the stuffy telephone booth with the classified directory on his lap, and wrote down the numbers of a large building-supply house and a glass company. Time was getting short. That section between the two windows would have to be sawed out, and some sort of sash put in before the glass could be put into place. The whole affair became urgent. Midnight was a deadline.

He dialed the first number, and heard the phone ring a dozen times. If there was a night watchman at the building-supply company, it apparently wasn't his job to answer telephones. The same lack of response greeted his attempt to rouse the glass company. It was, after all, Christmas Eve.

Then he remembered the party which he was supposed to be attending, and Big Bill Carnahan, the builder. He dialed again, and the receiver went up on merry sounds and a jovial and hearty voice answered, "Bill Carnahan speaking."

"This is Johnny Greer. Look, I need your——"

"Where've you been, boy?" boomed the man who wanted to be mayor. "What's holding you up? I've got two county supervisors and some other important people out here, and we're whipping up an organization and waiting to see Santa fall off the Christmas tree. Come on out!"

"Sorry," Johnny said. "I can't make it tonight. Could you get a store to open and sell me a sheet of plate glass, eight by five?"

"Tonight? What the devil, Johnny, it's Christmas Eve! Come on out and have a drink!"

"I've got to have a big window put in before midnight," Johnny said.

Carnahan laughed. "Oh, been out busting windows already, eh? Tell 'em I'll bail you out, and tell 'em they'll have to wait."

"It's for a little crippled girl, Mr. Carnahan," Johnny said. "A Christmas present for her. How about lending a hand?"

"Well, now you know I'd like to help, Johnny, but I've got guests here, and it's Christmas Eve, and——Well, the thing is impossible tonight, anyway. You couldn't get it done."

"The hell I can't!" Johnny flared, and hung up.

He looked at his watch. Somebody ought to know the people who owned those stores where they sold glass. Members of the building trades, perhaps. And who would know the right person to contact in the building trades? He sat up with a flash of inspiration—the *Gazette's* labor editor, Wade Mason!

He looked up Mason's home telephone, smiling to himself, thinking how wrong a man can be. Hardly two hours before, he had told Dominick that the power of the press no longer existed. He had said that only once in five or ten years did a really good story come along. Now that story was in his hands, to be shaped and built and made complete, and a curious, warming pride filled him as he knew he had found the way to do it. The power of the press.

Wade Mason answered, and Johnny quickly outlined the problem, beginning with Dominick and the glass. He told it as an experienced leg man would tell a story to the rewrite desk, and Mason grunted now and then to show that he understood the problem. Mason had been in the business a long time too. He didn't say much, but Johnny knew the contagion had caught.

And now both of them were pretending,

as newspapermen have done for years, that they were doing all this for the story. Mason said, "Okay, I'll call Joe Gallagher. He's the head of the Carpenters Local, and he'll be able to get the glass and round up a crew. You go on back and stand by. What about pictures?"

"I'll get a photographer," said Johnny, who had forgotten about pictures. "But are you sure Gallagher and his men will do the job?"

"It's Christmas, isn't it?" asked Mason. Then, as if ashamed of having put it on that sentimental basis, he added, "Besides, they want their names in your column now and then, don't they?"

Giannina was still sleeping when the truck and three cars parked at the curb below, and if she didn't sleep through the sawing and hammering that went on behind the closed door of the front room, she did a very good job of pretending, even when a couple of flash bulbs went off.

But she heard the bells. All over the city the

Big Bill Carnahan, the builder, dreamed of being the big man of the town. As the Man with the Plan, he was designing to win the mayoralty of San Francisco in the next election.

bells began at midnight, and those of Old St. Mary's sounded very near as they chimed "Adeste Fideles." She sat up in bed, her big eyes shining.

"It is Christmas, Johnny!" she said. "And papa has come home with my present."

"Yes," Johnny said, watching the closed door. "It is Christmas, Giannina. Your papa will be late, like I told you, but the present is here, and in just a minute——"

Wade Mason opened the door. He said, "Okay, Johnny, it's ready."

Johnny held out his arms, and the child put hers around his neck. He lifted her, thinking how tiny and fragile she was; he carried her into the front room and put her into the big chair.

"Merry Christmas, Giannina!" he said then, and everybody joined in a chorus.

"Merry Christmas, Giannina!" said burly Joe Gallagher, the workmen and Wade Mason.

She clapped her hands. "I want to see my present!" she said excitedly.

Joe Gallagher reached up and pulled aside the blanket that had been hung over the window. Wade Mason turned out the light. The bells were chiming "Oh, Little Town of Bethlehem."

A lump caught in Johnny Greer's throat. There was the big window, framing darkened rooftops and the glow from the street lamps, and a clear midnight sky. Almost centered in it was the lighted cross on Old St. Mary's, and farther on, above the brilliant symbol of everything that Christmas stands for, was a single bright light on the top of some tall building.

Giannina pointed to this. "It is beautiful," she whispered through the silence that held the room. "It is like the star the Wise Men followed."

Johnny remembered that quote an hour later when he sat down at his desk and picked up the telephone. The first number he dialed was that of the city's most famous orthopedic surgeon, and the conversation with him was most satisfactory. The second number was one he had called earlier, and the voice answering was annoyed.

"Carnahan," Johnny said, "I've been thinking it over. I've decided that, with the proper help, you can be defeated. Good night."

He hung up and rolled a sheet of paper into his typewriter. At the top he typed A Line of Cheer From Johnny Greer. Then he lighted a cigarette and began to write steadily. (1949)

John Collins Harvey

The Christmas Gift

Christmastime at our hospital is one of the best times of the whole year. The usually busy and bustling corridors are quieter. The wards are almost empty of patients, for most, who can be, have been discharged. Few new patients come in; only those who are really sick. One half of the resident staff of doctors and nurses is given a three-day holiday. Those remaining can take a breather and relax somewhat from the grueling daily routines followed during the rest of the year. Best of all, though, the spirit of Christmas invades the place.

During the week preceding Christmas the corridors and wards are decorated. Patients, doctors, nurses, aids and orderlies all give a hand. Hidden talents come to light. Christmas scenes are painted on the omnipresent glass partitions and windows. Camels, Wise Men, sheep and shepherds are marching ceaselessly around the wards. Sometimes they are hard to identify, but then everyone is kind to those whose spirit is willing, but whose hand and eye aren't. Wreaths of pine, holly and mistletoe are hung over doorways and in the halls. A Christmas tree, gay with dyed bits of cotton and gauze and other hospital-made decorations, is put up in the center of each ward.

To my mind the most beautiful effect of this face lifting is achieved by the Administration Building, a hideous old Victorian structure of rather ugly proportions with marble floors and heavy oak woodwork. The building, four stories in height, has a central, octagonal-shaped rotunda extending upward from the ground floor to the large glass dome. The main entrance to the hospital opens into this rotunda. In the center, facing the door, is a larger-than-life-sized statue of Christ, with its cold white marble arms warmly lifted in an embrace. Appropriately at the base is this inscription, "Come unto me, all ye that are weary and heavy laden, and I will give you rest." The main stairway to the upper floors is opposite the

front entrance. The four floors form four inner balconies about this central rotunda.

On the walls of the main stairway are hung huge wreaths of pine and holly. On the old heavily ornamented and multi-branched brass candelabra at the foot of the stairs are placed two huge pine wreaths with red-ribbon bows. The heavy oak bannisters and posters which give a feeling of solidarity to the balconies about the rotunda are wrapped in pine-and-holly garlands. The simplicity of these decorations adds even more grandeur to the awe-inspiring figure of the "Merciful Comforter."

Since the opening of the hospital in 1889 the choir of Brown's Memorial Baptist Church has come each Christmas Eve to sing carols for the staff and the patients. Many of the choir members are employees of the hospital, but almost all have been patients in the hospital at some time or other. By now some of the members who came originally as youngsters are grandparents; yet each year they return on Christmas Eve to give their present to their beloved hospital.

The choir always begins caroling in the rotunda. There, grouped about the figure of Christ, after brief prayer, they sing the best-loved carols and Negro spirituals. They finish with the "Hallelujah Chorus" from "The Messiah."

The doctors and nurses who can slip away for a few brief minutes from the wards, some patients in wheel chairs or on stretchers, and many friends of the hospital arrange themselves on the

The only life Irene had ever known was the hard and humble life of a farm on the Eastern Shore.

balconies to listen to the carols. It is a glorious occasion and one not easily forgotten. I know, for I have been part of the group listening each Christmas Eve for many years.

The most memorable Christmas Eve for me, however, was my first one, when I was a house officer in the hospital. This year, known as the internship, is the first year of practice for a newly graduated doctor. The theories of medicine have been learned in the long hard years of medical school; the practical experience in medicine has now begun.

It is only in the practice of medicine that the full realization dawns of the tremendous responsibility for human life placed in the hands of the physician. Believe me, this is quite frightening for the young physician. Many grave doubts arise in an intern's mind about his own knowledge, ability and worthiness for such a sacred trust. Wise and gentle guidance from more experienced physicians, coupled with the appreciation and affection shown him by the patients whom he has helped care for, builds self-confidence in the intern. However, the process is a slow and sometimes seemingly endless one.

Certainly I was no exception as an intern in having grave doubts about my abilities and worthiness for a medical career. These doubts were so great in the fall of my internship year that I had just about decided to leave medicine and enter another field. I figured I just could never be a good doctor. But Fate has a way of intervening in the affairs of most people, and it did with me in the person of Irene "S."

One Saturday morning in early September I was "covering" for a few hours in the Accident Room for another intern who was sick. I was at the time assigned to the female ward, but found time to spare to give a hand in the Accident Room. A thirty-nine-year-old Negro woman was brought in by her family. They had brought her to Baltimore from their small farm on the Eastern Shore of Maryland. They had driven the long way around the bay in their twenty-year-old truck because they didn't have the money to pay the ferry toll. They started about five o'clock that morning and reached the hospital about ten o'clock. A twenty-year-old broken-down farm truck doesn't make a fast ambulance.

Irene's brother, sister, eldest daughter and cousin were with her. They were obviously very poor, simple farm people who were turning to the hospital for help as a last resort. They had been told that Irene was crazy and should be put away, but they decided to bring her to Baltimore to see if she couldn't be helped.

She was a pitiful creature, emaciated, woebegone, and looking twice her age. She was talking irrationally at times and, when she could muster the strength, would struggle feebly with those supporting her. She fidgeted with the bedclothes and pulled at her hair. Her family reported that she had been getting "peculiar" for some time. She had been losing weight, for she didn't eat, complaining that food made her sick. She vomited what she ate, and retched frequently when she didn't eat. She had become so weak that she had taken to her bed and showed no interest in her surroundings. A doctor had been called to see her, and told her family that she was mentally ill and should be committed to the state mental hospital.

I proceeded to examine her. She was extremely pale. She was quite emaciated and she had great muscle weakness. Her facial expression was dull and listless. She was short-winded and had signs of dropsy. I didn't know what was wrong with her, but I did think she was seriously ill. I made arrangements to admit her to the hospital; she was brought to the ward where I was assigned as intern. Thus the responsibility for her care in the hospital fell partly on me.

That afternoon the resident physician and I examined her more closely and performed some laboratory tests. We found she was bleeding from her bowels and that this blood loss had caused a profound anemia. It became obvious that her nausea, vomiting and refusal to eat were associated with abdominal pain. The muscle weakness and nervousness seemed to be linked to severe overactivity of the thyroid gland. A basal metabolism test was performed which showed a result consistent with that diagnosis. She was started on iodine drops, the proper medication for Graves' disease, or hyperthyroidism. Digitalis was given for her heart condition. The X ray of her stomach, taken the next day, showed a large ulcer. Proper anti-ulcer treatment was instituted. She was given blood transfusions and was fed intravenously for a

few days until the medicine could take effect.

Gradually Irene began to respond to our therapy. She became quiet and subdued, so that sedation could be discontinued. She began to eat. Her heart began to function more efficiently. The abdominal pain disappeared. Her anemia disappeared. She became quite a different person.

All of this treatment necessitated long and close observation. I got to know her well during this time. She had little formal schooling, but she was endowed with a great deal of common sense and she was rich in her love for other people. This began to show immediately as improvement occurred.

I enjoyed talking with her and would spend spare moments at her bedside, listening to her talk about life on the farm, crops, cooking or her family. She dearly loved flowers, and since she could not use the little land the family had for growing anything other than food, she would pick wild flowers and tree blossoms in the fields. One of her favorites was holly, which grew in profusion around her home. She knew little of current events and virtually nothing about the world beyond the Eastern Shore. She had never been to Baltimore before the time she was brought to the hospital by her family.

She improved steadily, and finally the day came for her to be discharged. She said good-by to the nurses, to the other patients with whom she had

A large dose of Christmas cheer—a likely prescription for every patient.

become friendly during the time she had spent on the ward, and to the doctors. She shook hands with me and said simply, "Thank you, Doc."

We arranged for her to be cared for by a physician in a town on the Eastern Shore, since she had no money to come back for periodic check-ups at our hospital. She thought traveling from her home and getting about in Baltimore would be too confusing for her anyway. The physician sent word on several occasions that she was doing well. I did not think much about Irene in the press of work.

Then Christmas approached with all its excitement. The wards were decorated. Patients had been discharged. The doctors and nurses who had Christmas holiday were gone. The quiet of Christmas Eve descended. In the dining room that night there were lighted candles on the tables. They furnished the only light in the room except for the twinkling lights on the gaily decorated Christmas tree in the center of the room. It was pleasant and cozy, and the usual hospital meal actually tasted good!

Soon the time came to go over to the rotunda for the carols. The choir assembled. The group of listeners became quiet. There was the sparkle of anticipation in the air. Here most of the people away from home and loved ones, each quite alone with his own problems, yet bound together in the common work of treating and caring for the sick, stood or sat on the balconies waiting for the music. Below, the choir, gowned in cassocks, prayed softly around the statue of Christ and then burst into song. The singing was magnificent. The whole situation was more beautiful than I had been led to believe by those who had told me about it.

Yet I was terribly sad. This was my first Christmas away from home. Always before, during school, college and medical-school days, I had managed to get home for Christmas. Now I seemed to be terribly alone even in the midst of friends! Doubts in my own ability, dissatisfaction with my own efforts, and a feeling of unworthiness overcame me. Self-pity is inexcusable and terribly destructive. I tried to concentrate on the singing, so as to drown my sadness. Soon the choir was singing the "Hallelujah"—a final burst

of heartfelt song, and it was over. The choir was now moving behind the stairs and on into the main corridors to the wards. I still felt depressed.

I turned to go downstairs and back to my ward when I caught sight of the porter at the front door, beckoning to me. I walked down the stairs and across the floor to him. He handed me a box wrapped up in brown paper tied with a knotted piece of red string. He said that during the caroling a Negro woman had slipped in the front door and asked him if he would find me. He told her he thought I was up on one of the balconies listening to the caroling, and that when it was finished he would call me, but he couldn't do it while the caroling was on. She said she couldn't wait, and asked him to give me the box she was carrying. He said she told him she had only twenty minutes before the last bus left for home, and since he couldn't call me she would have to hurry along. He said he tried to explain to her that a bus left from in front of the hospital about every fifteen minutes. He couldn't understand her worry over missing the bus.

I took the package up to my room and opened it. Over the old brown paper were pasted Christmas decorations cut from newspapers. On one of the flaps of the box was pasted one half of an old Christmas card which had a printed name lined through with red crayon and my name printed crudely on it instead.

I opened the box, and inside were pieces of holly branches obviously freshly picked. I knew immediately who the donor was and what the hurry was. She had a four-hour trip back to the Eastern Shore to get home for Christmas!

Freshly picked holly in a crudely decorated carton tied with a knotted piece of red string. A simple present from a poor, uneducated woman? Not at all—the greatest gift I have ever received!

I looked out the window into the dark sky with its shining stars. And I thought of that night some nineteen hundred years ago. From another part of the hospital I heard the choir singing, ". . .bearing gifts we traverse afar. . . ."

I knew then what I had wanted to know for some time. (1958)

Lt. Col. Melvin Russell Blair

A Christmas Story from Korea

On the south bank of the Imjin River, Korea, the 25th (Tropic Lightning) Infantry Division was dug in, waiting for the Chinese Army to attack. Three battle-hardened regiments —the 24th (Eagles), the 27th (Wolfhounds) and 35th (Cacti)—were holding the sector near the confluence of the Imjin and Han rivers where the Chinese were expected to strike. As the soldiers listened to the peculiar, high-pitched wail of the wind that came in from the Yellow Sea, whipping up little twisters of snow as it bit into the north bank where thousands of North Korean refugees were huddled, one GI mirthlessly commented, "Wind's singing us a carol." It was December 24, 1950.

Our biggest nightmare was the refugees. Between the 25th Division and the Chinese were some 40,000 North Korean civilians. It was an ironic paradox that these people feared the Chinese communists—their "allies" —more than death itself, and fled from their approach. They were mostly women, children and very old men—for the North Korean Army had conscripted all of the able-bodied males.

There we were—an outnumbered army in a tactically indefensible position, with thousands of refugees in our line of fire.

What we saw across the river was hard to take. The refugees were starving, and we had no food to give them. They were dressed in cotton rags in weather that dropped to five degrees below zero; yet, if they lit a fire, our patrols were forced to put it out, for fires would attract the enemy.

The meager roads became choked with refugees who crossed the Imjin, creating a security hazard. Finally, 8th Army headquarters ordered that no more North Koreans be permitted to cross the river.

The men of the 25th were confused about these people. They had no love for them, for they knew of the savageries perpetrated by North Korean civilians upon our wounded and captured soldiers. Yet, as they silently watched the ragged, starving women and children pass through their lines before the embargo was clamped on, they were reminded of their own women and children back home. They wanted somehow to help. But they didn't know exactly how.

The answer came on this day before Christmas.

It had been a rather special day. We had expected the Chinese attack to come on Christmas Day, so headquarters had ordered that we feed our men Christmas dinner a day early. The quartermaster worked a minor miracle and brought a hot turkey dinner right up to the front-line troops. Turkey and all the trimmings—including stuffing, cranberries, sweet potatoes, rolls and real butter—even candy and mince and pumpkin pie.

What really tickled the men, though, was that packages from home came through, just in time for Christmas. Expecting the Chinese to strike, no one heeded "Do Not Open Until Christmas" instructions. Front-line foxholes bulged with cakes, tinned delicacies, socks, mittens and the like.

I happened to be at the front lines that afternoon in connection with my duties as Division G-2 (Intelligence officer). I stopped in the area held by the 35th Infantry, leaned over a foxhole and asked the soldier occupying it who he was and how he was doing. He hopped out and told me he was Pfc. Stanley Crowley, of Birmingham, Alabama, and that he was doing all right. He was a red-haired, freckle-faced rifleman, nineteen years old. He was not particularly chunky, but he looked enormous because of the six layers of clothing he was wearing in the subzero weather.

"Let me show you what I got for Christmas, colonel," Crowley drawled. First, he produced a wool scarf; then, commencing an odd sort of strip-tease, he pulled back layer after layer of clothing, finally coming to the object he had next to his skin. It was a fruit cake. "Got it here to keep it from freezing," he explained.

Just at that moment there was a diversion. A band of refugees, utterly desperate, decided—orders or no orders—to cross the river.

The stampede—and hundreds came across before we could stop it—was led by a woman with three children. It was low tide. She waded through the ice-clogged water that came above her waist. With one arm, she carried a child of about three; with her other arm, she supported a second child of about five so his head was above water. The third—a boy of about seven—had to make out for himself.

These four were the first to reach the south bank, and they started running right through the 35th's position. When they reached Private First Class Crowley's foxhole, they stopped, for Crowley was standing in their path.

He looked at the woman. She returned the gaze from black, sunken sockets. He looked at the children. Their lips were cracked and bleeding; their fingers bluish with frostbite. The oldest boy had slipped and gone in over his head in crossing; his hair was frozen into icy wisps.

Slowly, from around his neck, the red-haired boy from Alabama unwound his Christmas scarf. "Here, take it," he said to the woman.

She drew back in fear. Crowley kept holding it out, and finally she took it. She looked at her children to see which needed it worst. She settled on the oldest boy, who was shaking so violently he hardly could stand.

Then Crowley again began his curious strip-tease with the six layers of clothing. He brought out his fruit cake and handed it to her. Again she hesitated. Then she took it.

She broke off three small pieces and handed a piece to each of her children. None for herself. She handed the cake back to Crowley. By gestures, he conveyed that she was to keep it all. She stood expressionless, then bowed to Crowley, and motioned for each of her children to bow.

While this was going on, other refugees were watching. So were the men of Private First Class Crowley's company. Silently, spontaneously, a sort of spiritual chain reaction began. Crowley had shown what to do about the refugees.

Out of their foxholes came the soldiers, bearing gifts for the North Koreans. They gave gloves, mufflers, food from their own rations, cakes and delicacies from the U.S.A. Some of the soldiers made second trips and came back with blankets and shoe-pacs; others peeled off jackets and draped them around wet, shivering children.

The whole thing was done almost in dead silence, though some of the boys said things like "Merry Christmas, Joe," or "Happy New Year, little girl," as they passed out their presents.

In the middle of it all, up raced the battalion commander in an open car, ready to chop off heads for the flagrant security breach. What the hell was going on, he wanted to know. He found out. Before he left, he passed out a pocketful of hard candy to Korean kids. He also turned his head when his driver gave away the blankets they had been swathed in when they drove up.

"Sure cold today, colonel," said the driver cheerfully.

"Drive on," said the colonel.

Slowly, Operation Santa Claus subsided. South Korean police stopped the refugee flow. Those who had come over were directed to a railroad track and told to start walking south—fast.

Then the soldiers returned to their foxholes. Materially, they were poorer; militarily, they had done a risky thing. The only thing about it was that the men of the 35th, holding their sector of the 25th Division's battle line, all felt so good that evening. There was no peace, but there was considerable good will, on the south bank of the Imjin on that Christmas Eve, 1950.

(P.S.: In April, 1951, Pfc. Stanley Crowley was reported killed in action.) (1951)

Olaf Ruhen

Christmas on the Island

A little grinning lad came up the track as MacGregor began to climb the tall, upthrust boulder they called the Fishermen's Rock, his bare toes digging into the ancient footholds. In one hand the boy carried three hen eggs carefully wrapped in a lily leaf; in the other a mud crab, its claws pinioned with a strip of palm frond.

"Where are you going?" he wanted to know.

MacGregor stopped and looked at him. The boy's grin was from ear to ear.

"I'm going to the top of the rock," MacGregor said carefully.

"Just to see about?" asked the boy.

"Just to see."

"All right. You see plenty."

From the top of the rock, MacGregor saw plenty, indeed. He saw the whole beautiful world, and in the middle of it, in the water almost directly beneath him, a ketch setting sail, ice-white, immaculate and curiously remote in spite of the muted rattle of blocks, the groaning of the anchor winch which came as an undercurrent to the screaming of the parrots in the trees. The departure of the little ship disturbed him—the setting out of someone he had never known for a destiny he could not guess at. It was like his own farewell to civilization six months before—it was emotionally cold. Like himself, for that matter. Or at least that was what Kathleen had told him.

"Underneath, you're as cold as a fish," she had said when she gave him back the ring. "Nothing ever warms you. You're too good, Mac. You're clinically exact. And it isn't good for you. It won't get you anywhere."

"I don't make mistakes, anyway," he said.

"Perhaps that's what I mean," she told him.

He had regretted Kathleen, but it was the pursuit of his painting career rather than her dismissal which had brought him to this island of

Owelaka, an outlyer of the Trobriand group which is itself an archipelago set in the Coral Sea. And he stayed, though the island is not of itself beautiful. It is simply a coral plain, a little tip tilted by forgotten earthquakes, with a vegetation that differs hardly at all from that of any coral island. But from his perch on the Fishermen's Rock, where traditionally the canoemen climbed to shout their successes to the expectant village, he could see the ocean's loveliest waters, studded at a little distance by islands that are dead volcanoes; and islands beyond islands, mountainous, symmetrical, tinted with the shades of sea distance.

He had been induced to stay by some furious necessity to master the problems presented by his art. He had found a home with old Frank Richards, the trader, in a great cool barn of four chicken-wire walls and a sago-leaf roof which served as storehouse, living quarters and trading post in the village of Lamari, on the east coast; and here he kept himself firmly applied to painting when he was not looking after Frank's interests during the trader's frequent absences. He was looking after them now, paying his weekly call at the district office in Papatalu, where a safe anchorage and adjacent copra plantations constituted Owelaka's sole commerical assets.

He was barefoot, because that was the best way to negotiate the three ragged ridges of abruptly upthrust coral that, under heavy forest, divided Lamari's lovely coral beaches, its populated villages and fertile garden land, from Papatalu. In four places he had had to balance on slippery peeled trunks of trees no more than six inches in diameter. Once he had crossed a rock bridge.

Perhaps beneath Mac's cool exterior ran warm currents.

There were two cliff faces, not high, but rugged, that had to be climbed with handholds; and everywhere except directly on the foot-wide, smooth-worn trail, the rock was jagged with razor edges. But he had all the time in the world, and the way was beautiful with flowers and butterflies and water-flecked green ferns.

The weather was hot. It was ten days before Christmas in the northwest monsoon, and MacGregor stayed on top of the rock resting and watching until the ketch had beaten northeast round the coral, heading, as he guessed now, for the main Trobriand group, which was in the north. He scrambled down to the track again and headed for the district office.

Stevens, the patrol officer, saw him coming, and threw a yellow envelope on the counter.

"Radiogram for you," he said.

MacGregor tore it open. "Three days old?" he complained. He wasn't really surprised.

"Yes. Well, there was no hurry," Stevens said. "You can't get a message out in reply. The radio's broken down."

"When are you going to have something urgent of your own so you'll fix it?" MacGregor inquired nastily, but Stevens only grunted and turned his back. He threw a bundle of letters—mostly for Richards—on the counter. The radiogram was from Richards too. It read:

DELAYED THREE WEEKS BROKEN PROPELLOR SHAFT STOP SOME DAMAGE STOP SLIPPING SAMARAI STOP PLEASE MEET LAYONI AND EXPLAIN WHY NO CHRISTMAS STOP LOOK AFTER HER STOP SORRY TO TROUBLE YOU. FRANK

Well, that was Frank all over, MacGregor thought. He had the ends all tied up, but, somehow or other, nothing went right for him. He had made a special trip to get Christmas stock for his store, and now he wasn't going to be home for Christmas. Layoni was his ten-year-old half-caste daughter and the apple of his eye, and Layoni's mother had died at her birth. MacGregor had never seen the child. He felt, at any rate, that he had no special affinity for small children. They bored him.

One of the letters, he saw, had the name of Layoni's mission school on the envelope, so he tore it open. It contained Layoni's school report and the news that the mission schooner would land her at Papatalu on Owelaka on December twenty-first. He looked up, reminded of something.

"Beautiful ketch just left the bay," he said. "Whose is it? No trader, I bet."

"You're safe," Stevens told him. "That was Innstrom's Tanagra. If I had his money I wouldn't be bucketing round these waters in a wind ship, that's for sure. Even though it's got everything that opens and shuts."

"Sir Gordon Innstrom?" MacGregor asked.

Stevens nodded. "The same," he said.

Sir Gordon was the one man above all others MacGregor would have liked to meet. He was the only one of the Australian millionaires, as far as he knew, who took any interest in painting. More than that, in MacGregor's view, it was an informed interest. Innstrom knew his subject.

"I'd have liked to meet him," MacGregor said.

"You'll get your chance," said Stevens. "He's coming back. He spent a few days with the Allisons, and they've asked him back for their Christmas party."

The Allisons had the biggest copra plantation. There were only a dozen Europeans on the island, and the Allisons comprised the self-appointed aristocracy. MacGregor avoided them whenever he could. Mrs. Allison got on his nerves more than just a little.

"So charmed to welcome an artist to our little community," she said when she met him first. "I paint myself, of course. But in my first year here I painted everything, absolutely everything paintable. One can't go on painting the same coconut palm." None of her efforts hung upon her walls, and the few prints there, while they were good, seemed to bear no relationship to one another.

MacGregor himself was engaged in a period of searching introspection. When he got home he went through his paintings again, stacking them up three or four at a time in the best light. They were not what he wanted.

He had left Sydney with no very impressive reputation, but in all honesty he did not know why. His work was modern. It had flow and rhythm; and in particular, a series of portraits that almost approached caricature had deserved, he felt, a public recognition. His techniques were good. He was a young man going places, and he had undertaken the visit to the Trobriands for publicity purposes as much as anything; it was a vivid place where no other artist had been. And then the islands had intrigued him, entangled him, and finally, he had to admit, defeated him. For the exaggerated color and the exotic forms of the tropics mated badly with his exaggerated technique.

He sorted out the portraits of Doraima, a Lamari village adolescent who, on a whim, had her head shaved entirely bald. The girl's figure was exquisite. The dainty conformation of her completely naked head mated wonderfully with her fine-cut features and her regal bearing. She painted designs of happiness on her face—eye-encircling curves of shining black and enameled white in pigments of charcoal and lime and coconut oil.

MacGregor's first painting of her, in his usual style, was so bad he destroyed it. The others now faced him: two or three representational treatments in assorted surroundings that offered a flat and clinical result, and a slightly better version, with an almost Egyptian flavor. This one had drawn praise from Mrs. Allison, but he felt it lacked something.

Over-all, he was very disappointed. His work

seemed alien to the land and to himself. The more immediate reason for his inspection, however, was to decide whether the quality of his work was sufficient to intrigue such a patron as Innstrom. If he could achieve Sir Gordon's patronage, his fame and future would be assured.

Several days later, when a native boy arrived at Lamari with an invitation to the Allison Christmas party, he was delighted to accept. He put the latest Doraima portrait back on the easel and added a few finishing touches, planning to present it to his hostess. Brought to the party, it would inevitably form a topic for conversation among the guests — conversation into which Sir Gordon must be drawn. Thus he would make his chance.

The Allison children and four or five others— the patrol officer's two and a Sanderson and two Emmets—were on the mission schooner with Layoni when he came to meet her. She was a slim child, primly dressed, with pipestem legs and neat polished shoes, and she stood a little behind the others, ignored by them, clutching her case in both hands, with her head downcast.

Her voice, when she spoke, was tiny but musical.

Mrs. Allison, having gathered her brood about her, nodded a bright farewell. She was a big, heavy woman, briskly pleasant.

"We'll expect to see you on Christmas Day then, Mr. MacGregor," she said. "Come in the afternoon. The children will be having their party then, and we'll expect you to stay for ours in the evening." She looked at Layoni. "Someone at Lamari can look after Frank's child," she added. "I doubt that she'd get on too well with our lot."

The little girl dropped her chin on her chest again and looked at the ground. MacGregor felt her register the snub, brutal and direct. He took her absurdly small case, made his farewells, and they started up the track. When they paused at the summit and sat in the sun by the Fishermen's Rock, Layoni waited awhile before she asked, "Will my daddy be home for Christmas?"

"I'm afraid he won't be," MacGregor said absently. "He'll have to stay in Samarai until his boat is fixed. A couple of weeks, maybe."

He suddenly sensed Layoni's disappointment, and looked at her closely. For the first time he noticed the dusky glory of dark hair, the smooth olive complexion, the incredibly beautiful liquid brown eyes. There was something a little pathetic, he thought, in the way she looked down at her toes. Suddenly realizing she was at home, on her own ground, away from the disciplined days of mission school, she reached forward, undid her shoe fastenings and stripped off her shoes and socks. MacGregor thought, uncomfortably, of another disappointment.

"I'm afraid there won't be any Christmas presents either," he said. "And no party. Your daddy was going to bring all the things back with him, and now he can't."

There was a long pause this time, while the movements of her hands were arrested, and then she said gently, "Oh, it doesn't matter." She looked up. "We did have a

party at the mission, and it was nearly Christmas," she said. "Some of the girls there don't have any parties but the mission parties." Later on, when they were walking down the track, she said, "The girls that have parties will tell us all about them when school starts."

"I thought Mrs. Allison might have asked you to come to her party," MacGregor said, and Layoni shook her head.

"She never does." She had the utmost composure and poise. "Maybe daddy will bring a party back with him," she said. "It won't be very far from Christmas, will it?"

She looked up at him, and her beautiful eyes belied these Pollyanna sentiments, for they were close to tears. He began to feel a real interest in this little scrap of humanity. Suddenly he made a resolve that she should have her party.

At night, after he had sent Layoni to bed, MacGregor sat and smoked his pipe. *What on earth does one do*, he thought, *to please a child at Christmas?* Most of his memories came from the commercial art work he had done in student days for city stores. There would have to be a tree— well, that was simple. He could manage that. But there were no toys, no ornaments, no strings of lights. Playmates would be no problem. And he could keep the party a surprise—last-minute invitations would not worry the native children of the village. There should be an angel for the top of the tree. He tried to remember what else.

The village of Paladau, in the south of the island, was renowned for its wood carvers. They were simple artisans who cheerfully tackled the job of making, say, a three-legged table; chopping it with most intricate design out of a heavy solid tree trunk, using tiny adzes of their own manufacture, smoothing the cuts with the sandpaper skin of a stingray, and adding the final polish with a boar's tusk. Their main products were beautiful wooden bowls, simply and handsomely carved, but when a Paladau villager had nothing else to do he carved little fish or pigs, and instruments for the daily work of the people. None of the island natives cared to use any artifact that had not been given some ornamentation of beauty, but a Paladau man would neglect his gardens for his carving, with the enthusiastic approval of his wife and family.

Timothy, the old village councilor, was sharpening an adz in front of his hut, and looked up, smiling, when MacGregor walked in. The artist came straight to the point.

"I want you to carve me an angel, Timothy. You know this something, an angel?"

"No, sir."

"A woman then—a woman that has wings on her back like a bird's wings; a woman this high"—he gestured with his hands about fifteen inches apart—"and in her right hand she holds a stick that has a star, like this, on the end of it." With the point of a knife he scratched a star-tipped scepter on the ground.

"A woman with wings and a stick?" asked Timothy. "This is an angel?" He pronounced the word three times over, trying to get it right.

MacGregor caught himself quickly. "Why, no," he said. "An angel is like a woman, truly, but she must be something more. She is the meaning of all giving, the cause of all happiness; she makes your heart light."

"Like a new bride?" asked Timothy.

MacGregor searched his mind. It seemed urgent that Timothy should have exactly the right idea.

"Like a new bride and a new mother," he said. "Like the bride and the mother of all the world." He wondered whence the image came, and thought it over. It did not sound ridiculous at all.

"And she looks like this," he added. He drew three quick little sketches of the angel while the councilor watched him intently, his curiosity growing.

"I want it quickly," warned MacGregor. "The day after tomorrow." Absently he added a halo to the front-face figure.

"All right," Timothy said. "I'll bring it to Lamari."

"Something else," MacGregor remembered. "I want some things for a child to play with. There should be three wise men with camels, and shepherds with their sheep, and a crib for a Baby. You know sheep? Or camels?"

"Are they like pigs?" asked Timothy.

"Like pigs," MacGregor said. "Only more like this." He drew a sheep and watched the old man's eyes when he looked at it. "Never mind," he said. "I guess pigs will do. They are for Layoni, for her Christmas presents."

The old man nodded. "I know this Christmas," he said. "That is when the government holds the sports at Losuia."

MacGregor drew a deep breath. "Christmas is more than that, Timothy," he tried to explain. "Christmas is when everybody thinks of other people, to make them happy. At Christmas the white man thinks of God, and pleases Him by making His children happy."

I sound like a preacher, he thought. *I have never thought these things before.*

Timothy smiled. "I have heard of these things, but not seen them," he said. "I will be glad to help. But Mr. Richards will bring toys."

"Not this Christmas, Timothy," MacGregor said. "His boat has broken down. That's why I want you to make these things. And not you only. Tell the others that I need toys for the children and that I will pay them well."

"The day after tomorrow I will bring them to Lamari," the councilor promised.

Once he had committed himself to give Layoni the party, MacGregor went about it enthusiastically. Layoni had renewed friendships amongst the children of the village, though in the year she had been gone she had almost forgotten the Boyowan language of the island; and most of the day she spent on the beach or in the water, and was never underfoot. MacGregor saw her only for meals, which he sometimes got himself, but oftener left to the hired boys Richards kept in the store. At night Layoni would look briefly at her books, which were few; then go to bed to sleep dreamlessly. MacGregor's affection for her grew with each meeting, and in the two days of preparations she was much in his thoughts.

It was easy, without her knowledge, to find a she-oak tree with the necessary symmetry and the desired size, and to install it in a corner of the store, concealed by burlap sheets and cartons of goods. He was also able to recruit a few of the village women to help him by making strings of shell beads and raucous trumpets made from the coiled leaves of the coconut palms. They caught his enthusiasm and by Christmas Eve other villagers to whom he had not spoken were bringing in gifts—a beautiful little canoe with mast, butterfly-wing sail, and tiny paddles; a set of tops made from coconut shells doweled with wooden pegs; a cord carrying bag in five colors.

Timothy and three men from Paladau came late on Christmas Eve with their carvings. The angel was a triumph, queerly modern in design, with a long body and short, thick legs; and, in place of the halo that Mac-Gregor had drawn, she carried a cooking pot on her head. She had long almond eyes and a straight, unsmiling mouth. But she was nevertheless beautiful, with an air of proud kindliness most suitable for an angel. MacGregor handled the carving for a long time, turning it over and over. Then he looked at the other things, spread about him on the ground.

There were at least twenty little pigs, each round and fat, and standing stockily on four absurd short legs. There were three little figures of men. There was a short trough, shaped like a Phoenician galley—"Something for the baby," Timothy said. MacGregor recognized it. It was an ancient baby bath, just big enough to admit a mother's fingers, holding just enough water to clean a baby. It was the only Trobriand article made for babies. MacGregor set it down carefully. Then he saw the thing.

It was a big carving a foot long. It was cut from some golden timber, and it had a long body, six short legs and a tail that was a dragon's tail, except that it curved upward and back, its frill of broad spines soaring like a banner, and joined in two places to the thing's back. The neck balanced the tail, but carried an enormous head with two pointed ears, four round eyes and rows and rows of bared teeth. MacGregor picked it up.

"What is it?" he asked.

"It is a camel," said Timothy, and MacGregor put back his head and laughed.

"I think it is a camel. I have never seen a camel," Timothy added. He seemed affronted, and MacGregor stopped laughing.

"It is not quite a camel," he said. "But it is a very good something. I am truly pleased with it."

"Yes, it is a very good something," Timothy said complacently.

MacGregor paid the men well in tobacco and goods from the store, and they left. He looked at the angel a long time; then he took his paints and, with some compunction at hiding the beautiful grain of the wood, painted it in the colors of life. He painted the pigs, too, and the little men who represented shepherds; and when that was done, he turned to the decoration of the tree, tying in place the brilliant crimson globes of fruits and golden oranges, and all the colorful things he could think of. He could not add the angel or the

painted toys until the morning, when the colors would be dry, but even so it was long past midnight when he went to take a final look at the sleeping Layoni.

She was lying quietly, an olive-skinned doll, her dark hair spread about the pillow, her thin arms carelessly outside the single sheet that covered her. In her sleep she looked a little sad and a little lonely, and he felt a great rush of affection for the child.

He took a long time to go to sleep himself, thinking not of Layoni but of the Allison party. He was excited about it, and in a way disgusted with himself for being excited, because he certainly condemned Mrs. Allison for her rejection of Layoni. It would have been easy for her to be kind to the child, who was, after all, the only person on the island alien to both the natives and the whites. At least on Christmas Day she could have given her the companionship of the other English-speaking children, MacGregor felt. On the other hand, he felt the prospects of the Innstrom contact to be enormously important. Sir Gordon's was an acquaintance which MacGregor could develop with, he felt, the happiest of results when he returned to civilization. From the starting point of the Doraima painting, which Mrs. Allison would certainly have in a place of prominence, he might even secure Sir Gordon as a kind of patron, and that, combined with his own abilities as an artist, would be quite sufficient to insure the success of his whole career.

So his thoughts went, on and on into the night, and it was quite late when he awoke.

"Where will you go this morning?" he asked Layoni at breakfast.

"Just swimming, I think," she said, and he nodded. He would be able to find her when he wanted her. So he said nothing about the waiting Christmas tree. Better to keep it really a surprise. In an hour or two it would be ready.

It took even less than that to set the painted angel at the top of the tree, to wrap in concealing leaves the painted pigs that should have been sheep and the funny little men that should have been shepherds, and the toys—the tops decorated now with bands of bright red and blue—and to arrange them all in their places. But when that was done, Layoni and her friends were nowhere to be seen.

It would be a four-hour walk to the Allisons—maybe three if he hurried—but MacGregor did not particularly worry about his schedule. A little later never mattered in the islands. The children would turn up by lunch; he could start the party and still get to the Allisons' in plenty of time. But it was early afternoon when Layoni appeared, and he felt aggrieved.

"We've had a lovely day, Uncle Mac!" she cried. "We found a cave——"

"Well, go and find all the other kids again," he said. "Bring them here just as fast as you can."

He looked at his watch as she ran off. It was one. He pulled down the burlap barriers and the pile of crates, and revealed the Christmas tree. Even in his impatience he was pleased with the result. The tree was beautiful, its branches gracious under the offerings. From the top twig the angel, proud and lovely, looked indeed as though she offered her benediction.

When the little girl came again to the doorway of the store, she just stood still and stared. Behind her, children pushed their way in, until they, too, could see the tree and the angel.

"Merry Christmas, Layoni," greeted MacGregor. She didn't hear him until he had said it twice more. Then she ran, not to the tree, but to him, clutching his legs and looking up at his face; and he felt the strong unselfish love of a man for a child welling up in him. It was new to him and took him by the throat and left him weak.

"Thank you, thank you, thank you," she cried.

"Just for you," he said, "and your friends."

She walked slowly over to the tree, picked her way daintily, and there was that in her eyes that dimmed the radiance of the angel enthroned there. It was a look of beauty, of complete adoration, reflecting the kind of sheer happiness that can bring tears. MacGregor watched her for long minutes; he sat there watching while she called the others; he sat on and on. And suddenly it was urgent that he should keep forever the memory of that look and that happiness; and almost

unconsciously he reached for his sketch pad.

Working swiftly, he captured the moment. Quickly he made sketch after sketch—the face, the uplifted eye, a hand outstretched—not coldly and clinically, but in a fever of excitement that somehow intertwined with his other emotions.

Suddenly she was lifting up the animal that Timothy had carved—the six-legged monster.

"What is it?" she asked.

"It's a something," he told her. "Timothy said it's a camel." She dissolved into laughter.

From there it went on as a children's party does, except that the creator of the party sat there amongst them, his pencil flying, stabilizing and holding forever the moments in which a fat brown baby sat in ecstasy, fingering a spotty painted pig; or the whirl of movement with which a lucky lad raced to the water with a toy canoe. And when, at last, MacGregor retrieved the angel from the top of the tree and Layoni took it and sat with it in her arms, with her face molded into a pure testimony of love and happiness, he sat and drew that, too; his lines swiftly conspiring to produce, not merely the features, the waving black hair, the liquid brown eyes, but the configuration of love itself—of love and happiness and the true recipient spirit of Christmas.

When he had finished he realized that the afternoon was gone, and that the Allisons would see neither him nor the portrait of Doraima. There was no time to go, and no excuse. He could never explain such a late arrival.

Instead he stayed with Layoni, and when the village children went, read to her a little while, and watched her sleep at last; the painted wooden angel clutched in her arms, its cooking-pot halo against her shoulder. He realized he had probably made an enemy of the Allisons—his explanation about Layoni's party would certainly not be acceptable to the woman who had refused to invite the girl herself. The Allisons didn't matter, but he regretted missing Innstrom.

The day after Christmas was like any day after Christmas, MacGregor thought moodily as he cleared away the tree and the debris. He worked slowly, absorbed in thought, and was surprised by a stranger at the door, a tall gray man, a little red in the face from walking, dressed in correct tropical whites and carrying an ebony stick. The stranger held out his hand.

"My name's Innstrom," he said. "You're MacGregor. I heard some talk about you last night, and I wanted to see for myself how an artist would treat all this magnificent material."

MacGregor could hardly believe his luck. They talked for a while, and he showed his paintings; some of the lesser ones first. But as Sir Gordon looked at painting after painting, MacGregor's spirits sank. The visitor was politely appreciative, no more. When at last the Doraima portrait was shown, MacGregor knew with certainty that his work hadn't passed the test.

"Interesting," said Sir Gordon, fingering a gray mustache. "A really interesting solution, and I can see the problems you're up against here."

MacGregor made tea, and managed with difficulty to keep up a conversation. Whatever it was the millionaire had come hoping to see, he had not found it, and the artist reacted with disappointment almost to the point of despair. But as he turned to go, Sir Gordon idly picked up the sketch pad with the drawings of the children at the party. Carefully he went through them, then, with the pad, seated himself at the table.

"Now these?" he asked. "They're recent?"

"Yesterday's." MacGregor laughed. "They're the reason I didn't meet you at the Allisons'."

"Obviously," said Sir Gordon, "you found something better to do." He pointed to the Doraima portrait against the wall. "You see the difference? That one's good—good technique, good balance, a fine subject—but it's cold. It lacks emotion. You felt nothing. You had nothing to feel. These"—he took up the drawings again—"these are different. They have feeling. They are alive. Here your hands were directed through eyes altered by your own emotions. You were emotionally involved, you see. You are forever involved. And I think you will never be the same as you were before." He reached in his pocket and found a card. "I must go, young man. I'm glad I came. I'd like to see more of your later work. Look me up when you come to Sydney."

MacGregor walked with him to the Fishermen's Rock at the top of the hill. He had a feeling he might never see Sir Gordon again, for suddenly he knew with certainty that he didn't need him. When he returned, Layoni came racing from the beach and threw herself into his arms. The angel hit him on the head, but he didn't care.

"Thank you! Thank you, Uncle Mac!" cried Layoni. "Thank you for the party!"

"Thank you, little girl," he said. "Thank you for everything." She didn't really understand him, but

he didn't bother to explain it.
(1956)

Rupert Hughes

Mrs. Budlong's Christmas Gifts

The morning after Christmas Eve is the worst morning-after there is. The very house suffers the headache that follows a prolonged spree. Remorse stalks at large—remorse for the things one gave—and did not give—and got.

Everybody must act a general glee which can be felt only specifically if at all. Everybody must exclaim about everything: Oh! and Ah! and How sweet of you! Isn't it perfectly dear? The Very Thing I wanted! How did you EVER guess it?

Christmas morning in the town of Carthage is a day when most of the people keep close at home, for Christmas is another passover. It is Santa Claus that passes over.

People in Carthage are not rich and the shops are not grandiose, and interfamily presents are apt to be trivial and futile—or, worse yet, utile.

The Carthaginian mother generally finds that father has credited the hat she got last fall to this Christmas; the elder brothers receive warm underthings and the young ones brasstoed boots, mits and mufflers. The girls may get something ornamental in their stockings, and their stockings may be silk or nearly; but then girls have to be foolishly diked up anyway, or they will never be married off. Dressing up daughters comes under the head of window-display or coupons and is charged off to publicity.

Nearly everybody in Carthage—except Mrs. Ulysses S. G. Budlong—celebrates Christmas behind closed doors. People find it easier to rhapsodize when the collateral is not shown. It is amazing how far a Carthaginian can go on the most meager donation. The formula is usually: "We had a lovely Christmas at our house! What did I get? Oh, so much I can't remember!"

Mrs. Ulysses S. G. Budlong, however, does not celebrate her Christmases behind closed doors—or, rather, she did not;

for a strange change came over her last Christmas. She used to open her doors wide—metaphorically, that is; for there was a stormdoor, with a spring on it, to keep the cold draft out of the hall.

As regular as Christmas itself was the oh-quite-informal reception Mrs. Budlong gave to mitigate the ineffable stupidity of Christmas afternoon—that dolorous period when one meditates the ancient platitude that anticipation is better than realization.

On Christmas Day Mrs. U. S. G. Budlong took all the gifts she had gleaned and piled them on and around the baby-grand piano in the back parlor. There was a piano lamp there, and it was about as large and as useful as a date palm tree. Then she invited the neighbors in. It looked like hospitality, but it felt like hostility. She passed her neighbors under the yoke, gloated over her guests, and seemed to overgloat her gifts.

She got the gifts though, no question about it. By hook or by crook she saw to it that the bazar under the piano lamp always gleamed.

One of the chief engines for keeping up the display was the display itself. Everybody who knew Mrs. Budlong—and not to know Mrs. Budlong was to argue oneself unknown—knew that he or she would be invited to this Christmas triumph. And being invited rather implied being represented in the loot.

Hence ensued a curious rivalry in Carthage. People vied with each other in giving Mrs. Budlong presents. Not that they loved Mrs. Budlong more, but they loved comparisons less.

The rivalry grew to quite ridiculous proportions, but of course Mrs. Budlong did not care how ridiculous it grew; for it could hardly have escaped her shrewd eyes that people gave her presents in order to show other people that some people needn't think they could show off before other people without having other people show that they could show off too, as well as other people could—or something like that. The psychology must be correct, for it is incoherent.

Mrs. Budlong herself was never known to break any of the commmandments; but in her home her neighbors made flitters of the tenth—against coveting thy neighbor's son and so on.

As Mr. and Mrs. County Road Supervisor Detwiller were walking home from one of these occasions Mr. Detwiller was saying: "Well, ain't Mizzes Budlong the niftiest little gift-getter that ever held up a train? How on earth did we happen to get stung?"

"I don't know, Roscoe. It's one of those things you can't get out of without getting out of town too. We've gone and skimped our own children to buy something that would show up good in Mrs. Budlong's back parlor; and when I laid eyes on it in all that clutter—

why, if it didn't look like something the cat brought in I'll eat it!"

Mr. Detwiller's one and only consolation—and he grinned over it—was:

"Well, there's no use cryin' over spilt gifts; but did you see how she stuck old Widower Clute for that Japanese porcelain vase? She called it vahs!"

"Porcelain?" sniffed Mrs. Detwiller. "Paper-musshay!"

"Well, getting even a paper-what-you-said from old Clute is equal to extracting solid gold from anybody else. He's the stingiest man in seven states. He doesn't care any more for a two-dollar bill than he does for his right eye. I bet she gave him ether before

Mrs. Ulysses S.G. Budlong— the busybody of Carthage, creator and champion of Carthage Christmases.

he would let go."

"Oh, she works all the old bachelors and widowers that way," said Mrs. Detwiller with a mixture of contempt and awe —"invites 'em to a dinner party or two round Christmas marketing time, and begins to talk about how pretty the shops are and how tempting everything she wants is; says she saw an imitation bronze clock at Strouther & Streckfuss that it

almost broke her heart to leave there. But of course she couldn't afford to buy anything for herself now when she's got to remember all her dear friends; and she runs on and on. And the old bach growls, 'Stung again!' and goes to the store and tells Mr. Streckfuss to send Mrs. Budlong that blamed bronze clock she was admiring. That's how she gets things. I could do it myself if I'd a mind to!"

Mr. Detwiller felt that there was more envy than truth in this last remark, and he was rash enough to speak up for justice.

"You could if you'd a mind to? Yep!—if you'd a mind to. That's what somebody said about Shakespeare's plays—'I could 'a' wrote 'em myself if I'd a mind to!" says he; and somebody else said, 'Yes— if you'd a mind to,' he says. And that's about it. Anybody could do what Mizzes Budlong does if they had the mind to; but the thing is, she's got the mind to. She goes after the gifts—and gits 'em! She don't almost git 'em and she ain't just agoin' to git 'em—she gits 'em! And what gits me is how she gits 'em!"

"Roscoe Detwiller, if you're goin' to praise that woman in the presence of your own lawful wife I'll never speak to you the longest day I live!"

"Who's praisin' her? I was just sayin'——"

"Why, Roscoe Detwiller, you did too!"

"Did what? Why, I was roastin' that woman to beat the band!"

"And to think that on Christmas Day, of all days, I should live to hear my own husband, that I've loved and cherished and worked my fingers

to the bone and never got any thanks—other women keepin' two and three hired girls—and after him denyin' his children things to get expensive presents for a shameless creature like that Budlong woman——"

All over Carthage on Christmas afternoon couples were similarly celebrating Mrs. Budlong's annual triumph.

Now, of course Mrs. Budlong did not get all these presents without giving presents—not in Carthage! It might have been possible to bamboozle these people one Christmas, but never another. Mrs. Budlong gave lots of presents. Christmas was an industry with her—an ambition. It had long ago lost its religious significance for her as for nearly everybody else in Carthage.

Even Mr. Frankenstein, the Pantatorium magnate, is one of the most ardent advertisers of Yuletide bargains, while Isidore Strouther and Esau Streckfuss are almost persuaded every December. They might be entirely persuaded if it were not for the scenes they witness in their aisles during the last weeks of shopping and the aftermath of trying to collect from the Carthage husbands.

Mrs. Budlong's Christmas presents were of two sorts—those she made herself and those she made her husband pay for. He was the typical husband who never fails to settle his wife's bills so long as he may raise a row about them until his wife cries and looks like an expensive luxury which only a really successful man could afford. Then he subsides until the first of the next month.

II

Mrs. Budlong's Christmas campaign was undertaken with the same farsightedness as a magazine editor's. Along about the Fourth of July she began to worry and plan. By the second week in August she had her tatting well under way. By the middle of September she was getting in her embroidered doilies. The earliest frost rarely surprised her with her quilts untufted. And when the first snow flew her sachet bags were all stuffed and smelly.

She was very feminine in her sense of the value of her own time. At missionary meetings she would shed tears over the pathetic pictures of oriental women who spent a year weaving a rug that would sell for a paltry hundred dollars and last a mere century or two. Then she would happily devote fifteen days of incessant stitching at something she toted in a sort of drumhead.

In the end she would have compiled a more or less intolerable piece of colored fabric which she called a "bureau cover" or a "drape" or a "throw." It could not be duplicated at a shop for less than one dollar and seventy-five cents, and it would wash, perhaps three times.

Mr. Budlong once figured that if sweatshop proprietors paid wages at the scale Mrs. Budlong established for herself all the seamsters and seamstresses would curl up round their machines and die of starvation the first week—but he never told Mrs. Budlong this. Fancy stitching did not earn much, but it did not cost much and it mysteriously contented her. She was stitching herself to her own home all the time.

The Christmas presents Mrs. Budlong made herself were not all a matter of needle and thread. Not at all! One year she turned her sewing room into a smithy. She gave Mr. and Mrs. Colonel Tisnower the loveliest hand-hammered brass coal-scuttle that ever was seen—and with a purple ribbon tied to it. They kept flowers in it several summers until one cruel winter a new servant put coal in it and completely scuttled it.

The same year she gave Mrs. ex-Mayor Cinnamon a hammered-brass version of a C. D. Gibson drawing. The lady and gentleman looked as if they had broken out with a combination of yellow fever and smallpox, or suffered from enlarged pores or something. And the plum-colored plush frame didn't sit very well on the vermilion wallpaper; but Mrs. Cinnamon hung it over the sofa in the expectation of changing the paper

some day. It stayed there until the fateful evening when Mr. Nelson Chur called on Miss Editha Cinnamon and was just warming up a proposal that had been held over almost as long as the wallpaper, when bang! down came the overhanging brass drawing and bent itself hopelessly on Mr. Chur's cranium! Mr. Chur said something that may have been Damocles—but he did not propose. Mrs. Budlong was weeks wondering why Mrs. Cinnamon was so snippy to her.

The hammered-brass era gave way to the opposite extreme of painted velvet. They say it is a difficult art; and it must be. Mrs. Budlong's first landscape might as well have been painted on the side of her Scotch collie.

Her most finished roses had something of the look of shaggy tarantulas that have fallen into a paintpot and emerged in a towering rage. It was in that velvetocene stratum that she painted for the

Christmas according to Mrs. Budlong meant presents made by her own hand.

Haskell Coffin

church a tasseled pulpit cloth that hung down a yard below the Bible. Doctor Torpadie was a very soothing preacher, but no one slept o' sermons during the reign of that pulpit cloth. Mrs. Budlong was so elated over the success of it, however, that she announced her intention of going in for stained glass. She planned a series of the sweetest windows to replace those already in the church; but she never got nearer to that than painted china.

The painted-china era was a dire era. The cups would break, the colors would run; they never came out what she expected after they were fired. She knew the pigments must suffer alteration in the furnace—but such alteration!

She soon became accustomed to getting green roses with crimson leaves, and deep blue apple blossoms against a pure-white sky; but when she finished one complete set of table china in fifty pieces, each cup and saucer with a flower on it, the result looked so startlingly like something from a medical museum that she never dared give the set away. She lent it to the cook to eat her meals on.

During this epoch, Master Ulysses Budlong, Junior, was studying, at school, a physiology ornamented with a few color pictures representing the stomachs of alcohol specialists. They were meant, perhaps, to frighten children from frequenting saloons during recess or to warn them not to put whisky on their porridge.

It was at this time that Mrs. Budlong spent two weeks' hard labor painting Easter lilies on an umbrella jug. When it came home from the furnace her husband stared at it and mumbled:

"It's artistic—but what is it?"

Little Ulysses shrieked: "Oh, I know!" And darting away he returned with his physiology opened at one of those gastric sunsets; and—well, it was this that impelled Mrs. Budlong to a solemn pledge never to paint china again—a pledge she has nobly kept.

From smeared china she went to that art in which a woman buys something at a store, pulls out half of it and calls the remnant drawnwork. A season of this was succeeded by a mania for sofa cushions. It fairly snowed sofa cushions all over Carthage that Christmas; and Yale, Harvard and Princeton pillows appeared in homes that had never known even a nightschool alumnus.

There ensued a sober period of burnt wood and a period of burnt leather, during which excited neighbors with a keen sense of smell called the fire department out three times and the board of health once. And now Indian heads broke out all over town; the walls looked as if a shoemaker's apron had been chosen for the pennant.

There were other varied spasms of manufacture, each of them fashionable at its time and foolish at any time. But, foolish soever, Mrs. Budlong was fair. A keen sense of sportsmanship led her to give full notice to such people as she planned to honor with her gifts. She knew how embarrassing it is to receive presents from one to whom no present has been sent; and she made it a point of

Somewhere between firing and final product, Mrs. Budlong's china underwent drastic changes.

Calls returned promptly meant "be prepared" at all times to those being called upon.

honor somehow to forewarn her prospective beneficiaries betimes. Her favorite method was the
classic device of pretending to let slip a secret. For
instance:

"Yesterday morning, my dear, I had the
strangest experience. It was just ten o'clock. I
remember the hour so exactly because for the last
few days I have made it a rule to begin work on your
Christmas present just at ten——Oh! but I didn't
mean to tell you! It was to be a surprise. No; don't
ask me—I won't give you an inkling; but I really
think it will please you. It's something you've
needed for such a long time."

And she left the victim hopelessly to writhe from
then on to Christmas, trying alternately to imagine what gift was impending and what would be

an appropriate countergift to give Mrs. Budlong.

III

In more ways than one Mrs. Budlong kept Carthage on the writhe. Christmas was merely the
climax of a ceaseless activity. All the year round she
was at work like yeast alert in a soggy dough.

She was forever getting up things. She was one of
those women who return calls on time—a little
ahead, in fact. That made it necessary for you to
return hers earlier. If you didn't she called you up
on the telephone and asked you why you hadn't.
You had to promise to come over at once, or she'd
talk to you until your ear was welded to the telephone. Then, if you broke your promise, she called

you up about that. She got in from fifty-two to one hundred and four calls a year, where one or two would have amply sufficed for all she had to say.

It was due to her that Carthage had such a lively social existence— for its size. Once she fell ill and the people felt as passengers might feel when a street car is suddenly braked back on its haunches—all Carthage found itself wavering and poised on tiptoe and clinging to straps; and then it sagged back on its heels and waited. Mrs. Budlong was the town's motorman—or "motorneer" as they say in Carthage. Before she was up she had invitations out for a convalescent tea; and everybody said: "Here we go again!"

If strangers visited Carthage Mrs. Budlong counted them her clients from the moment they arrived. Of course the merely commercial visitors she left to the hackmen at the station, but friends or relatives of prominent people could not escape Mrs. Budlong's well-meant attentions. It was sometimes embarrassing when relatives appeared—for everybody has somewhere concealed some relatives he is perfectly willing to leave forever in concealment.

Mrs. Alex—pronounced Ellick—Stubblebine never forgave Mrs. Budlong for dragging into the limelight some obscure cousins of her husband's who had drifted into Carthage to borrow money on their farm. Mrs. Stubblebine was always bragging about her people—her own people, that is. Her husband's people, of course, after all, were only Stubblebines, while her maiden name was Dilatush— and the Dilatushes, as everybody knew, were related by marriage to the Tatums.

These were Stubblebines that came to town, however. Mrs. Stubblebine could hardly slam the door in their faces, of course, but she would fain have locked the doors after them. She would not even invite them out on the front porch. She told them the back porch was cozier and less conspicuous. Then Mrs. Budlong had to call up on the phone and sing out in her telephoniest cheer:

"Oh, my dear, I've just this minute heard you have guests—some of your dear husband's relatives. Now they must come to me to dinner tomorrow. Oh, it isn't the slightest trouble, I assure you! I'm giving a little party anyway. I won't take no for an answer."

And she wouldn't. Mrs. Stubblebine fairly perspired excuses; but Mrs. Budlong finally grew so suspicious that she had to accept or leave the impression that the relatives were burglars or coun-

terfeiters in concealment. And they were not—they were pitifully honest.

The result was worse than she expected. Mr. Stubblebine's cousin was so shy that he never said a word except when it was pulled out of him, and then he said: "Yes, ma'am!" And not another syllable.

In Carthage when you are at a dinner party and you don't quite catch the last remark, you don't snap "What?" or "How?" or "Wha' jew say?" Whatever your home habits may be, at a dinner party or before company you raise your eyebrows gracefully and murmur: "I beg your pardon?"

Mr. Stubblebine's rural cousin, however, said "Huh?"—like an Indian chief trying to scare a white general. And he was perfectly frank about the intimate process of mastication.

And when he dropped a batch of scalloped oysters into his watchpocket he solemnly fished them out with a souvenir after-dinner coffee spoon having the Statue of Liberty for a handle and Brooklyn Bridge in the bowl.

The wretch's wife was so nervous she talked all the time about people the others had never seen or heard of. And she wasn't ashamed of what she was chewing either. And she said she "never used tomattus."

Mrs. Stubblebine would have felt much obliged to Fate if she had been presented with an apoplectic stroke, but she had to sit the dinner out. And from what she said to her poor husband afterward you would have thought he picked out those relatives just to spite her, when, as a matter of fact, he had always loathed them and regretted them; and the next day he borrowed money to lend them and send them back to the soil.

Mrs. Budlong had constituted herself an entertainment committee for all sorts of visitors. If a young girl came home from boarding school with a classmate the real hostess had hardly time to show her to the spareroom and say, "This is the bathroom round here; watch out for the steps—and if the water don't run just wait——" when the telephone would go br-r-r-r! And there would be Mrs. Budlong brandishing an invitation to a dinner party that evening.

When the supply of guests ran low she would visit the sick. If a worn-out housewife slept late some morning to catch up, Mrs. Budlong would hear of it and rush over with a broth or something. It is said that old Miss Malkin got out of bed in spite of the doctor's orders, just to keep from eating more of Mrs. Budlong's renowned wine jellies.

In Carthage one pays for the telephone by the year. The company lost money on Mrs. Budlong's wire. She was an indefatigable telephonist. She would spend a week-end at the instrument while the prisoner at the other extreme of the wire shifted from ear to ear, sagged along the wall, postponed household duties, made signals of distress to other members of the family and generally cursed Mr. Alexander Graham Bell.

Three wall telephones were changed to table 'phones on Mrs. Budlong's account, and Mrs. Talbot had hers put by the bed. She used to nap while Mrs. Budlong talked, and trained herself to murmur "Yes, dear!" at intervals in her sleep.

By means like these, Mrs. Budlong kept Carthage more or less under her thumb. Carthage squirmed, but it could not crawl out from under. This, then, is the history of how the thumb was removed for good and all. It was Mrs. Budlong that removed it. Carthage could never have pried it up.

And the thumb came off because it grew popular.

Hitherto Mrs. Budlong had never been truly popular. People were afraid of her. She was a whipper-in, a true social bush-beater—driving the populace from cover like partridges. She would not let the town rest. The merchants alone admired her, for she was the cause of much buying of new shoes, new hats, new clothes, fine groceries, olives, Malaga grapes, salted almonds, raisins, English walnuts and other things one eats only at parties. She was the first woman in Carthage who ever gave a luncheon and called it breakfast as, years before, she had been the first hostess to give a dinner at any time except in the middle of the day. She was also the first to say "Come to me" when she meant "Come to our house." It had a Scriptural sound

and it was thought shocking till Carthage grew used to it.

It was due to her that several elderly men were forced into their first evening dress. They had thought to escape through life without that ordeal. Old Clute would have preferred to be fitted for a pine box and would have felt about as comfortable in it. He tried to compromise with the tailor on a garment that would serve as a "Prince Albert" by day and a "swaller-tail" by night; but Mr. Kweskin could not manage it, even though he struggled valiantly.

So Mr. Clute blamed Mrs. Budlong for yet another expense. Husbands all over town were blaming Mrs. Budlong for running their families into fool extravagances. Mothers were blaming her for dragging them round by the nose and never letting them rest. They never dared trust themselves about the house in a wrapper, for Mrs. Budlong might happen in as like as not—rather liker than not. Everybody in town resentfully obeyed Mrs. Budlong. Roscoe Detwiller, for his part, wanted to organize a Homekeepers' Union, and strike.

And then, just as the town was fermenting for revolt, Mrs.

Another gown, another Budlong affair.

Budlong came into a lot of money.

IV

That is, Mr. Budlong came into a lot of money. Which meant that Mr. Budlong would be permitted to take care of it while his wife got rid of it. One of those relatives very common in fiction, and not altogether unknown in real life, finally let go of her money at the behest of her impatient undertaker; and the Budlongs had the pleasure of seeing the glorious news of their good fortune in big headlines in the Carthage paper. It was the only display Mr. Budlong ever received in that paper without paying for it—except for the time when he also ran for mayor on the opposition ticket and was referred to in letters an inch high as "Candidate Nipped-in-the-Budlong."

Now the cornucopia of plenty had burst wide open on the front porch. It seemed as if they would have to wade through gold dollars to get to their front gate *when* the money was collected.

And now it was Mrs. Budlong's telephone that rang and rang. It was she who was called up and called up. It was she who sagged along the wall and shifted from foot to foot, from elbow to elbow and ear to ear.

After living in Carthage all her life she was suddenly, as it were, welcomed to the city as a distinguished visiting stranger. And now she had no need to invite people to return her calls. They came spontaneously. Sometimes there were a dozen calling at once. It was a reception every day. There were overflow meetings in the room that Mrs. Budlong called Mr. Budlong's "den." It was a place where she kept the furniture she did not dare keep in the parlor.

People who had never come to see her in spite of her prehensile telephone dropped in to pay up some musty old call that had lain unreturned for years. People who had always come formally, even funereally, rushed in as informally and with as devouring an enthusiasm as old chums. People who used to run in informally now drove up in vehicles from MacMulkin's livery stable; or if they came in their own turnouts they had the tops washed and the harness polished, while the gardener and furnaceman who drove had his hat well-brushed, was not allowed to smoke, and was also urged to sit up straight and keep his foot on the dashboard.

People who had been in the habit of devoting a day or two to cleaning up a year's social debts, and walked down the streets dropping doleful calls like wreaths on headstones, walked in unannounced of mornings. It was now Mrs. Budlong that had to keep dressed up all day. Everybody accepted the inevitable invitation to have a cup of tea, until the cook struck. Cook said she had "conthracted to cuke for a small family, not to run a continurous bairbecue!" Besides, she had to answer the doorbell so much she couldn't get her hands into the dough before they were out again.

And dinner was never ready. The amount of tea consumed, and bakery cake, and the butter, began to alarm Mrs. Budlong. And Carthage people were so nervous at taking tea with a millionairess that they kept dropping cups or setting them down hard.

Mrs. Budlong had never a moment, the whole day long, to leave the house; and she suddenly found herself without a call returned. She had so many invitations to dinners and luncheons that her life became a hop, skip and jump.

During the first ecstasy of the good news Mrs. Budlong had raved over the places she was going to travel to—Paris—now pronounced Paree—Westminister Rabbi, Vienna, St. Mark's, the Lion of Lucerne! She talked like a handbook of Cook's Tours. To successive callers she told the story over and over until the rhapsody finally palled on her tongue. She began to hate Paree, St. Mark's and the Lion of Lucerne. All she wanted to do was to get out of town to some quiet retreat—for Carthage was no longer quiet. It simmered to the boiling-over point.

Once it had been Mrs. Budlong's pride to be the social leader of Carthage. Now that her husband was worth—or to be worth—a hundred thousand dollars, Carthage seemed a very petty parish to be the social leader of. She began to read New York society notes with expectancy, as one cons the Baedeker of a town one is approaching.

She lay awake nights wondering what she should wear at Mrs. Stuyvesant Square's next party and at Mrs. Astor House's sociable. She fretted over the choice between taking a letter from her church to St. Bartholomew's, or to Grace, or St. John the Divine's. And all the while she was pouring tea for the wives of harnessmakers and druggists, dentists and grocers! All the more reason for not appearing before them in the same clothes incessantly. With a dinner or a reception or a tea or a ball every night, her two dressy-up dresses became so familiar that she could hardly afford to trot them round much more. And she could hardly afford to get new ones; for, after all, she had not come into the money. She had just come at it or toward it or, as her husband began to say, "up against it."

Mr. Budlong was kept on such tenterhooks by lawyers with papers to sign, titles to clear, executors and executrices to consult, and waivers, deeds, indentures and things, that he had no time for his business.

Like housemaids' knee and painters' colic is millionaires' melancholia. And the Budlongs were enduring the illness without entertaining the microbe.

It is almost as much trouble to inherit money nowadays as to earn it in the first place. Mr. Budlong was confronted with such a list of postmortem debts that must be prepaid for his deceased Aunt Ida that he almost begrudged her her bit of very real estate in Woodlawn. And they began to think that funeral monuments were in bad taste if ostentatious.

They had always accounted Aunt Ida a hard-fisted miser before, but now she began to look like a slippery-palmed spendthrift. They began almost to suspect the probity of the poor old maid. Worse yet,

The changes brought about by the money-yet-to-come caused Mr. Budlong to despair that it ever would.

they feared that some later will might turn up, bequeathing all her money to some abominable charity. She had been addicted to occasional subscriptions during her lifetime.

The Budlongs themselves were beginning, even at this distance from their money-to-be, to suffer its infection, its inevitable reaction on the character. Those who live beyond their means joyously when their means are small become small themselves when their means get beyond living beyond. The Budlongs began to figure percentages on sums left in the bank or put out on mortgage. They began to think money—and money is money, large or small. Mrs. Budlong began to feel that she had been unjust to Aunt Ida. What she had called miserliness was evidently prudence and thrift, and some other pleasant sounding virtues.

When it came to the point of deciding that she must give a large dinner to wipe off a number of social obligations all at once, and she found that the olives, the turkey, the Malaga grapes, the English walnuts and a man from the hotel to wait on table would total up twenty-five dollars or so, she found herself figuring how much twenty-five dollars would amount to in twenty-five years at compound interest.

She grew frantic to be quit of Carthage—to rub it off her visiting list. Unconsciously her motto became Cato's ruthless *Delenda est Carthago*; but she could neither wipe Carthage off her map nor free her feet from its dust. Her husband's business required him yet a while. Even to close it up took time; and he would not and could not borrow on Aunt Ida's estate until he was sure it was his.

All the while, however, the festival reveled on. People in Carthage, to whom New York was an inaccessible Carcassonne, were now planning to visit Mrs. Budlong there at the palatial home she had described. Some frankly told her they were coming. Wealth took on a new discomfort.

Mrs. Sally Swezey afflicted the telephone with gossip: "Mrs. Talbot was saying yesterday, my dear, so many people have threatened to visit you in your home on Fifth Av'noo, that you'll have to hang hammocks in your yard."

That was the discomfort of the morrow, however. Today was busy enough. One morning she was called to the telephone by the merciless Sally Swezey with a new infliction. There was something almost ghoulish in Mrs. Swezey's cackling glee as she sang out across the wire:

"We're all so glad that the next meeting of the progressive euchre club is to be at your house."

Mrs. Budlong's chin dropped. She had quite forgotten this. Sally chortled on:

"And, say, do you know what?"

"What?"

"Everybody says you're going to give solid gold prizes, and that even the booby prize will be handsomer than the first prize was at Mrs. Detwiller's."

"Ha-ha!" laughed Mrs. Budlong in a tone that sounded just like the spelling.

Mrs. Budlong's wealth seemed to be accepted as a sort of general legacy. All Carthage assumed to own it and to enjoy it with her. Her walls rang with the hilarity of her neighbors; but her laughter took on more and more the sound of icicles snapping from the eaves of a shed.

She became the logical candidate for all the chief offices in clubs and societies and circles. She suddenly found herself seven or eight presidents and at least eleven chairwomen. The richest woman in town heretofore was Mrs. Foster Herpers, wife of the pole-and-shaft manufacturer. He owned about half of the real estate in the county, but his wife had to distill money out of him in pennies. With a profound sigh of relief she resigned all her honors and privileges in Mrs. Budlong's favor.

Being president chiefly meant lending one's house for meetings, as well as one's china and tea and sandwiches, and being five dollars ahead of everybody else in every subscription. Mrs. Budlong was panicstricken with her own success, for there is nothing harder to handle than a dam-break of prosperity.

Worse yet, Mr. Budlong was ceasing to be the meek thing of yore. Every day was beginning to be the first of the month with him.

It was well into November when he flung himself into a chair one evening and groaned aloud:

"I don't believe Aunt Ida ever left any money! If she did I don't believe we'll ever get any of it. And if we do I know we'll not have a sniff at it before January. One of the lawyers has been called abroad on another case. We've got to stay in Carthage—at least over Christmas."

"Christmas!" The word crackled and sputtered in Mrs. Budlong's brain like a fuse in the dark. The past month had been so packed with other excitements that she had forgotten the very word. Now it blew up and came down as if one of her own unstable Christmas trees had toppled over on her, with all its ropes of tinsel, its eggshell splendors and its lambent tapers.

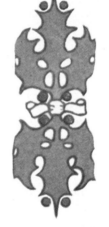

V

First, Mrs. Budlong felt amazement that she could have so ignored the very focus of her former ambition. Then she felt shame at her unpreparedness. She caught the evening paper out of her husband's lap to find the date. November ninth and not a Christmas thing begun! Yet a few days and the news-stands would apprise her that Christmas was coming; for in the middle of November all the magazines put on their holly and their Santa Clauses, as women put on summer straw hats at Easter. Mrs. Budlong's hands sought and wrung each other as if in mutual reproach. They had been pouring tea and passing wafers when they should have been Dorcasing at their Christmas tasks. And now, at the eleventh hour, she found herself without a single present tatted or painted or hammered or fired. It had been left for her husband—of all people—to warn her that Christmas was imminently approaching!

If he had been a day later the neighbors would have anticipated him as well as the magazines. The Christmas idea seemed to strike the whole town at once. Mrs. Budlong became the victim of her own classic device of pretending to let slip a secret. The townswomen shamelessly turned her own formula against her.

Mrs. Detwiller met her at church one Sunday and said:

"Yesterday morning I had the most curious presentiment! I remember the hour exactly because I've been making it a rule to begin work on your Christmas present every morning at——Oh, but I didn't intend to let you know. No, I won't tell you what it is. But I can't help believing it's just what you'll need in New York."

Myra Eppley, with whom Mrs. Budlong had never exchanged Christmas presents at all, but with whom an intimacy had sprung up since Mrs. Budlong came into the reputation of her money, had the effrontery to call her up on the telephone one morning and say:

"Would you mind telling me, my dear, the shade of wallpaper you're going to have in your New York parlor, because I'm making a——Oh—but will you tell me?"

Poor Mrs. Budlong almost swooned from the telephone. She did not know what the color of her wallpaper would be in New York. She did not know that she would ever have wallpaper in New York. She only knew that Myra Eppley, too, was calling her "My dear!" Myra Eppley also was going to give her a Christmas present—and would have to be given one.

Mrs. Budlong had received fair warning, but she

felt just about as grateful as a wayfarer feels to the rattlesnake that whizzes: "Make ready for the coroner!"

Next, Mrs. Chur—Editha Cinnamon that was, for she had finally landed Mr. Chur in spite of the accident, or because of it—called up to say:

"Oh, my dear, my husband wants to know what brand of cigars your husband smokes; also, deary, what size bath-slippers do you wear?"

When Sally Swezey came to the progressive euchre fight at Mrs. Budlong's she noted with joy that her hint had borne fruit. The prizes were, indeed, of solid gold. Mr. Budlong did not learn it until the first of the following month, when the bill came in from the jewelry store.

As if she had not done enough in forcing solid gold prizes on Mrs. Budlong, Sally had to say:

"I'm just dying to see your back parlor, my dear, this next Christmas afternoon! It has always been a sight for sore eyes; but this Christmas it will be a perfect wonder, for I do declare everybody in town is going to send you something nice."

This conviction was already chilling Mrs. Budlong's marrow. Of old she would have rejoiced at the golden triumph; but now she could only realize that if everybody in Carthage sent her something nice it was because everybody in Carthage expected something nicer. And she had not tatted or smeared or hammered a thing! As usual, too, the excess of work on hand had a paralyzing effect. At a time when she should be half done she could not even begin!

The realization that Christmas was near shocked the normally over-active Mrs. Budlong into in-action.

VI

Days and days went by in a stupor of hopelessness. Thanksgiving came and the Budlong turkey might as well have been a crow. In desperation she decided to make a tentative exploration of the shops now burgeoning with Christmas.

The length of the list sent her to the cheaper counters, but she was not permitted to browse among them. At Strouther & Streckfuss' Mr. Strouther said with reeking unctuousness:

"Vat makes Mees Bootlonk down here amonkst all this tresh? Come see our importet novelties."

And he led her to a region where the minimum price was MBBA-BDJA, which meant that it cost twelve dollars and twenty-five cents and could be safely marked down to twenty three dollars and seventy-five cents.

She eluded him and got back to the 25¢ realm, only to be apprehended by Mr. Streckfuss, who beamed:

"Ah, nothink is here for a lady like you are! Only fine kvality suits, such a taste you got!"

By almost superfeminine strength she evaded purchasing anything there. She went to other shops, only to be haled to the expensive counters. Storekeepers simply would not discuss cheap things with the millionairess-elect.

Sympathy was last on Mr. Budlong's list.

She crept home and threw herself on her husband's mercy. He had none and she lighted hard. It was the first of December; and, in addition to his periodical rage, Mr. Budlong was working himself up to his regular pre-Christmas frenzy, when he felt poor and talked poorer in order to keep the family in check.

His face was a study when he heard his wife's state of mind. He delivered the annual address on Christmas folly, that one hears from fathers of families all round the world at this time.

"Christmas has quit being a sign of people's affections!" Mr. Budlong thundered. "It has become a public menace. It's worse than Wall Street. Wall Street is supposed to have started as the thermometer of the country's business, and now it's gone and got so goldurn big that the thermometer is makin' the weather! When Wall Street feels muggy it's got to rain; and the sun don't dare shine without takin' a peek at the thermometer first off.

"Christmas ain't any longer an opportunity to show good will to your neighbors. It's a time when you got to show off before your neighbors. You women make yourselves and us men sick the way you carry on all through December! And the childern!—they're worse'n the grown-ups!

"Old-fashioned Christmas was like old-fashioned circuses—mostly meant for the childern. Nowadays circuses have growed so big and so improper that nobody would dast take a child to one—or, if you do, they get crazy notions.

"When I was a boy, if I got a drum and a tin horn I was so happy I couldn't keep quiet; but last Christmas little Ulie cried all day because he got a 'leven-dollar car when he wanted an areoplane big enough to carry the cat over the barn.

"This Christmas Trust business ought to be investigated by the Gov'ment and dissolved! Talk about your tariff schedules! What we need is somebody to pare down this Christmas gouge. It's the one kind of tax you can't swear off.

"And as for you—why, you're goin' daffy! Other years I didn't mind so much. You spent a lot of time and some money on your annual splurge; but I will say you took in better'n you gave. But now you're on the other side of the fence. These Carthage women have got you on the run. You'll have to give 'em twice as good as they send or you're gone. You're gone anyway! If you gave each one of 'em a gold platter, full of diamonds, they'd say you'd inherited Aunt Ida's stinginess as well as her money!"

Mrs. Budlong went on twisting her fingers.

"Oh, of course you're right, Ulie. But what's the use of being right when it's so hateful? All I can think of is that everybody in town is going to give me a present! Everybody!"

"Can't you take your last year's presents and pass 'em along to other folks?"

"Everybody would recognize them and I'd be the talk of the town!"

"You're that anyway, so what difference would that make?"

"I'd rather die!"

"You'd save a lot of money and trouble if you did just that."

"Just look at the list of presents I must give!" She handed him a bundle of papers. He pushed up his spectacles, put on his reading glasses and snorted:

"Say! What is this—the town directory?" He had not read far down the list when he missed one important name. "You've over-looked Mrs. Alsop."

"Oh, her! I've quarreled with her. We don't speak—thank Heaven!"

"It would be money in your pocket if you didn't speak to anybody. Gosh!" he slapped his knee. "I have an idea! Stop speak-ing to everybody."

"Oh, don't be silly. This is serious."

"But I'm not being silly. I'm quite serious."

VII

Ulysses S.G. Budlong was a man fertile in re-sources and unbending in their execution. Other-wise he would never have attained his supremacy as the town's leading hay-and-feed merchant.

"It's as easy as falling off a log!" he urged her. "You women are always spatting about something. Now's your chance to capitalize on your spats."

"Men are such im-boo-hoo-ciles!" was Mrs. Budlong's comment as she began to weep.

Her husband patted her with a timid awkward-ness, as if she were the nose of a strange horse.

"There! there! We'll fix this up fine! What did you quarrel with Mrs. Alsop about?"

"She told Sally Swezey—and Sally Swezey told me—that I used my Carthage presents to send to relatives in other towns."

"She flattered you at that," said Mr. Budlong un-consolingly. "But don't you ever dream of for-giving her until after Christmas."

Mrs. Budlong was having such a good cry and en-joying the optical bath so heartily that her grief became very precious to her. It suggested what a beautiful thing grief is to those who make a fine art of it. She smiled wet-liddedly.

"There is nothing in your idea, Ulie; but I have a good one. I'll announce that I can't celebrate Christmas due to our great grief for Aunt Ida!"

"Great grief!" Mr. Budlong exclaimed. "Why, you couldn't have celebrated Aunt Ida's finish more joyous without you'd serenaded her in Wood-lawn with a brass band!"

"Ulysses Budlong! You ought to be ashamed of yourself for saying such a thing!" But she suddenly heard—in fancy—the laugh that would go up if she sprung such a pretext. She gave in.

"We'll have to quarrel with somebody, then; but what excuse is there?"

"Women don't need any real ex-cuse. You simply telephone Sally Swezey that a certain person told you—and you won't name any names—that she had been making fun of you, and you'd be much obliged if she never spoke to you again!"

"But how do I know Sally Swezey has been making fun of me?"

"Oh there ain't any doubt but what everybody in the town of Carthage is doing exactly that!"

"Ulysses Budlong! Why, how can you talk so?"

"If people without money couldn't make fun of people with, what consolation would they have? Anyway, it's not me but the other folks you're supposed to quarrel with. You spend an hour at that telephone and you can get the whole town by the ears."

"But I can't use the same excuse for everybody."

"You'll think up plenty, once you put your mind to it." And with that a perfect excuse came in pat—came in howling and flagrant.

Ulysses, Junior, burst into the room as if he had forgotten the presence of the door. He was yelping like a coyote and from his tiny nose an astonishing amount of blood was spouting.

"What on earth is the matter?" the startled mother gasped. "Come here to me, you poor child —and be careful not to bleed on the new rug."

Ulysses' articulation was impeded with sobs and the oscillations of three semi-detached teeth that waved in the breeze as he screamed:

"Little Clarence Detwiller licked me. And I on'y p-pushed him off his sled into a puddle of ice-wa-wa-water; and he attackted me and kicked my f-f-fa-face off!"

Mr. and Mrs. Budlong were so elated with the same idea that they forgot to console their heart-broken offspring with more than Mr. Budlong's curt: "First teeth anyway—saves you a trip to the dentist." He nodded to his wife. "Just the excuse we were looking for."

"Sent direct from Heaven!" nodded Mrs. Budlong. "You call up Roscoe Detwiller this minute and say his son has criminal tendencies, ought to be in jail, and will undoubtedly die on the gallows. Then he won't speak to you tomorrow."

"You bet he won't! He'll just quietly do to me what his boy did to Ulie. No, my dear; you tell all

ly!—Boys will be——Oh, I'm sorry you punished him. He's such a sweet child!——Oh, don't think of it! I'm sure it was all Ulie's fault. It will teach him next time. He's so rough! ——Oh, how awfully sweet of you! Good night, dear."

She stuck the receiver on the hook and then looked for a hook to hang herself on. Her eyes were shifty with shame as she mumbled: "I couldn't get a word in edgeways. She apologized."

"She apologized!" Mr. Budlong roared. "And you ate out of her hand! And you were going to show me what a coward I——Butter wouldn't have melted ——Say, why didn't you kiss her?"

Mrs. Budlong was suffering a greater dismay than remorse.

"What d'you suppose that cat of a Clara Detwiller's going to do?" she moaned. "She's going to make her boy send Ulie a nice Christmas present! And now we shall be obliged to buy one for Ulie to give to him!"

"Well, of all the——Oh, you're a great manager, you are! You call up a woman to get rid of giving one Christmas present and now you've got to give two! Here! Where you going?"

"I'm going to that 'phone and tell Mrs. Detwiller what I think of her."

"You keep away from that 'phone. Before you could ring off again her husband would have a Christmas present wished on to me!"

that to Mrs. Detwiller yourself."

Mrs. Budlong tossed her head with an air of fine contempt.

"What cowards men are!—always shielding themselves behind women's skirts! Well, if you're afraid, I'm not. I'll give her the biggest talking to she ever had in her born days!"

She rose with fortitude and started to the telephone—sneered at it and glared at it. Her husband stood by her to support her in the hour of need. He watched her ask for the number and snap ferociously at the central. Then she felt panicky again and held the transmitter to him appealingly. He waved her away scornfully. She set her teeth hard and there was grimness in her tone as she said: "Is this you, Mrs. Detwiller? Oh, yes, thank you; I'm very well. I wanted to tell you——Oh, yes, he's well too. But what I started to say was——Yes; so Ulie says! Yes, right in the face!—Oh, of course——Natural-

VIII

The next morning Mrs. Budlong arose from dreams of finding bargains after all. She felt a spirit in her feet that led her to the Christmas-window street; but the crowds and the prices and the servility of the salesfolk drove her out again.

On her laggard way home she saw Sally Swezey, lean and lanky, and reminding her of a flamingo. Mrs. Budlong remembered her husband's suggestion. She made a quick resolution to do or die. Her cheek was cold and white, and her heart beat loud and fast; but she tried to set her chin into a square jaw, and she passed Sally Swezey as if Sally Swezey were a lamp-post by the curb—just a common lamp-post by the curb, and nothing more.

She heard Sally's gush of greeting stop short, as if someone had turned a faucet in her throat; she heard a gulp; then she heard a strangled silence. Then she heard Sally call her name tentatively, tenderly, reproachfully. Then she heard no more.

And she knew no more until her feet somehow carried her home; but she had hardly time to flop into a rocker and utter a prayer of gratitude and pride for having been vouchsafed the courage to snub a Carthaginian before—br-r-rr!—the terrible telephone was rattling at her. She knew just who it was and she braced herself to meet one of Sally's sharp-tongued assaults. Sally said, in part:

"Oh, you poor darling dear, is that you? And how are you now? I was so alarmed for you. You looked so ill and worn; and——Aren't the Christmas crowds awful this year? And nothing fit to buy, and such prices! And——You must be just worn out! You really must spare yourself; for do you know what you did, dearest? You went right by me without seeing me or answering me. Yes, you did. I was so startled that I didn't have brains enough to run after you and assist you home. I'm so glad you got there alive. I do hope you're feeling better; and I'm so ashamed of myself for letting you go all that way alone in that condition. Can you ever forgive me?"

When Mr. Budlong came home for luncheon Mrs. Budlong told him the whole story. He glared at her with an I-give-you-up expression and growled:

"And when she said all that what did you say?"

"I don't know," Mrs. Budlong faltered. "All I know is she's coming over this afternoon with a lot of that wine jelly I gave her the recipe for."

"Well, what do you intend to do this time?" Mr. Budlong demanded. The skeptic in his tone stung her to revolt. She could usually be strong in the presence of her husband. She looked at least like Mrs. Boadicea as she said:

"I intend to tell her what you told me to. And I will accept no apologies—none whatever."

When Mr. Budlong came home to dinner she avoided his gaze. She confessed that she had changed her program. She hadn't the heart to insult Sally, she had admitted she was a bit dizzy and qualmish, and she had—Well, she—

Mr. Budlong finished for her fiercely:

"I know! You ate a lot of her wine jelly, told her she was a love and kissed her goodby; and would she excuse you from coming to the door, because you were still a little wobbly!"

Mrs. Budlong looked at him in surprise. "She told you."

"Nah! I haven't seen her."

"Then how on earth did you ever guess?"

"It was my womanly intuition!" he snarled; and that evening he went downtown and sat in the hotel lobby for a couple of hours. He usually did this anyway—in summer he sat on the sidewalk; but this evening he did it with a certain implication of escape. On the way home Mr. Budlong was busy with schemes. His mind turned again to his son.

In a smallish town a growing boy is an unfailing source of *casus belli*. As an inciter of feuds there was something almost Balkan or Moroccan about Ulysses Budlong, Junior. Nearly every day he had come charging into the house with bad news in some form or other. Some rock or snowball he had cast,

Made of snips and snails and puppy dog tails, full of the devil, all boy—such was Mrs. Budlong's darling little Ulie.

Carthage, no longer subjugated, was overwhelming.

with the most innocent of intentions, had gone through a window or a milk wagon or somebody's silk hat. Or he had pulled a small girl's hair or taken the skates away from a helpless urchin. He had bad luck, too, in picking victims with belligerent big brothers.

Mr. Budlong recognized these desperado traits and he fully expected Ulysses, Junior, to make him the father of a convict. Suddenly now despair became hope. Let Mrs. Budlong capitalize her spats; he would promote Ulie's. The Affair Detwiller had turned out badly, but Mr. Budlong would not yield to one defeat. He watched eagerly for the next misdemeanor of his young hopeless. He relied on him to embroil, as it were, all Europe in an international conflict.

The dove of peace, however, seemed to have alighted on Ulysses' shoulder. He even began to go to Sunday-school—the Methodist this year, because they had given the largest cornucopias in town the Christmas before. He talked nothing but golden texts; Mr. Budlong began to think he would one day be the father of a clergyman.

Meanwhile Mrs. Budlong grew belligerent again. She snubbed people right and left, and they imputed it to absent-mindedness. She failed to go to the dinner party the Teeples gave in her honor, and she sent no excuse. This was the unpardonable sin

in Carthage and the Budlong chairs sat vacant through the dinner.

Mrs. Teeple, however, assumed that she was ill and sent her cut flowers. And she hoped Mrs. Budlong would feel better soon.

A few days later Mrs. Budlong's pet Maltese kitten was done to nine deaths at once by the Disneys' fox terrier. She mourned the kitten, but there was consolation in the thought that she could now cut the Disneys off her list; but before she could get the kitten decently interred in the back yard Mrs. Disney was at the front door. She flung her arms round Mrs. Budlong and wept, declaring that she had resolved to give the murderous terrier to a farmer, and had already sent away for a pedigreed Angora to replace the Maltese. It would arrive the day before Christmas.

As if that were not enough for one day, in the afternoon Myra Eppley called. She saw Mrs. Budlong at an upper window and waved to her as she came along the walk. When the cook arrived upstairs, like a grand piano moving in, Mrs. Budlong said in an icy tone:

"Not at home."

"But I told her you was. And she seen you there at the windy."

"Not—AT—home!"

"But I'm afther telling her——"

Mrs. Budlong could be as stern as steel with her husband or her servants. She cowed Brigida into lumbering downstairs with the message. Mrs. Budlong went to the window to watch her victim's retreat.

Instead, she heard a light patter of footsteps and Myra Eppley hurried into the room.

"Oh, my dear, are you ill? Pardon my coming right up, but I was so worried for fear you were—but you aren't, are you?"

Mrs. Budlong was at bay. She glared at the intruder and threw up her chin. Myra Eppley stared at her aghast.

"Why, you aren't mad at me, are you?"

Mrs. Budlong smiled bitterly and said nothing. Myra Eppley shrilled:

"Why, what have I done?"

As a matter of fact, what had she done? All that Mrs. Budlong could think of was her husband's suggestion for a war with Sally Swezey. She spoke through her locked teeth:

"It's not what you've done but what you've said!"

"Why, what have I said?"

"You know well enough what you've been saying behind my back, and you needn't think that people don't come and tell me! I name no names; but I know—oh, I know!"

Now, of course, everybody says things behind everybody else's back that nobody would care to have repeated to anybody. Through Myra Eppley's memory dashed a hundred caustic comments she had made on Mrs. Budlong. She blushed and sighed, turned away and closed the door after her, like the last line of an elegy.

A surge of triumph swept over Mrs. Budlong. Success at last!

Then the door opened and Myra Eppley reappeared with a look of angelic contrition.

"I hardly know what to say," she said. "Of course I must admit I did rather forget myself. It was at the last meeting of the progressive euchre club. Before you came everybody was criticizing you for having solid gold prizes when they were at your house. They said it was vulgar ostentation. I didn't say anything for the longest time; but finally, when they all said your money had gone to your head and asked me, 'Hasn't it?' I admit I did mumble: 'It seems so.' But it is only what everybody else says all the time, and I assure you I didn't really mean it. Of course nobody can behave just the same after they are a millionaire as they did before. But I am awfully fond of you; and—and——"

"It was most disloyal!" said Mrs. Budlong. "And to think that, after tearing me to pieces behind my back, you could come and call on me!"

It was a fine speech; but after she heard herself say it Mrs. Budlong had a sinking feeling that if she herself had never called on anybody she had criticized she would have stayed at home all her life. Myra Eppley took another line, however. She threw herself on Mrs. Budlong's mercy—and if

Cut flowers were not easily obtained in late December—but Mrs. Budlong deserved only the best.

Mrs. Budlong boasted of one thing more than another it was her mercy.

"I have just been at the church," said Myra, "helping to decorate it for Christmas week; and I was hanging up a big motto, Peace on Earth, Good Will to Men!—and I think it ought to apply to women too. I grovel in apology and I pray you to forgive me. You can't refuse to forgive me when I ask you to, can you?"

Mrs. Budlong wanted to but could not, and the two women fell about each other's neck and exchanged tear for tear. As they were comfortably dabbing each other's tears from their cheeks and sniffing their own, and laughing cozily after the rain, Myra Eppley giggled and sobbed all at once:

"The idea of your thinking I didn't just love you—and me working my fingers off making a Christmas present for you!"

IX

The day before the Day Before Christmas found them in a panic. The Day Before found them grimly resolved to stand siege.

On the blessed Eve they sat by their cheerless fire-front and stared at the packages that had been pouring in all day long. The old postman had staggered under the final load and hinted so broadly for a Christmas present that he got one—the first breach in their solemn resolve. They had excepted

Guardians of gratitude—Christmas gifts were the only way Carthaginians could express their true feelings.

Ulie, of course, from the embargo; but they had been in such a flurry that they had postponed him until they forgot him entirely.

The doorbell was rung so incessantly throughout the evening that the cook sat on the hall stairs to be handy. She piled the packages up on the piano until they spilled off. The piano lamp was gradually sinking beneath the encroaching tide. Presents were brought in wagons, carriages, buggies, carts, by coachmen, gardeners, cooks, maids, messenger boys, and children of all ages and dimensions.

On any other occasion Mrs. Budlong would have been running here and there, peeking into parcels and restraining her curiosity until the next day, out of sheer joy in curiosity. Now she opened never a bundle. She could only think of the morrow, when all of these donors found that reciprocity had gone down to defeat! The Budlongs avoided each other's eyes. They were thinking the same thing.

The strain endured until it tested their metal to the breaking point. When two enormous packages were brought to the door by the Detwillers' hired man Mrs. Budlong broke out hysterically:

"I just can't stand it!"

"Hell!" roared Mr. Budlong. "Get on your hat and coat, we'll go buy everything left in town!"

X

Holiday bargains in Carthage were not brilliant. After being pawed over for several weeks they were depressing indeed. When the Budlongs strode into Strouther & Streckfuss' it was nearly ten o'clock at night. The sales-wretches, mostly pathetic spinsters of both sexes, were gaunt and jaded, and held on to the counters. Even Messrs. Strouther and Streckfuss had the nap worn off their plushy sleekness.

When the Budlongs made their irruption they were not received cordially. Word had gone abroad that the Budlongs were buying all their Christmas presents out of town. They must be, for they bought none in. This treachery to home industry was bitterly resented. Then Budlong galvanized everybody with a cry like a flash of lightning:

"I want to buy nearly all you got. Get busy!"

It was too late to select. Mr. and Mrs. Budlong, with their lengthy list in hand, sprinted up one aisle and down another, pointing, prodding, rarely pausing to ask, "How much?" but monotonously chanting: "Gimme this! Gimme that! Gimme two of these! Gimme six of them! Gimme that! Gimme this! Gimme them!"

They bought glaring garden jars and ghastly vases, and scarfpins that would disturb the peace, silly bisque figurines for mantels and what-nots, combs and brushes that would raise the hair on end instead of allaying it, oxidized-silverized leadpencils, buttonhooks, toothbrushes, nail files, cuticle knives, pincushions, inkstands, paperweights, picture frames, bits of lace and intimate white things with ribbons in them—Mr. Budlong turned away as his wife priced these.

The town clock was striking midnight as the Budlongs dragged themselves home. There was much yet to be done. Parcels must be opened, price tags removed, gifts done up in pink tissue paper and gold twine, cards must be inscribed and inserted, and the parcels rewrapped and addressed. The Strouther & Streckfuss driver had been hired at an exorbitant cost to sit up and deliver the many gifts. The horses had not been consulted.

The Budlong parlor was soon a hideous scene. The husband would open a bundle and sing out:

"Who's this big, immense, pink-and-purple cuspidor for?"

"That's a jardineer! It's a return for that horrible cat those odious Disneys are going to inflict on me. Here's the card, it's all ready."

She handed him a holly-wreathed pasteboard on which she had written: "For Mr. and Mrs. Disney, with most affectionate Yuletide greetings."

She indited cards as fast as she could think up phrases. She sought for variety, but the effort was maddening. She wrote: "Very merry Christmas." "The merriest of Xmases." "A merry, merry Yuletide." "A Happy Christmas and a Merry New Year." "Christmas Greetings." "Xmas Greetings." "Yuletide Greetings." "Wishing you a——" "With loving wishes for——" "Affectionate——" And so on, and so on, and on and on. She scribbled and scrawled until slumber drugged her and her pen went crazy. When she fell asleep she was writing: "A Yuly New-mas and a Hapry X-Year to Swally Sezey!"

The delivery man pounded on the door and, wild-eyed, Budlong let him in from the night. The man whispered that he'd have to start at once if he was to make the rounds before his horses laid down on him.

Mr. Budlong called his wife but she did not answer. He shook her and she proceeded to roll off the chair on to a divan. Mr. Budlong straightened her out and stared at her in hopeless pity. He stared at the chaos of bundles. He seized the pack of cards from his wife's fingers and ran here and there jabbing pasteboards into bundles haphazard.

This is how Sally Swezey acquired an ashtray lined with cigar bands and why old Mr. Clute was amazed to receive a card offering him Mrs. Budlong's "loving and affectionate greetings!" He was

more amazed when he opened the bundle. There were ribbons in it!

As fast as Mr. Budlong stuffed cards into bundles he loaded bundles into the driver's arms as if they were sticks of wood. The driver stacked them up in his wagon. He made seven trips in all, and some of the cards fell out and were stuck in still longer bundles than before; but both the driver and Mr. Budlong were too sleepy to care. The driver finally mounted his seat and called out from the dark:

"Say, Mr. Budlong, where do I leave these packages—on the porch or do I ring the bell?"

"Chuck 'em through the windows! The more glass you break the better I'd like it!"

"All right, sir. Get ap! Good night, sir—and wishing you a Merry Christmas!"

"Merry——" said Mr. Budlong, reaching for a rock; but even the stones were frozen to the ground and the driver escaped. As Mr. Budlong closed his front door a thread of crimson broke out in the east.

An hour or so later Ulie awoke and sat up with a start. To his intense confusion he bumped his little skull on the bottom of his bed. He realized that he had fallen asleep in his ambush. He peered forth to see if he had snared Santa Claus.

The stockings were empty.

With a shriek of disappointed rage Ulie dashed into his parents' room to protest.

Their bed was empty.

He ran through the house, stumbled downstairs and into the back parlor. His father was snoring on a mattress of Yuletide parcels. His mother was curled up on a divan under the smoking piano lamp. Her hands were clutching strands of gold cord, and her hair was pillowed in pink tissue paper. She was burbling in her sleep.

Little Ulie bent down to hear what she was saying. He made out faintly:

"Mishing you a Werry Muschris and a Nappy Hoosier!" (1911)

May Wilson Preston

Gene Coughlin

The Wonderful Merry-Go-Round

There would never again be a November dusk like this one. Soft and satin-smooth, it had settled on the four of us as we turned away from the scrubby bank of Cicero Creek and our exploration of hillocks that, we knew, were Indian burial mounds, no matter what the older inhabitants of Tipton, Indiana, had to say. Our elders contended that Indians definitely had never lived nor even camped in our part of the state; they insisted that the nearest authentic mounds were at Tippecanoe, which was several hours distant on the swift electric cars of the Union Traction Company.

We didn't intend to argue with our elders, but we had the evidence to prove they were wrong. Jody O'Beirne had a piece of flint that must have been an arrowhead; Bob Glass had uncovered something like a clamshell that had served some brave as a spoon; Tommy O'Toole kept fingering a dozen beads that undoubtedly had graced the swanlike throat of a beautiful princess. I carried a clump of feathers, a little moldy and decomposed, stained with something that had to be war paint. To make the outing complete, we had located a tree loaded with papaws, supersweet in their green and yellow jackets. We used plenty of red haws, tiny and tart, to take away the cloying effect of the papaws, and we were a quartet of surfeited nine-year-olds when we turned into what could be called the outskirts of Tipton.

On Mill Street several bonfires of sycamore and maple leaves had been touched off. We loitered in the low-hanging smoke, coughing but happy in the knowledge that the odor would cling to coats and sweaters and make us smell like frontiersmen who hunkered nightly over campfires.

We had plenty of time to beat it to the unguarded grade crossing, but we waited for the Lake Erie & Western freight, its oil-burning headlight jiggling in the gloom, its fireman painted in bronze as he hurled coal into the bright maw of the firebox. The downdraft of smoke brought tears to our eyes, but still we were able to call off the initials and the numbers of the boxcars and gondolas as they clattered past, and also identify Mr. Higgins, the conductor, standing on the rear platform of the caboose.

"Goin' to the railhead," Jody announced solemnly. "Pushin' steel west, night and day!"

We nodded, knowing the train was going south and then only to Indianapolis, forty miles away. Jody had certain privileges in such matters, since his father was a passenger conductor on the road, a circumstance that kept us from mentioning in his presence that many people said the initials L. E. & W. really meant "Leave Early and Walk."

There was a Panhandle freight just pulling out of the siding down toward The Junction, but we didn't wait for that; we were loyal to the Lake Erie, and the Panhandle was part of the Pennsylvania system.

"Well," Tommy O'Toole sighed, "best head for home."

The others turned on East Street, but I didn't. I had special permission to stop off at the coal yard and walk home with my father when he locked up at six o'clock. I hadn't mentioned it, but Bob Glass sensed my destination.

"You going to see The Invention?" he asked quickly, and I said, "I might. For a minute."

"We could go along," Jody suggested. "Just for a minute."

"Not tonight," I said. "It's nearly done, and you know how people are. If somebody got ahold of the patent——"

Whether for work or pleasure, horses were a common sight early in this century, indispensable to daily living.

"That's right." They all nodded, and we parted. My route took me past the power-and-light plant and up the wagon track between the coal bins and the big barn that, occasionally, contained ice that was retailed by the Coughlin Coal & Ice Company.

Old George, the huge Percheron, heard my feet crunching the cinders, and turned around to look, moving the wagon just as Delt McGill, the deliveryman, flung up a scoop of coal, some of which hit the wagon side.

"Hold still, you big galoot," Delt yelled, "or I'll whack you!"

I had two handfuls of red haws and crab apples. George made a vacuum of his massive muzzle, swooshed them down and thanked me by nudging me with his nose, knocking off my cap and leaving a glob of froth on the shoulder of my Mackinaw. I headed for the coal office.

The office was a frame box about nine feet square, with small windows on three sides and a row of sliding panes on the side next to the scales. My father would slide back a window to hand out a receipt to Delt or to receive money from him after he had made a delivery. He did the same thing usually to converse with cronies or customers who called in person; not that he was inhospitable, but there was almost no room at all for adult visitors in that little office, what with The Invention and its original wooden model, plus a desk, one chair, a little potbellied stove and a padlocked cabinet containing drawings and blueprints and other papers having to do with the patent.

I stood up on tiptoe on the beam between the scale floor and the sliding panes, and the first thing I saw was The Invention, which was to make us rich. As usual, it looked mean and ominous to me, its black and ugly hulk taking up more than the corner originally assigned it. It had gear teeth that gleamed and flickered in the uneven light of the kerosene lamp hung from the low ceiling.

I had a vague idea of what it did, or was supposed to do, but I considered it vastly overrated for its size, weight and the attention it got and the effort it had cost my father, who had made all of its parts by hand. And yet it held a tremendous fascination for me. It would accept a little nut a half-inch square that was fed to it, let it rattle down a slot all the way to its innards and then, after my father grunted and turned a crank, it would eject the nut with threads cut on the inside.

"Of course," my father would explain after a demonstration, "that was just a rough example of what this Nut Tapping Machine can do. Driven by steam, this machine will tap, or thread, more nuts in an hour than any other machine on the market today can do in a day."

When he talked like that I admired The Invention, and it was a pleasure to help wipe it with an oily rag. But there were times when I resented it as a selfish monster, content to sit there on its cast-iron bottom and settling that section of the office deeper and deeper into the Indiana soil. This resentment came after I had overheard aunts and uncles, among others, remark that The Invention, through the patent attorney, was devouring money that we could have used for food and clothing, with no end in sight.

My father was sitting at the desk, his derby on the back of his head, using his left hand to stroke the full mustache that was in need of another application of walnut oil to disguise the graying roots and tips. He wore the Celluloid collar, Size 17, and the sleeve garters that were part of his business costume, along with the glasses that came from the five-and-ten and which he did not need but affected because most Tipton merchants wore spectacles as symbols of solidity.

I eased quietly through the door just as he started writing the receipt for Mrs. Board's half ton of coal that Delt McGill was loading. He wrote a beautiful flowing hand, much better than I could ever hope to achieve with the Palmer Method. What made his penmanship even more distinctive was that he held the pencil between the stubs of the first two fingers of his right hand. He had lost parts of these fingers while switching bars on the Chicago & Alton. I was at his elbow as he signed, "Owen J. Coughlin."

"What does the J stand for?" I asked.

He started a little, took off the glasses, and his dark-brown eyes twinkled as he answered my question with one of his own. "What does the D stand for in John D. Rockefeller?"

I admitted I didn't know, and he nodded. "An initial," he said, "is something any man can own. Rich or poor."

"But rich men have more initials than poor men," I pointed out. "Look at J. P. Morgan——"

"And F. W. Woolworth," he put in. "I think that what happens is a man starts out with just a plain first name, like John or Jim, and then, when he becomes a success, he adds an initial or two to make his signature more dignified, I suppose. The J doesn't stand for anything. But it might come in handy."

He winked and looked at The Invention. I followed suit, and we were both dreaming when Old George walked onto the scales, making the office shake. My father weighed the coal, handed Delt the receipt and told him to put horse and wagon away and go home after the delivery. We were wiping the machine with oiled rags when the big bell boomed in St. John's steeple, two blocks away, and we stood erect, reciting the *Angelus* to ourselves. He clapped his hat back on his head, and I shook him a bit with another question. "We didn't get the church contract this year, did we?" I asked.

He stopped the breath that would have extinguished the lamp and gave me a quick look. "Who told you that, Eugene?"

I told him, "Lots of people."

But my main informant had been Delt McGill, who had been bitter in giving the reason. He blamed some of the wealthy farmers who made up the bulk of the congregation of St. John's Catholic Church, where the three of us Coughlin boys served Mass and where we rented a pew. Delt said these farmers had got into the habit of driving their grain wagons to town and loading their own coal at our yard. But they had the sly

Around 1911, coal delivery was a slow business, yet a lucrative one—if the big contracts came through.

habit of using only the fork, thus getting the big lumps of the soft coal and leaving the small pieces and slack for the town customers served by Delt. My father had chided them gently at first, pointing out that *he* had to pay for *all* the coal and slack in a car and that they should take some of the fat along with the lean. But they had persisted until the matter finally became an issue, and the self-serving farmers were told that the Coughlin Coal & Ice Company didn't want their business any longer.

Some of these ex-customers were trustees of the church and, when it came time to award the contract for coal to be used in church, parsonage and school, gave the plum to an outsider whose bid was very little lower than ours. Since several carloads were involved, the contract meant the difference between a success and a failure for a year for my father's business.

The key rattled in the lock, and he tried the office door twice before he said softly, "No, Eugene, we didn't get the contract. What all did you do today, and where did you go?" I told him, and the tension lifted as we walked home.

Round steak, a quarter's worth, was sizzling in two skillets, and the potatoes were boiling on the cookstove. Joe, eleven, and John, thirteen, were at the kitchen table, Joe writing a composition and John figuring collections on his paper route. My mother reigned in her rocking chair near the oven. She was slight and pretty, a gentlewoman whose folks—the Mullarkeyes—had owned hundreds of acres of lush farm land near Tipton.

A talented pianist, Ellen Bridget Mullarkey had been sent to a conservatory of music in Indianapolis, and there had been talk of a concert career until, on a visit to a cousin in Joliet, Illinois, she had met Owen at a Switchmen's Ball and married him with the stipulations that he give up railroading before he lost any more fingers or any limbs and become a merchant in

Tipton. Now she was content with her husband, her three sons, an upright piano she played occasionally and a firm belief in the basic goodness of her fellow men. Her gray eyes widened as I told about our exploration of the Indian burial mounds, and she was properly horrified when I displayed my tuft of feathers. The others of our group gathered around and were sure the stain was war paint, and I went to bed happy, full of steak and potatoes and the conviction that The Invention would take care of all of us.

This mood continued through Thanksgiving and well into December. And then, a couple of weeks before Christmas, everything went wrong. People stopped buying coal—or stopped paying for it—and hints were dropped to the effect that "Santa might be late this year—if he gets here at all." I still had high hopes that I would get a Flexible Flyer sled and maybe a pair of ice skates—until one night, when I was supposed to be asleep upstairs, I heard my father and mother murmuring in the kitchen. He told her the patent attorney had to make further search in Washington and that would take more money, and he didn't know where it was to come from. Her assurance that the Lord would provide seemed sort of faint.

On top of that I was suddenly notified to stay away from the office for a few days—some ultrasecret work had to be done on The Invention.

The outlook was very bleak when, two days before Christmas, the three of us were doing the dishes, and John asked if I had written my letter

The letter to Santa Claus gets harder to compose as the writer grows older and the legend loses credibility.

to Santa Claus yet this season.

"No," I said, "and I don't think I'll write one this year. Won't do any good."

I was too cautious to say I no longer believed in him. I had my doubts, but I was willing to give him a chance—if business had been a little better.

"Well, now," John said. "Old Santa has been pretty good to you and to all of us, Eugene. He'd feel hurt if you forgot him all at once."

I gave in and wrote the letter which followed a pattern that, apparently, had been handed down in the family. I don't recall being prompted; it just seemed to take form, and it went:

Dear Santa: I know you are very busy, and I will not take much of your time. I want you to take care of the poor boys and girls first and see that they get warm clothes and food. If there is anything left, I would like a Flexible Flyer sled and a pair of ice skates. There is a piece of mince pie and coffee for you on the kitchen stove. Thank you, Santa.

Christmas Eve I went to bed early and had a restless night, as befits a martyr. It seemed that I had just dozed off when the sound of tinkly music filled the house, and the three of us rushed downstairs. All the lights were on, the base burner was a cherry red, and in the warm glow glittered the most fascinating toy I had ever seen.

It was a merry-go-round, complete with concealed music box and a ringmaster with curled mustache, tipping his high silk hat every time he passed the tiny ticket box. Boys and girls rode the prancing horses; ladies and gentlemen sat sedately in the circling tubs, all dressed in clothing of every hue. At first glance it seemed huge on its packing-box platform although it turned out to be about thirty inches in diameter. I don't know how long I crouched in wonderment before I figured it out that this was the reason for my being barred from the premises. I looked at my father, beaming and wiggling his good fingers, a sure sign of excitement, and my mother, in her dressing gown, holding his hand in both of hers.

When it was my turn to wind it up I announced, "Santa Claus didn't make this! He couldn't!"

"Well, then, Eugene," my mother said, "who did make it?"

I found out I couldn't talk. I pointed at my father, and he swung me up higher than his great shoulders, and when he rubbed the bristles of his mustache

The first glimpse of the tree and toys—Christmas in all its glory—is overwhelming.

against my cheek they were moist from a sudden tear—I guess it was. Then he ordered us gruffly to get ready for Mass, which we did.

Usually on Christmas our various gangs took turns visiting homes and inspecting gifts, but we hardly got out of the house that day. Jody and Bob and Tommy, plus pals of Joe and John, descended on us to watch the merry-go-round. Each demanded the privilege of winding it up.

Grownups came too, and Mr. Glass, who made regular trips to Chicago, paid the supreme compliment. "You can't get anything like that at Marshall Field, even," he said. "And if you could, I bet they'd want $100 for it!"

Getting ready for bed that night, the three of us wondered at the skill and the patience represented in the masterpiece, and John asked me, "Are you still mad at The Invention?"

I said I didn't see what that had to do with the merry-go-round, and he explained. "Well, pop never had any manual training, never knew how to do anything with his hands but pull switches and give signals. He didn't know the first thing about carving or carpenter work until he got the idea for The Invention four, five years ago. Then he taught himself how to do things with

wood and iron. He carved that wooden model down at the office, and he cut the metal parts for the working model. So, when he had to do something extra special for this Christmas, he knew how to do it. He made a merry-go-round that the best carpenter in Indiana couldn't make."

I understood his point, and I relented somewhat in my attitude toward The Invention. But it was still on probation until, on New Year's Day—my birthday—I got the Flexible Flyer after all! (The skates could wait.)

After that I never entertained a mean thought regarding The Invention. It never did make us rich; it didn't even get into production. When, seven years later in 1918, the power-and-light company took over the coal yard, it still squatted there, sinking into the soil and smiling benignly as it showed its teeth.

In those seven years, as far as I was concerned, it was just as much a member of the family as Old George, who hauled the coal faithfully even when hay and oats were hard to come by, or Prince, the collie, who sometimes figured we were having too many meatless days and would deposit not one, but two freshly killed chickens on the back porch. (1961)

CHRISTMAS SCENES OF THE PAST

Author Unknown

Christmas at the White House 100 Years Ago

Christmas at the White House one hundred years ago was a remarkably gay and festive occasion. Thomas Jefferson was then President, and hospitality was dispensed at the mansion with a freedom which found no subsequent parallel until the arrival of Mr. Roosevelt, whose ideas on that subject seem to be remarkably like those of the author of the Declaration. Then, as now, every agreeable stranger who "dropped in" at the White House was invited to make himself at home, and it is a matter of historical record that as many as fifty persons at a time were sheltered under the Executive roof-tree—though how it was managed nobody can say for sure!

Contemporary, and still-extant, descriptions of the White House in those days, its family and its domestic doings, make it easy to give a fairly accurate account of the way in which Mr. Jefferson and his household spent Christmas Day one hundred years ago. For one thing, it is known that his two daughters, Mrs. Randolph and Mrs. Eppes, came up to the capital to spend the holiday, bringing with them their husbands, both of whom were Virginia Congressmen; and Mrs. Randolph also brought her six children, who were their grandfather's very particular pets.

Jefferson introduced the first children into the White House. He was a widower, having lost his wife twenty years earlier; but his daughter, Martha Jefferson Randolph, spent the bulk of six years with him in Washington, and her sister, Mrs. Eppes, came now and then, bringing her children, so that there was no lack of family atmosphere. Mrs. Randolph, indeed, was the mother of the first child ever to be born in the White House, the happy event occurring in the winter of 1805-6.

Mrs. Randolph cared little for social pleasures, in the fashionable sense of the term, and could not be persuaded to assume the responsibilities of mistress of the White House. She was a very motherly sort of woman, and devoted to the children, for whom a schoolroom was fitted up at the west end of the second floor, she herself acting as teacher. Upon Mrs. Dolly Madison devolved the serious duties of entertaining, and it was she who presided at the Christmas dinner, as well as on all other formal occasions.

To make the picture of the Christmas vivid, one must recall, in imagination, the striking figure of Jefferson—tall and distinguished-looking, with red hair and spindle-shanks, his face much freckled, his hands and feet large, and his teeth noticeably fine and perfect. Extremely simple in his habits, and unaffected in manners, he often

Jefferson had his own brand of "open door policy."

Family ties were important to Jefferson, a widower.

market on the morning of that Christmas Day, a century ago, and picked out the geese for the dinner. He was fond of good cheer, and liked to exercise his judgment in the choice of a bird or a joint. Nowadays the White House steward, rather than the President, attends to all that sort of business. But those were days of greater simplicity in ways of living, and it was not considered (as now would be the case) that the President was derogating from his dignity in purchasing his own provisions.

It is chronicled that on the afternoon of that day Mrs. Madison took four of Mrs. Randolph's little girls to ride, and on the way back, over the old Georgetown Road, she bought boughs of mistletoe from an old Negro, decking the carriage with them. Doubtless gifts were exchanged—for the Jeffersons, being Virginians, believed, as the New England Adamses did not, in celebrating Yuletide in this and other ways—but, of course, the principal event was the dinner, which was held in the state dining-room, the private dining-room being too small to accommodate all the guests.

There was, indeed, quite a large party. Besides the President and his two daughters and their husbands, there were Mr. and Mrs. Madison, half a dozen other persons of distinction, and a number of relatives and neighbors from Virginia—not to mention at least six children, for each of whom a special cranberry tart was provided. Mr. Jefferson never forgot the little ones, and the tart, placed at each small plate, was considered indispensable to the happiness of the occasion.

The requisite illumination was furnished by eight large silver candelabra which stood on the table, holding dozens of wax candles, and the viands were dispensed with the aid of a dozen Negro servitors.

offended people by the frankness with which he expressed his opinions, which were certainly not modeled after anybody else's.

The White House, one hundred years ago, stood in the midst of a rough-looking and uncultivated area, which as yet had not been brought under subjection by the skilled gardener. Its principal entrance was at the south front (now closed to the public), and its interior had a rather bare and unfurnished appearance. The East Room was used only as a laundry, and the furniture of the other apartments was scanty.

Mr. Jefferson himself went to the old Marsh

John Adams established state dinners at the White House, their stiff formality delighting his highly conventional soul, but Thomas Jefferson abolished them. He preferred to entertain in a different style, and, being a very hospitable man, he made everybody welcome to his board. As above stated, he took great pleasure and pride in selecting viands for his own table, and those who dined with him were always sure of enjoying good cookery, along with first-rate wines.

There were no clergymen present at that Christmas dinner one hundred years ago. Jefferson, as is well known, had no affinity for the cloth. But, on the other hand, painters, Bohemians, adventurers, and deadbeats generally, foreign and domestic, were at home in the White House during his rule. He was easily imposed upon, and people whom he scarcely knew would quarter themselves upon him for indefinite periods. One family of casual visitors, from Europe, stayed ten months.

Presided over by Mr. Jefferson the Christmas feast could not be otherwise than a jolly affair. Of everything eatable there were huge quantities— and all of the viands were placed on the table at one time, the appropriate fashion of those days. The guests were encouraged to stuff themselves, and choice wines, in both decanters and bottles, were freely offered. Thomas Jefferson, a temperate man, abstemious for

those bibulous days, when it was considered almost a duty for a gentleman to get intoxicated after dinner, enjoyed a social glass, and was by no means lacking in the convivial impulse.

The heavy drinking, however, was not begun until after the ladies, at a signal from Mrs. Madison, had left the table. Then a huge punch-bowl was brought on, and toasts were proposed, each one requiring to be duly honored with a brimming glass. Truly, what wonderful constitutions and capacities the gentlemen of those times must have had!

It may be taken for granted, then, that on this occasion, at all events, the men preserved a reasonable measure of sobriety; for presently they were obliged to join the ladies in the Oval Room, which is known to-day as the Blue Room, where much gaiety followed. There were round games, forfeits and various other frivolous pastimes for the grown-ups, the children having been sent to bed. By ten o'clock in the evening it was all over, and the guests were taking their departure—those of them, that is to say, who were not staying in the house.

Life was much simpler in those days than now, and late hours for entertaining were unknown. Such hospitality as the President dispensed was generous, but without attempt at any sort of display. Mr. Jefferson's salary was only $25,000 a year, and out of it he paid his own Secretary, as every President did up to Jackson.

It is worth mentioning that Dolly Madison presided at no fewer than fourteen Christmas dinners at the White House during the Jefferson and Madison administrations. One such celebration was missed because Mr. Jefferson spent Yuletide that particular year at Monticello, and another was missed (in 1814) because the British had driven Mr. and Mrs. Madison out of their official residence. (1903)

Tray upon tray of delectable fare—the Christmas feast.

René Bache

Christmas with Ben Franklin

Christmas, 1785, was probably the most enjoyable holiday Benjamin Franklin had ever spent. By that time, after his return from France, he had settled down to a peaceful existence in Philadelphia, and, realizing that now his struggles and anxieties were at an end, was enabled to devote his time to pursuing, in a leisurely way, the occupations most congenial to him, in the bosom of an affectionate family, cared for by a loving daughter, and finding special pleasure in the society of six grandchildren, four of whom had been born during his last absence abroad.

Marie Antoinette

The gentle sentiments belonging to Yuletide were always held dear in that household, and Franklin's children and grandchildren had been brought up to celebrate the festival with the giving of gifts, the hanging-up of stockings for Kriss Kringle to fill, and all the other modes of merrymaking appropriate to the old-fashioned holiday. This, too, notwithstanding the fact that his earliest years were spent in Boston, where (as was the case in all of New England in those times) Christmas was almost wholly neglected, the great feast day in that part of the country being Thanksgiving.

Richard, the baby, was only a year old in the winter of 1785. His sisters, Deborah and Eliza, were four and eight respectively. Louis was six, William twelve, and Benjamin Franklin Bache, the eldest (who had been abroad with his grandfather for eight years), was sixteen years of age. It had been unreasonably expected of Louis, by the way, that he would be a girl, and his mother had written to Doctor Franklin for a list of the various names of Marie Antoinette to choose from; but the child turned out to be a boy, and was named after the King instead of after the Queen of France.

So many young people in the house must have made it a pretty lively Christmas. Doctor Franklin's wife had been dead for some years, and his household was managed by his daughter Sally, who, with her husband, Mr. Richard Bache, lived with him. The dwelling, on Market Street, which was fairly spacious, had been planned by the philosopher himself before he went for the second time to England as agent for several of the Colonies, and was built by his wife during his absence. After his return he added a library to it, which was his own particular "den" and snuggery.

The house stood on a patch of land which ran through from Market nearly to Chestnut Street, and in front of it was a considerable area of lawn, with a great mulberry tree, under which Franklin delighted to sit in warm weather, receiving his friends and drinking with them a cup of tea. He had acquired this habit of sitting outdoors during his long residence in Paris. There were flowerbeds of the old-fashioned kind, and a vegetable patch; but the latter, it seems, was eventually wiped out, for Doctor Franklin writes (in May, 1786): "Considering our well-furnished and plentiful market as the best of gardens, I am turning mine into grassplots and gravel walks." The market to which he refers was a wooden, shedlike structure extending along the middle of Market Street for several "squares," and endured, in a shabby and much-decayed condition, up to

Louis XVI

After the church service, which probably lasted a couple of hours, worshipers headed home to Christmas dinner.

within approximately twenty-five years ago.

Such were the surroundings in the midst of which Franklin spent the Christmas of 1785, and, with the data accessible, it is not difficult to fill in the outlines and to compose a reasonably accurate picture of the holiday as it was enjoyed by the famous philosopher and his family.

The sage himself was an early riser, and breakfast was served at 7:30 o'clock, by which time the young folks had emptied their stockings—veritable "horns of plenty," filled for the occasion by their mother—and exchanged felicitations on the gifts received. These cheerful formalities past, the church bells rang out their notification of a more serious duty to be done, and all the members of the family put on their best "bib and tucker" and made ready for church.

The Franklin residence was on the south side of the street, between Third and Fourth. Christ Church, where the family had a pew, was only a few "squares" away, on the west side of Second Street above Market. One can readily picture in imagination the little procession churchward on that Christmas morning—the Doctor walking ahead, holding a child by either hand, his daughter and son-in-law following, and the other young people bringing up the rear. With due solemnity, doubtless, did they file into the sacred edifice and walk up the aisle to the ninth pew from the front, on the left, which to this day is occupied by some of Franklin's descendants.

It is a fact worth mentioning incidentally, that, when George Washington came to live in Philadelphia, as President, and rented the house at No. 190 Market Street, a block below the Franklin residence, he attended Christ Church, and it was proposed to put him in the front pew on the left, moving everybody else one pew back. This plan would probably have been carried out but for an objection by Sarah Bache, who said that it "would be just as preposterous as if a person should take an occupied corner house, and thus force everybody to move up." Accordingly, Washington was obliged to accept the use of Bishop White's pew, which was the third on the left of the aisle, six pews ahead of the one belonging to the Franklin family.

Doctor Franklin used sometimes to go to sleep at church, and possibly he did so on this Christmas Day, during the sermon of the rector, Bishop White. The service, which was that of the Church of England, was simple and bare of rites, as was usual in those days, with no exhibition even of cross or candles. Probably it lasted a couple of hours, and the children were glad enough when it was over. As for the philosopher himself, he did not attend divine wor-

ship merely for the sake of an outward show of respectability. He believed that it was right and useful to go to church. Notwithstanding an impression to the contrary that is somewhat widespread in these days, he was a profoundly religious man—though nonsectarian—and an earnest believer in an overruling Providence.

By the time the family had reached home again the hour for dinner had nearly arrived, and soon the guests, of whom there were a number, began to appear. Including the family, about thirty people sat down to table; for Doctor Franklin kept open house, his hospitality being always lavish, and the most distinguished persons who happened to pass through Philadelphia—statesmen, men of letters, and strangers of note in other walks of life—usually called on him, and were invited to break bread with him.

On such an occasion Franklin did much of the talking, and his daughter most of the carving. She was a fine-looking woman, and wore on her head a dainty white cap, while about her neck and shoulders a white fichu was folded becomingly. It was a huge roast of beef, solid and juicy, that she carved, and she stood up to do it, tucking up her sleeves to get them out of the way of the gravy. There were other meats on the table, including fowls, nearly everything being put on at once, after the manner of those times. The waiting was done by Negroes. Many people in the North owned slaves at that period, but the Doctor had manumitted the few he once possessed.

Half a dozen of the guests, perhaps, were men of noteworthy distinction—one or two of them Frenchmen whom Franklin had met while he was abroad. They all found much enjoyment in listening to the quaintly humorous remarks of the sage, who, while caring little for the more substantial pleasures of the table, dearly loved to talk to people who knew how to appreciate his discourse. He was a man with a good many hobbies, and when fairly set going on one of them he could keep on indefinitely. But he was so witty and amusing that his many companions were always delighted with

Franklin's varied interests, homespun philosophies and quick wit made him a popular part of any gathering.

his conversation, no matter what the topic on which he chose to speak.

The furniture of the table included only a few articles of silver, such luxuries being rare in those days. There was a set of china (a few of the cups and saucers are still in existence) which had been given to the Doctor by his great friend and admirer, Madame Helvetius, widow of a famous Frenchman whose house in Paris he had frequented. The knives were of steel, and the forks of the same metal, with three tines—the height of elegance at that period, and so precious that they were kept, together with the knives, in a

pair of inlaid mahogany boxes made for them.

For supplementary refreshments there were mince pies and plum-pudding, both compounded by Sally herself; for at that epoch it was a matter of course that a good housewife should understand and practice all the domestic arts, including that of cookery. When the pudding was brought on brandy was poured over it and ignited, burning with a lambent and appetizing flame; but for the special benefit of the Doctor himself had been prepared a dish of "floating island"—a favorite dessert on state occasions. And, to embellish the feast at its conclusion, there were almonds, Madeira nuts, raisins, oranges and lady-apples—these last not very good to eat, but rosy-cheeked and pretty.

For drinkables there were on the table Madeira wine, port and curacoa; also ale, home-brewed by the hostess. In later years, when the brewing business had become a great commercial industry, it was cheaper and easier to buy ale in casks than to make it at home, and thus, like many another ancient occupation of the good wife, the manufacture of fermented beverages departed from the household. But at that period "home-brewed" was still a luxury, and Sally Franklin's hand was not least expert in its production.

For no great length of time did the gentlemen, on this festive occasion, linger over the walnuts and wine after the ladies and children had left the table. The host, with his son-in-law and the other men, soon retreated to the library, where he took advantage of the opportunity to exhibit to them his electrical apparatus—a veritable marvel in those days, you may well believe—and to administer a mild shock or two to those of them who were inclined to submit to the operation. Two of the machines which he used still exist, and are in a tolerable state of preservation.

About this time, probably, a couple of Negroes brought in the ingredients for a punch, together with a most curious punchbowl, which was one of the good Doctor's favorite possessions. It had the shape of a cask, though made of china, and held about two gallons. The ingredients were put in through the bunghole of the cask, and the punch was drawn off into glasses by means of a spigot. It is hardly necessary to say that the punch was a rum punch—rum being the favorite drink of the time—though fortified with a liberal modicum of brandy. Doubtless it was strong.

Franklin knew how to compound a first-rate punch. One can imagine him reciting for the entertainment of his guests, as he began to mix the punch, a bit of verse which he himself had composed on the subject:

Boy, bring a bowl of china here!
Fill it with water, cool and clear.
Decanter with Jamaica ripe,
And spoon of silver, clean and bright;
Sugar, twice fin'd, in pieces cut,
Knife, sieve and glass in order put;
Bring forth the fragrant fruit, and then
We're happy till the clock strikes ten.

The Doctor took but little of the punch himself, though it is not unlikely that some of his guests, tempted by the appetizing quality of his brew, may have become a trifle mellow. It was the fashion to drink hard, and none the worse was thought of a man who took a drop more than was good for him. Besides, this was Christmas.

Though in his youth he had been extremely abstemious, Franklin in later life held somewhat more liberal views. In his exquisitely humorous vein (while living in Paris) he wrote to his friend the Abbé Morellet: "*In vino veritas,* says the wise man. Truth is in wine. Before the days of Noah, then, men, having nothing but water to drink, could not discover the truth. Thus they went astray, became abominably wicked, and were justly exterminated by *water.*"

But to return to the little Christmas afternoon party in the library:

Doctor Franklin had composed a number of drinking songs, and he knew how to sing one when his audience was likely to be appreciative. It is not unreasonable to suppose that on this occasion he may have been inspired by a glass of the punch to render one of his own composition.

Well, what happened next? It is all a surmise, but it is not unlikely that the Doctor played, for the amusement of his guests, on the harmonica —an instrument of his own invention, which was a modification of the so-called musical glasses. The latter consisted of a series of glass receptacles containing different quantities of water, and by reason of that fact yielding different notes in the scale; but in Franklin's contrivance the glasses were of different sizes, containing no water, and the notes were produced by passing a moistened finger around their edges successively.

On that Christmas evening, after supper, several friends doubtless dropped in, and tables were set out for cards. Franklin toward the end of his life (he died in 1790) greatly enjoyed chess, and cards also. "I have, now and then, a little compunction in reflecting that I spend time so idly," he wrote to a friend; "but another reflection comes to relieve me, whispering, 'You know that the soul is immortal. Why, then, be a niggard of a little time, when you have eternity before you?' "

To another friend, at the same period, he wrote: "It is true that I enjoy here everything that a reasonable mind can desire—a sufficiency of income, a comfortable habitation of my own building, having all the conveniences I could imagine, a dutiful and affectionate daughter to nurse and take care of me, a number of promising grandchildren, some old friends still remaining to converse with, and more respect, distinction and public honors than I can possibly merit."

Doctor Franklin was very devoted to his family, no member of which was ever forgotten by him at Christmastime. His gifts on such occasions were always useful ones. To his younger sister, Jane Mecum, a widow who lived in Boston, he would send two or three barrels of best quality flour, which was accompanied by a draft for a round sum of money.

Much as he preached of economy and saving, he could be nobly generous, and the opportunity of which he most liked to take advantage for the bestowal of substantial tokens of his regard and affection arrived once a year, at Christmas—a festival which, for the sake of the kindly and cheerful sentiments associated with it, had a strong interest for the most sympathetic and good-humored of philosophers. (1904)

Rebecca Harding Davis

Some Old-Time Christmases

What usually happens when you uncover your real past to strangers? You show, for instance, to your neighbor a photograph of the old farmhouse where you were born. When you look at it you can smell the clover in the fields, you hear the cows lowing, you know that your mother is weeding in the garden yonder. You see yourself and Jack—two big, freckled boys, leaning from that attic window at night planning your lives out in the world, full of fighting and glory.

Just beyond that hill are the trees under which your mother has slept this many a year.

Jack lies dead in California. And your glorious life——?

All of these things are in that photograph for you. But your neighbor sees in it only a common frame house and barn that need repair badly.

The glories of the Christmases of my childhood, so splendid in my remembrance, would no doubt seem poor and cheap to this generation. For life was simple then as Charles Wagner would have it now, and bare of show and glitter. The nation was not as yet drunk with prosperity. The exchange of costly and beautiful things among friends and acquaintances—the gay, burdensome duty which now amuses and bores the whole country once a year—was then unknown. Then, only the few who loved you brought you gifts to remind you of the day when Christ was born. But what love went into the homely things! How you hoarded them!

Christmas trees then were unknown in this country outside of Pennsylvania. In Virginia we never had heard of Santa Claus. The stockings were hung in a row over the great fireplaces. But it was the fairies, we believed, who filled them so miraculously. We were told that they, too, rejoiced at the Infant's birth as did all living things. We believed that at sunrise the cows in the stable and the wild beasts in the mountains knelt, and even the dead arose and praised God that the Babe was born in Bethlehem. It was thought, too, that the sinner who left this world on Christmas morning was given a kindly greeting beyond the darkness, and that the gate of Heaven stood ajar for all comers during that hour in which the Son of God had passed through it on His way to save the world.

These superstitions belonged to the Scotch-Irish settlers of the Southern and Middle States. None of them, I think, ever penetrated into New England. Even Christmas itself was regarded by the descendants of the stern old Puritans there as a superstition, and, with Good Friday, Easter and all days set apart to commemorate religious events, was denounced as a remnant of "Popish idolatry." They rated the observance of them with gambling, dancing and other carnal delights. Even Sunday—under that name—they abjured and flouted. The Jewish Sabbath, a grim season of self-denial, they kept scrupulously. Thanksgiving was the one human festival of their year.

"I like Christmas," Henry Ward Beecher once said. "I can see the use and beauty of its observance. But it is new and foreign to me. I did not know it when I was a child, so my heart never warms to it as to Thanksgiving."

In fact, the day never has been acclimated in that chilly section of the States. I know at the present time large and important towns in New England in which Christmas is as foreign a festival as the *Jour des Morts*.

Hallmark Cards, Inc.

In New England, the time for merry-making and feasting was Thanksgiving. Christmas was virtually unknown.

In the South, to which the Cavaliers, with many ungodly habits, had brought a creed full of tender and holy superstitions, Christmas was always loyally kept. In the darkest districts of the slave-holding States that master was rated by his neighbor as hard and brutal who did not rejoice the souls of his people by gifts on that day.

In one of these South Carolinian or Georgian plantations the field hands would gather by daybreak in a ring around the lawn while the house servants, strutting among them, lofty and supercilious, drilled and ordered them about. The presents, given by the mistress or her children, usually were trifles—a red handkerchief, a pound of tea, or sugar or a lump of "baccy." "White meal," or wheat flour, was a highly coveted item, though no self-respecting Negro would eat the mawkish bread made of it. A loaf of this bread would fill the place of honor in a cabin for months. The proud possession of the luxury was held to raise its owner nearer to the social status of the whites.

More hearty kindness from one side and loyalty from the other went into these poor gifts than Northerners could understand. The day was given up on the plantation to idleness and fun, and that was a poor cabin that did not belch forth the fat smoke of 'possum and hominy as they

cooked over the fire for Christmas dinner.

In Catholic Maryland and in German Pennsylvania the day was always set apart and scrupulously kept, though with different customs. With the mass of Protestant Irish in Pennsylvania and Virginia it was observed more as a family feast, a time when it behooved us to be forgiving and jolly together, rather than as a religious occasion.

Peace and good will always found vent in heavy feeding and drinking. The housekeeper whose turkeys and mince pies then fell short of her own high standard vaguely felt during the whole year following that she had utterly failed in a religious duty.

"I hope," an old fire-eater said anxiously once in my hearing, "that the Christian faith of my household is beyond a doubt. Never in my remembrance has a Christmas morning dawned when egg-nog was not brought to our bedsides before we were awake. The rule is absolute, sir, absolute! Let others do as they may, we never neglect to honor the holy day."

This man's house and heart were homes always open to the poor and wretched. He lived to help, to give his money, his thought, his care, to the needy. But it never had occurred to him that this habit of his life had anything to do with religion. It was through the turkey and egg-nog that he professed his faith.

This queer alliance of soul and stomach is quite as firm and general now as in old times. We all have a vague sense of Christian duty done while we go through the courses of a modern Christmas banquet.

But it was from the Pennsylvania Dutch that we borrowed most of our Yule customs in this country. The Christmas tree came to us directly from them.

The Mennonites have a queer legend about it. Martin Luther, they say, was once lost in the forest in a frightful storm on Christmas Eve. He fell, and would have died but that he saw a strange gleam of white shining through the thick darkness.

It was the light from the door of a woodcutter's hut, falling on the branches of a pine tree, which were covered with rime. He crept to the door and so was saved.

The pious Dutch folk now hang glittering tinsel on their Christmas trees in memory of that hoar frost, and insist that the custom of dressing a tree had its origin in the gratitude of Lutherans for this rescue of the great reformer. This could hardly be the truth, as the Christmas tree has been known to the Germans for centuries, long before Luther was born.

But it is true that Christmas, with all its good cheer for soul and body, appeals to the Pennsylvania German more directly than to other men. His faith is simple and strong; he likes to be happy and he also likes to eat.

He spends ten months in storing away food for the remnant of the year that is left. Whether his home be the big farmhouse of some rich Mennonite, or the abode of an Amish, he has sufficient store in it to stand a siege. His great red-roofed barns crown every hill from the Delaware to the Ohio; his cellars are packed with hogsheads of salted meat and huge bins of vegetables and fruit. He is always ready for possible war or famine or whatever the future may hold.

The Pennsylvania German is a generous fellow, too, always on the lookout for a chance to feed and comfort his needy neighbors. There are so few chances of merrymaking in his life that even a funeral is made into a feast for him. He stays his tears in order to feed the entire countryside for a period of two or three days.

Naturally, to this hospitable, devout soul Christmas has always been a more important day than to less kindly folk.

I remember its approach one year in a small community of so-called Pennsylvania Dutch. They were all well-to-do folk. Each family owned a spacious modern brick house set in the midst of a skillfully tilled farm.

In the house was the usual complement of rooms: a large parlor, a dining-room and fine, great bed-chambers, all handsomely furnished and kept in exquisite order. They never were used except at a funeral, a wedding and on Christmas Day. The family lived in the kitchen and the room above it.

Over the roof of each house swung a large bell which rang out loudly long before dawn for breakfast, at eleven o'clock for dinner and at four for supper. Before sundown, while the birds still were singing, the family all were snugly tucked away in bed. I never saw such bells in any other community. They had been rejected by the fire department of Philadelphia, and a shrewd agent had persuaded these farmers that the possession of one of them was as sure a proof of aristocracy as a coat-of-arms or crest. Consequently they listened to the incessant frightful clangor going on overhead with much innocent joy.

Preparations for Christmas began in October. Heavy fruitcakes and puddings had been compounded a year before. Firkins of choice applebutter made rich by quinces, cans of pawn-haus and liverwurst, barrels of pork and hogsheads of loud-smelling sauerkraut, were set aside for *Kristkindtag.*

Two weeks before the holy day the master of the house went at night, candle in hand, through each barn and outbuilding, to whisper to every living thing, from the cattle and horses to the pigeons and pigs, the good tidings. He was coming. The hives were always visited first; the bees, as everybody knew, being a testy folk who held themselves to be the nearest friends of the family and would savagely resent any neglect.

The yearly love-feast was held in the square church on the hill a week before the great day. The men, dressed in decorous brown, the full trousers plaited into a belt around their stout waists, the tails of their coats touching their heels, sat in the pews on one side; the women in short petticoats, capes of blue, and black coal-scuttle sunbonnets were ranged on the other.

Prayers were made devoutly and hymns sung. Then women, with decorous lawn caps and aprons, carried trays of pretzels and shining tin mugs of scalding coffee to serve to everyone.

In any other circumstance of celebration, this would be the time for socializing; the time when an austere people could give in to high spirits and a festive mood. But such was not the case.

This eating and drinking was done in solemn silence. When they had finished the servers took back the mugs and the company rose, sang a hymn, and parted, after a solemn shaking of hands, the richest man in the county greeting the laborer as "Bruder." It was not the Holy Supper, but a "love-feast," to enforce the truth that all Christ's children are brothers.

As Christmas approached the house teemed with fat dainties peculiar to the Dutch: cheeses compounded of pork and molasses, luscious pies filled with raisins, or with apples smothered in cinnamon syrup, crisp doughnuts in every shape, and a little sugar-cake called *Heitig kuchen,* which was made in enormous quantities and sent in boxes from house to house. On the day the chief actors were a young man who personated Kristkind tramping from farm to farm bearing gifts, and the wicked Belsnickel, clad in skins and armed with a whip to lash bad children.

It is certain that when I was a child the great religious festivals had fallen into neglect throughout this country. There was a feeble echo in a few sects to the sound of Christmas bells or the victorious Easter trumpets. But the ordinary American was too busy in his first century of work here to pay much attention to religion beyond the saving of his own soul.

It was Charles Dickens who first taught English-speaking peoples the meaning of Christmas Day. Call him a cad, or his art bathos, if you will. That one thing he did. The story of Tiny Tim perhaps now seems to you forced and unreal. But it went around the world, bringing hot tears to the eyes of men and women, making their hearts throb with pity for their poor brother and setting their hands to work for him. The good day, as never before, was recognized as the expression of Christianity.

This new zeal for Christmas was fresh in the hearts of our people when the Civil War broke out. Naturally, the two things jarred. "Yank" and "Johnny Reb" had trouble to bring for one day in December the spirit of love and peace into their long years of bloody battering of each other and fury of murder and rapine. But it is a fact that they honestly did try to do it.

I remember countless little happenings during the Christmas seasons of 1861-2, which showed how human, after all, were the awkward machines in blue and gray who were marching in huge masses through the country—how glad each man of them would have been to hear that the great riddle was solved, that he could settle down into Joe or Tom again with his wife and children, to find, perhaps, a crony and good fellow in that other Joe or Tom yonder whom he was sent out to kill.

In '61, too, the country had not yet begun to feel the stress of want. The crops of that year were large beyond record. The army was fed lavishly, and when Christmas drew near the stay-at-homes spent their zeal and affection in packing boxes for the boys in camp. And every woman, were she Dutch frau or New York belle, gave her time to baking cakes or knitting woolen socks enough for an army of centipedes.

Christmas boxes never had more meaning than then, to these thousands of half-frozen fellows in camp. After all, they were not soldiers, but college boys, thin-blooded clerks, fat, easy-going fathers of families who probably never before in their lives had slept out of their own snug beds. They broke open the boxes, and inside were the fond, foolish trifles the women at home had sent—useless things, perhaps, at which the man playing soldier laughed as he took them out. But it was his old mother who had packed them—or his wife, or the children. As he looked up outside of the tent he saw the night, and beyond the fires of the enemy's camp. To-morrow—to-night might end it all, and he never would see mother or child again.

There was more meaning in these Christmas gifts than we shall find in ours.

I remember that an old Federal officer once told me of opening such a box on Christmas Day in '61. The camp was down in the mountains of West Virginia. There had been a fight between detachments under Generals Milroy and Johnson, of Georgia. The Union troops kept the pass. They buried the dead and took possession of an old barn for a hospital. One or two wounded Confederates were stretched in the straw alongside of their own men.

The box came at sundown, and the lucky owner opened it in the door of the barn so that the sick men could share in the fun.

"I really didn't think of the Rebs," he said. "They were nothing to me but two dogs who had tried to pull down the flag. They were mere filthy heaps on the floor; their old home-made clothes were stiff with mud and blood. I handed one of them a cigar along with the rest, but he shook his head and turned his back.

"But presently, as I was unpacking the bundles, I saw him up, leaning on his elbow, watching me, his eyes very bright.

" 'Cap'n,' he said—he had a low, womanish voice for such a huge fellow, 'thah's a picture thah—could I look at it? Just a minute. Thank ye.' It was a little photograph of one of the children. He handed it back with a long breath and then laughed. 'I thought it was my Jack. But it's a gell. My Jack's twice the size of her. He's bigger than other boys, let alone a gell.'

"I nodded and moved away from him. His filthy rags were ill-smelling, and he had

Traveling near and far to spend time with family and friends has become part of the Christmas Day agenda.

been justly shot down, busy at a bad work.

"Then it occurred to me that it was Christmas, and so——

"Well, I sat down in the straw beside him and asked about Jack, and we smoked together. He told me his name and the town in Georgia where he lived, and at last asked me, in case he did not get well, to send word to his wife and mother. I don't know why I felt as I did. He was dirty and ignorant, but there was something fine in the man that brought him near to you. He died that night. I kept my promise, and when we crossed into Georgia I hunted up his people. His boy Jack is a friend of mine now. And it's odd, but I have come to think of his father as if he had been one of my kin.

"That all grew out of its being Christmas Day, I suppose," he added. "There's something in it different from other days that is impossible to explain." (1904)

Alister Burford

An Old-Time English Christmas

When the night ended and the day began no man could tell; for over London lay the fog. Dank and dun, it blotted out the houses; dense and impenetrable, it barred the streets. The lamps along the road glowed sickly yellow in the smother, and here and there a smudge of red showed where a candle flared.

Through the muffled air the shouts and cries of the venturesome came strangely hollow, and their footsteps echoed in the empty streets as if they trod the flags beneath arched cloisters. With outstretched hands the city groped through all the morning, every greeting an imprecation.

But on toward noon the fog began to lighten, and bit by bit the sun fought through. Then came the wind, and the last drifting scud blew into shreds. It brought a snap and sparkle to the dead air, a frosty nip, that rapid walking turned to tingling warmth.

The people rubbed their eyes and looked about them. Then, reassured that London town had not been spirited away by the genii of the fog, with one accord they reached for wicker baskets and started out. For in those good old days, when steam was but the waste of housewives' kettles, before the world turned topsy-turvy, the buying of the Christmas cheer was no light thing. Then were there twelve long days of merrymaking, and honest men had honest appetites.

As the night drew on the streets became more thronged. In every window candles twinkled; in every room a cheerful blaze danced in the grate, and sent out ruddy streams of light into the dusk. And everywhere was holly hung, and mistletoe.

Fat turkeys and lean turkeys, Falstaffian gob-blers in all the bronze glory of their feathers, and plump hen-turkeys, picked clean to the white skin; rotund turkeys which had gorged the autumn away in Norfolk farmyards, and lean, blue birds which had scratched out a precarious livelihood on barren moors; turkeys piled high on every stall, and swinging head down from rows of hooks; turkeys before, behind, on both sides, wherever the eye rested; tons of turkeys, hills of turkeys, mountains of turkeys, that was Leadenhall Market on Christmas Eve. Nor was there lack of unctuous geese and Dorking fowl, of spicy brawn in rolls, and good roast beef in great, thick joints, the firm red flesh streaked and o'erlaid with yellow fat, all gay with greens and streaming ribbons, which fit the hearty tastes of those hearty times.

In and around the shops and stalls surged the whole quarter, jostling, crowding, pinching thin turkeys, prodding fat turkeys, and smelling suspicious-looking turkeys. There were round-paunched old papas, red-faced and jolly, dragging wondering children along on either side, with a porter, bowed under a roomy hamper, following on behind; there were fat old housewives, smiling all down their shining faces to their double chins, waddling from stall to stall, intent on the one great business of the moment.

On every side there rose the sound of bargaining, buying and selling, the shouts and laughter of the children and the more staid greetings of their elders. And here and there were ragged men and boys who cried out sheets of Christmas carols; and from a corner came the wheezing of a broken violin and the cracked voices of some

frowsy waifs bawling out the good old
God rest you, merry gentlemen,
Let nothing you dismay,
Remember Christ, our Saviour,
Was born on Christmas Day.

From end to end, the market smacked of Christmas. There was a breath of it in the pleasant smells that floated out from the shops where the fruiterers were entrenched behind barricades of oranges and apples and grapes and lemons; there was a jingle of it in the rattle of the canisters from which the grocers were weighing out the spices for the morrow's pudding; there was a suggestion of it in the piled-up sweetness of candied fruits and figs and plums; and everywhere there was the certainty of it in the greens.

At precisely one minute before ten the coachee of "the Fastflyer" came out of the tap-room of "The Bell and Hand," wiping his mouth on the back of a stubby paw, and gave a stolid stare around the inn yard. He was a short, stocky man, whom a swaddling greatcoat of rough blue stuff, with bright brass buttons, and a low-crowned hat, in which was stuck a sprig of holly, made shorter and stockier still. His face, what little of it showed below the hat, and above a gaudy "neckerchief," was veined and mottled red, like a map of an extensive system of lakes and rivers. And as he waddled toward the coach, he was surrounded by an admiring circle of stable-boys, and preceded and followed by a smell of gin.

The horses, with two hostlers at the heads of the leaders, were already in their places; the four insides, wrapped in traveling shawls, were snuggled down in theirs; the outsides, a fine, bluff, jolly old gentleman, to whom the coachee touched his hat deferentially, and three well-built, frank-faced schoolboys, were running back and forth alongside.

The top of the coach was covered and piled with boxes, baskets and hampers, and the guard and two porters were still stowing things away in impossible corners of the boot. There were barrels of oysters and hampers of game; there were hares and turkeys and geese swinging from convenient hooks. From a basket on top, the head of a great turbot stuck up and glared stonily at the snout of a stiff and stark sucking-pig that poked out from another.

"Up you go, now, young gentlemen," cried out coachee at last, and the three schoolboys bounced to the top like India-rubber balls. Up went the old gentleman, puffing and blowing, and then

the coachee, with surprising agility, jumped into his seat, just as the guard stowed the last bundle in the boot of the coach.

"Give 'em their 'eads, 'Arry," called the guard; and he grasped his horn.

There was a sudden shuffling of hoofs, and the hostlers fell back; there was a tightening of reins, and the leaders began to prance; there was a crack of the long-lashed whip, and the coach was off. Away they went, to the blast of the horn, hurtling along through the half-fog of the morning, and meaner vehicles turned from their way. Away they went, out of the smoke and soot of the city, along the winding country roads, where the air came clear and clean over the freshly fallen snow. Away they went, past lanes and hedges, down a long slope, over an old arched bridge, and then past a churchyard, where the rough gray

Twelve full days of merrymaking; holly and mistletoe abounding; markets overflowing with turkeys; street corners dotted with carolers— that *was an old-time English Christmas.*

stones were stuck through the snow at queer, unsteady angles.

And now the shrill horn piped the entrance to a village. To every gate ran the housemaid and the cook, and giggled, and simpered, and cried "Oh, lor'!" as the coachee winked at one and leered at the other. From every ale-house the loungers came out and stared in stupid wonder at the charging coach.

Outside the village, the coachee eased his horses down and turned half out to let a mad procession by. Three old post-chaises, packed full of home-bound schoolboys, came racing up, the postboys standing in their stirrups and lashing the lean old brutes beneath them. With flags streaming, trumpets blowing, missiles flying, they came on, leaning far out the windows, and waving their caps. A sudden shower of missiles, a yell of "*Dulce domum!*" and they were past.

So sped the miles away, until at last the steaming horses drew up before the Abbey Inn.

From the Abbey Inn to the Manor House, where the fine old gentleman lived, the pair of shaggy ponies, which had been standing waiting for him, frisked and romped in no time at all.

"Hooray!" cried the lads in chorus, as the panting ponies stopped. And then the stout hall door flew open, and out burst a merry throng, blown on a gale of shouts and laughter. From mother to grandmother, from sister to brother, from uncle to aunt, from cousin to second cousin, the lads were bandied about and hugged, until they cried out "Enough!" and squirmed free.

From room to room, greeting the servants and admiring the greens, from stables to kennels, patting the horses and petting the dogs, they ran through all the afternoon. But with the twilight they came trooping to the spacious hall, where their elders sat in the deepening dusk.

Then the fine old gentleman, looking rosier and jollier than ever, advanced on the blackness of the yawning fireplace, holding tenderly in one hand a charred fragment of last year's Yule log. With this, that custom might be satisfied, he kindled a blaze that curled up and licked the rough bark of the good oak log. And soon the leaping flame lit all the hall, and danced back from the time-stained oak that wainscoted the walls.

Wax candles now were lit in every room, and from the farms around the tenantry came in, the men all stiff and jointless in their Sunday best, the women simpering.

Squeak, squeak! the fiddler was tuning up. Twang, twang! the harper was testing his strings, and impatient toes began to tap the floor. Then both together, in an ambitious flourish, and, at the head of the set, the silk-stockinged calves of the jolly old gentleman stepped in and out in gay anticipation.

Already the children were making merry. Unchecked by any frowning elder, a boisterous game of hoodman blind was in full swing, and youngsters were burning their fingers at snapdragon or sousing their heads playing bob-apple.

And so with games and dancing the evening wore away, until the butler staggered in under a great bowl of wassail, from which a spicy steam wreathed up. Then came more dancing and games and singing, and at last, when everyone was hungry and breathless, the jolly old gentleman led a fierce charge on a supper of cold fowl and beef, of venison pasties and pigeon and mince pies, with steaming punch or brown October ale to wash it down. Nor did a guest get up to go, nor a sleepy child submit to being led away, until the bells chimed out for Christmas morning. (1898)

Wallace Webster

Christmas with Royalty

No royal personage is more stately and conscious of his own importance than the German Emperor, who on Christmas Day, nevertheless, knows how to unbend, joining gayly in the jollification of the Court. This year he will celebrate the Yuletide festival at Potsdam with all of his children about him, including the recently-married Crown Prince and his bride. For each son and daughter there will be a tree, specially cut for the occasion from the near-by forest on the imperial estate, and a table at the foot of it laden with gifts. An eighth tree—the Emperor has seven children—will be largest of all, for Wilhelm II and the Empress, and its branches will bear presents for the various officers and ladies of the household, and royal court.

Emperor Wilhelm's children didn't have to "share" a Christmas tree—each of the seven was generously provided with his own.

The idea of the Christmas tree seems to have originated in Germany—a goblin that brings good luck into the house is supposed to dwell within its trunk—and hence the conspicuous part it plays in the imperial celebration. In obedience to custom, the eight trees will be set up in a large reception room in the palace, and nobody save the Empress and half-a-dozen servants will be admitted until the morning of the twenty-fifth of December. Then, when all the members of the household have assembled, including the officials of the Emperor's immediate entourage and the ladies in attendance, all will take part in singing the beautiful choral of Luther, at the conclusion of which the doors will be thrown open and the

people will eagerly enter the great hall.

The scene, as may be well imagined, will be quite a brilliant one, the trees—forming a small forest, glittering with electric lights of different colors and hung with bright ornaments—being ranged along one end of the great room, with the presents laid out on tables beneath. As usual, they will be of different sizes, in a row from smallest to biggest, in direct proportion to the ages of the imperial princes and princesses, the tree of the Crown Prince being larger than any of the others, except that belonging to his father and his mother. Whether there is to be a tree for the new Crown Princess nobody knows; for all of the Christmas arrangements at Potsdam are kept very secret, in order that they may lose nothing of the charm of surprise.

When the gifts belonging to the princes and princesses and those of the Emperor and Empress have been examined and admired, her Imperial Majesty will proceed to distribute the presents intended for the various officials and ladies of the court, taking them one by one from the great tree. For the women there will be articles of jewelry, rare and beautiful laces, and other things dear to the feminine heart; and the men will get gold cigarette-cases and valuable trifles appropriate to masculine uses. But in each instance, where it is practicable, the object bestowed will have a personal significance in connection with its recipient—often jocular, too, as in the case of a chamberlain who (having been

The Emperor's gifts to his children were primarily practical— books, strings, tacks—plus a few frivolous toys.

engaged in collecting large sums of money for the churches of Berlin) last year received a cigar-case of silver in the likeness of a contribution-box.

It has never been the policy of William II and his wife to bestow costly gifts upon their young children. The Christmas presents of the princes and princesses have been, as a rule, of the inexpensive and substantially useful kind, including perhaps a box of candy, a toy or two, and a number of instructive books. It is said that on one occasion the Crown Prince received from his father, as a mark of affection at Yuletide, a hammer, a ball of string, and a paper of tacks. But each boy, on coming of age, gets one very magnificent gift, usually at Christmas: a completely equipped establishment of his own, for which an adequate revenue of maintenance is provided.

In the distribution of Christmas gifts at Potsdam nobody will be forgotten—not even the stable-boys and scullery-maids. There is something for everybody, and the list of people to be remembered is a long one, comprising over a thousand names. In order that presents may not in any case be duplicated, a book is kept—a sort of Yuletide register, which runs back for fifty years—showing just what each person has received. To the Kaiserin her husband usually gives a handsome article of bijouterie, almost invariably diamonds, while to each of half-a-dozen of his most intimate men friends he sends a coal-black charger. To the King of England, his uncle, he forwards a case of precious Johannisberger, with a few of his latest photographs for the ladies of the family.

If Christmas is an important occasion at Potsdam, it is a festival not less notable at Sandringham. In that great English country house, neither palace nor castle, Edward VII finds himself more at home than anywhere else in the world, and there he will spend the holiday this year in the bosom of his family. The Prince and Princess of Wales will be there, of course, with their children, and it is reasonable to expect that there will be great romps.

In Potsdam half the day will be spent in religious exercises, Wilhelm II being an earnest church-goer and believer, but in his uncle's establishment in England there is more jollity and less piety, and an effort is made at Yuletide to relinquish all cares both as to this world and the next.

Gifts fit for a queen—fine jewels, perfumes and laces—things other women only dreamed about.

There will be trees for the young folks—the Prince Consort, King Edward's father, who was a German, introduced them at the English Court—and the children will hang up their stockings on Christmas Eve. To his wife the monarch will give a dozen bottles of her favorite perfume, lavender water (his invariable contribution), and also a necklace of diamonds or some such trifle in the way of jewelry. Of course, Alexandra already possesses a vastly greater number of jewels than she can possibly wear; but a queen, after all, is a woman, and what woman ever had all the jewels she wanted? There will be presents, you may be sure, for all the family and for the lords and ladies in waiting, the gentlemen of the bed-chamber, the mistresses of the robes, the maids of honor, and so on down to the grooms and kitchen-maids. When Victoria was alive, every retainer who had belonged to the household during the lifetime of her husband received at Christmas a piece of plate, with a black-bordered card that read: "With the good wishes of her Majesty and the Prince Consort." She liked, you

see, still to associate the Prince with gifts conferred upon those who knew him.

But it is the Christmas dinner that will be the most important feature of the holiday at Sandringham. One hundred plum-puddings—just think of that, and smack your lips!—will be furnished by the kitchens, to make sure that everybody may have plenty and to spare. There is no fear of waste, for whatever is left over will be given to the poor. And such delicious plum-puddings, too! The recipe has been handed down as carefully as any substantial heirloom, from the time of King James I, who, indeed, is said to have been its originator.

On the sideboards in the great dining-hall, in obedience to ancient tradition and long-established custom, will be placed a huge boar's head crowned with holly, a vast woodcock-pie, and a cold "Baron" of beef weighing two hundred pounds. The beef must be from one of the King's own oxen. It will be cooked on the twenty-second day of December, so as to give it plenty of time to cool, the roasting being done over an enormous dripping-pan in front of an open fire; and finally, when sufficiently chilled, it will be served on an immense silver dish which once belonged to Henry VIII. There is a legend to the effect that Charles II, on a certain occasion, being overcome with delight by the flavor of a loin of beef, drew his sword and, with much solemnity, knighted it in due form —whence the term Sir Loin. Whether this be a true story or not, it is not recorded that a chuck of beef was ever made a Baron.

The Czar of all the Russias is not likely to have a very merry Christmas this year, but he may derive some timely consolation from a dozen quarts of the finest Scotch whisky which, in accordance with long-followed custom, King Edward will send him. A huge stone jar of marmalade, specially prepared by the Queen's cooks, went to him annually from Balmoral Castle when Victoria was alive, but it may be that this tribute has been discontinued. Anyway, the present of Nicholas to King Edward will undoubtedly be, as usual, a dozen boxes of Cuban cigars, of a brand manufactured and put up expressly for the Czar by a firm in Havana. Five hundred boxes of them are shipped every year from Havana, in time for Christmas, and are distributed among relatives and among members of the Russian Court circle.

Not infrequently the gifts picked out by the Czar on such occasions are decidedly odd. For example, he will sometimes present to a favored courtier a herd of deer. When Queen Victoria was alive he would send to her at Christmas a fresh-caught sturgeon, packed in ice, and it is said the royal lady greatly appreciated the luxury. For the imperial children bonbons and toys are ordered from Paris; but the baby heir to the throne, though already a full general, is as yet too young to eat candy or to appreciate the meaning of Christmas—a festival which, it should be realized, is celebrated twelve days later by the Russians, in obedience to the rules of their Church, which put the date at our Epiphany.

Emperor Francis Joseph of Austria, will gather all his grandchildren around him this Christmas, as usual, and will make the day as merry as possible for them. He is getting to be an old man now, and his life has held many troubles; but in the company of the young folks he is able to forget his sorrows, and nothing delights him more than to go shopping for toys and other things likely to give pleasure to small boys and girls. To his fellow-sovereigns, and likewise to a few intimate friends, he sends, as a token of good will appropriate to the festive season, the greatest imaginable luxury in the way of drinkables—a dozen bottles of Tokay from the royal cellars.

The Sultan of Turkey, of course, being a Moham-

medan and himself the Pope of that faith, does not celebrate Christmas; but, as a matter of politeness, he signifies his remembrance of the day by sending to each of his fellow-monarchs—well, what do you think? Why, nothing more nor less than a huge and beautifully-decorated box of candy, of the kind known as "Lokoom," or "Turkish Delight." In eating this candy, which is specially prepared by the Sultan's own confectioner, the recipients have the pleasure of knowing that they are partaking of the favorite sweet of the royal seraglio. A gift, specially appropriate to the person upon whom it is to be bestowed, is put into each box.

If common report does not belie the Belgian monarch, the opera-singers of Paris are often the beneficiaries of King Leopold's Christmas generosity, and to them he is liberal enough, though a notorious niggard otherwise. With most of his family he has quarreled, and his palace at Brussels this year is not likely to be the scene of any cheerful Yuletide festivities. But his choice of gifts, when he does bestow one upon a royal or other distinguished personage, is usually a handsome Brussels carpet.

Christmas Day in Madrid is a gloomy time, so far as its celebration by royalty is concerned. There is a great deal of religious ceremonial and very little fun. It is said that Queen Christine, when she was Regent, tried to introduce at court the Christmas tree, the sentiment connected with which had been dear to her heart when she was only a little Austrian princess in the nursery at Vienna; but the high clerical dignitaries frowned upon it as an emblem of heathen worship, and the idea had to be abandoned. The royal mother is a woman of simple tastes, and it is recorded that, a year or two ago, when her son, King Alfonso, asked her what she would like for a Christmas gift, she decided in favor of a white bison.

Little Queen Wilhelmina, of the Kingdom of Pays-Bas, as it is known in the language of the

Traditionally, stockings have been hung by the young—or the young at heart, such as Queen Wilhelmina.

diplomats—or of the Netherlands, as we should say it—though she has been a married woman for several years now, still has a Christmas tree and hangs up her stocking for Kriss Kringle to fill. She is very clever with her needle, and to her friends she sends at Yuletide numerous specimens of her own handiwork.

At Rome, as in Madrid, Christmas is a rather solemn holiday, celebrated by religious processions and by masses in the churches. However, in the evening, the King will give a grand dinner, which will be followed by a reception attended by a multitude of political and other dignitaries. The Pope will pass the day quietly at the Vatican, and the potentates and other per-

sonages who receive presents from him in recognition of the sacred anniversary will value them rather for the sentiment they convey than for their intrinsic worth. His personal blessing, with an autographed letter, and accompanied by a few jars of wine made from grapes grown on the Pincian Hill, comprise the only gifts which he feels able to bestow. His predecessor, Leo, sent snuff to Queen Victoria every Christmas, recommending it to her as a sovereign cure for catarrh and other such ailments, and thus it was that her faithful companion and factotum, John Brown, obtained his supplies of the article. But the consignments of sneezing tobacco, it is said, have been discontinued under Pius X. (1905)

Acknowledgments

Text Credits:

"The Christmas Hunt" by Borden Deal. Copyright © 1960 by The Curtis Publishing Company. Reprinted by permission of the Borden Deal Family Trust (Borden Deal, Trustee).

"The Christmas Racket" by Jim and Allan Bosworth. Reprinted by permission of Allan Bosworth.

"Hard-Rock Candy" by Mack Thomas. Copyright © 1964 by Mack Thomas. Reprinted by permission of The Sterling Lord Agency, Inc.

"How to be Santa Claus" by Nat B. Read, Jr. Reprinted by permission of the author.

"Johanna's Christmas Star" by M.G. Chute. Reprinted by permission of the author.

"Silent Night" by Paul Gallico. Copyright © 1962 by The Curtis Publishing Company. Reprinted by permission of Harold Ober Associates.

"Women Want the Oddest Things for Christmas" by Peg Bracken. Reprinted by permission of The Lescher Agency.

Photo Credits:

Page: 167, 185-189, 274, 278, 287, Hallmark Cards, Inc.; 220, American Airlines; 231, Sylvania/GTE Products Corp.; 273, Culver Pictures; 276, Cardavon Press.

An effort has been made to trace the ownership of other text and photographs included. Any errors or omissions will be corrected in subsequent editions, provided the publisher is notified.